T0368755

# THE TRUE ORIGIN OF MAN

# THE TRUE ORIGIN OF MAN

## KENNETH SMITH

iUniverse LLC
Bloomington

# The True Origin of Man

*Copyright © 2013 by Kenneth Smith.*

*All rights reserved. No part of this book may be used or reproduced by any means, graphic, electronic, or mechanical, including photocopying, recording, taping or by any information storage retrieval system without the written permission of the publisher except in the case of brief quotations embodied in critical articles and reviews.*

*iUniverse books may be ordered through booksellers or by contacting:*

*iUniverse LLC*
*1663 Liberty Drive*
*Bloomington, IN 47403*
*www.iuniverse.com*
*1-800-Authors (1-800-288-4677)*

*Because of the dynamic nature of the Internet, any web addresses or links contained in this book may have changed since publication and may no longer be valid. The views expressed in this work are solely those of the author and do not necessarily reflect the views of the publisher, and the publisher hereby disclaims any responsibility for them.*

*Any people depicted in stock imagery provided by Thinkstock are models, and such images are being used for illustrative purposes only.*
*Certain stock imagery © Thinkstock.*

*ISBN: 978-1-4759-8966-3 (sc)*
*ISBN: 978-1-4759-8967-0 (ebk)*

*Library of Congress Control Number: 2013908957*

*Printed in the United States of America*

*iUniverse rev. date: 07/24/2013*

# CONTENTS

# INTRODUCTION

## *"The Missing Link"*

This book is an instrumental field guide that supports the standardized study of genetic Science and Theology Policy, through the merging of the scientific method with religious spiritualism. Policy is the study of the administration, its functions and responsibilities, its general leadership, and its problems at hand, which affect the character and success of the total enterprise. Agree or not, science and theology are bound together through the historical and biological data, which surfaced throughout mankind's existence. The complete misalignment of science and theology has given rise to many lawsuits in the U.S. Supreme Court that to date, remain unresolved and abandon religious and political leadership to govern itself. Recently established laws in the constitution carry a neutral and non-offensive tone, whether printed in school textbooks or not. These problems need to be confronted and the point of view assumed and analyzed to deal with them—not brushed under the rug by neutral laws. This guide offers the ability to do just that.

People need something tangible with which to test, in order to believe in our true, transcendental beginning. Resolving problems in public affairs, molding of ideals, clearly defining an agenda, and mobilizing resources can unify science and theology to face the opposition. Because science presents us with a predestined theory in

DNA and religion presents an "individual choice" to pursue faith and break the bonds of our human inclinations, on the surface there appears to be an inherent and overwhelming contradiction that prevents the two from co-existing.

The Smith Chart utilizes proven mathematical calculations, to deliver accurate predictions within the DNA genome variation results. The data is extracted from the 100% human genetic normal conformation as the variation reference. Above these "mind over matter" hypothesis, deceptive concepts fed the public prior to this discovery. The human "genetic normal," patterned after God, has been discarded by over fourteen-hundred top scientist of the (HGP) Human Genome Project; who through assembled effort, perceive the view of God as a nonexistent myth in their logic-driven minds, while they trust in the strength of their own bionic engineered arms. Early in the twenty-first century, the scientific community celebrated a conclusion in the Human Genome Project that has caused a derailment in the advancement of biotechnology. This project boasted great promise in the progression of every aspect of human life: food, medical care, entertainment, health, bodies, and to even counter global warming—a complete facelift for the entire planet and its inhabitants.

While working at Central Reference Laboratory in Anaheim California, I held a great passion for the study of hematology and possessed a curiosity in understanding the reasoning behind defective cells. Exploration into defects led to one of the greatest discoveries of this century. As I centrifuged and processed blood samples, I collected cultural specimens for testing. Upon the completion of those results and after data entry, I reported the findings to area medical facilities around southern California. On impulse, these studies were furthered into a feasible theory of the human "genetic normal," which is also the missing link between man and ape. After much research, it became a billion to one shot that came true! The discovery of this concrete genetic law called GMB (Genetic Marginal Boundaries) proves no two species can produce outside of their GMB. Selecting the right timing to come forward was done prospectively, because of the old literature adage, "if you have something important to say, then put it in writing." I ironed out all the wrinkles in the developed linear scale, called the (Smith chart), which is referenced from the "human genetic normal." These original humans have been given a prestigious name, **"Imperial Humanus."** Because they are not homosapiens, which calculates the GMB mutated cell percentage in all human species—similar to Ohm's law pie chart that calculates voltage, resistance, and current values in an electrical circuit.

The Smithsonian Institute will have to contemplate removing all its evolutionary exhibits and declare that discovery of the genetic 'normal'—the missing link between man and ape, and the truth into man's Alpha past. Truth will put an end to the debate, for there can only be one truth; it must be absolute fact, and not a mere rationalization, which is conceived inside the human mind and strengthens one's own point, even in disagreement. The newly discovered genetic fact incorporated into a twenty-five page intellectual, scientific, and genetic thesis—abstracted from a highly detailed and larger manuscript source.

The purpose of policy in organized effort anywhere is neither clear and fixed, nor unchanging. The director of the National Institute of Health in Bethesda MD, and chief of staff over the globally led human genome project research—publicly funded by the (U.S. Dept. of Energy) teamed with Celera Genomics of Rockville MD. Celera Genomics is a private company and through valiant effort, put together material referred to as the human genome, regarded by many as the *book of life*. Not to be confused with the other Book of Life to which the Christian God refers. HGP documentation is considered a history book, a shop manual, a parts list, and a textbook of medicine more profoundly detailed than ever before and is considered a virtual atlas of the human body; however, it can misguide you from the true human genetic path in its course through history. Without certified testing confirmed by a board of medical peers, there are unresolved queries that remain in its inconclusive pedagogy. HGP scientist shied away from public policy and peer testing. Instead, they injected an unfounded and opinionated conclusion that rejected the concept of a human genetic normal. These announced findings came from the first comprehensive analysis of the human genetic code, following a gala at a White House function in June of 2000. Leaders of the competing public and private teams announced they had each determined the almost three-billion letters of biochemical code in the human genome strung together along six-foot strands inside of human DNA cells. These three billion letters spell out directions for creating and maintaining human life. Considering the program's three-billion dollar expense, the program equals out to about one dollar a letter. For all these claimed evolutionary mutation within species to have accrued and led to the modern-day human race, the actual findings show shockingly very little variation, which means all individuals are about 99.9 percent genetically identical, as indicated by this team's effort.

The human genome is much more complicated than previously perceived Celera (president and chief executive at the time) acknowledged. This lack of knowledge limitation is one reason the genome project cost tens of millions of dollars. Two new Venter institutes supported by a hundred-million dollar endowed funding will operate on nearly twenty-million dollars per year. These foundations are guided by unfounded principles in evolutionary theory. Analysis error arose as a direct result of improper DNA sample selection processes and the scientific bias toward evolutionary testing theories. The selection process included genes from six people, who were identified as Caucasian, Hispanic, Mexican, Asian Chinese, and Afro American. They indicated that the number of harmless variations nestled in the human genome varies by race, and on average Afro Americans carry more variations than Caucasian. This data implied African American had more mixed versions of Afro-American speciation varying from light skin, to dark skin, more so than the variances within Caucasian speciation mixes. It deemed this observation as evidence that African Americans have been around longer. This book clearly explains the scientific facts and presents mathematical DNA evidence. These facts alone will reveal the true history of the world and its creatures, sans injected personal opinion or superfluous conclusions.

# THE CONTROVERSY

Truth, though simple, is burdened to find its way into man's life, while a complicated lie easily gravitates into man's lifeworks. Truth undisputedly stands alone and doesn't need anyone to alter the facts to fit into place. Scientists claim that the finding of no human genetic normal, after the completion of the US-led Human Genome Project in 2003 that cost more than $3 billion, is a claim of major advancement. Or has it caused a derailment in DNA progress? Some genetic scientists seem to think they've degraded God into being a myth and trust in the strength of their very own bionic-engineered arms. Even though DNA testifies to the human genetic normal specie thorough the variations changes referenced here from scripture in the King James Bible.

Every so often in the history of man, a controversy arises that sparks a debate for centuries. Opinions have varied widely about the truth of the matter at hand, but truth is an inarguable absolute. There is only one truth, and the facts will point to it as they're discovered. On July 1, 1858, in England, a meeting of the Linnaean Society took place, and a mild-mannered man named Charles Darwin took center stage as he presented his thoughts combined with those of Alfred Wallace on the theory of evolution. (Source: Seminar in Cultural Anthropology: Darwin) at California State University, Chico www.csuchico. edu/-curban/ Darwin/DarwinSem-S95.html

The next year, 1859, Darwin published *The Origin of Species,* 230 pages long, which he called an abstract of his larger work. The book was an immediate publishing success, selling out the first day it was in print. The Creationists opposed the validity of the writings, which chiefly undermined the basis of their faith by insinuating that God did not create the Earth in seven days and that *Homo sapiens* was nothing special among species. Reason being, it is known few easily accept having their preconceived notions disturbed whether Creationist or Evolutionist.

Darwin was careful not to write about *Homo sapiens* in *Origin* in 1859, and all he had to say about "man" in the volume was this: In a distant future in open fields for far more important studies. Psychology will be based on a new understanding of the necessary acquirements of each mental power and capacity by gradation. Light will be thrown onto the origin of man and history as a recapitulation and conclusion. Darwin spoke figuratively, but also can the Evolutionist mind that claims being concretely grounded in scientific logical fact withstand scientific truth that supports creation or will their mind evolve to stand upon new grounds of shifting sands to continue an argument. (csuchico.edu)

In 1860 there was a church meeting at Oxford questioning evolution verses religion theories. Several English churchmen who were there later published an item titled *Essays and Reviews,* wherein they questioned certain orthodox religious doctrines. In the 1860s and 1870s other events occurred to make Darwin's ideals almost passable during his lifetime. It was certainly one of the most trying times in the existence of Christianity.

Then Bishop Colenso in 1862 started to publish his doubts about the Pentateuch. In 1863 Sir Charles Lyell produced his evidence on the antiquity of man, which seemed to be inconsistent with the account of creation in the *Bible.* Renan's humanizing work in 1863 *Vie de Jesus* appeared. In 1865 J.R. Seely of Cambridge then published another humanizing work on Christ called *Ecce Homo.* In 1870 The British Association at Exeter accepted evolution. In 1871 Darwin published his *Descent of Man.* Thus in these ten to twelve years orthodox religion received a series of body blows, which seemed to be aimed at its existence. (csuchico.edu)

When *The Descent of Man* was published in 1871, the controversy was almost over in Darwin's time. On his seventy-third birthday, Darwin wrote to a friend to say. "My course is nearly run." Then on Wednesday, April 19, 1882, he had a fatal heart attack and died.

At his death, twenty Members of Parliament immediately requested of the dean of Westminster that Darwin be buried in the Abbey, oddly in one of the holiest places in the British Empire, but the British know how to honor their scientists. Darwin's pallbearers were the president of the Royal Society, the American minister to the British Isles, a churchman, an earl, two dukes, and the three leading British biologists of the times, who were among his closest scientific friends: Thomas Huxley, Alfred Wallace, Sir Joseph Hooker, and noted supporter Herbert Spencer, all of whom had the general consensus about Darwin's internment at the Abbey as "Worthy enough—to attend—to suspend their objection to religious rituals." (csuchico.edu)

After Darwin's memorial service, one could imagine clergy and scientists were still in the constant debate of creation versus evolution; it became vocal at some points but not heated. Thomas Huxley was said to be the "bulldog" for aggressively taking the stance on the theory of evolution while they were all still in the graveyard.

"You people just don't give up, do you? You're beaten—Darwin's theory of evolution has stumped you. Your grand tree of Christianity has fallen. Admit it!" Huxley argued aggressively in the light fog that drifted ominously around them all.

"Even from a stump sometimes branches will sprout to bear seed, and with faith like that of a mustard seed, a new tree will rise forth in its place," a clergyman said.

"Bloody daft you all must be, to continue this holy charade. But I shall live my life to the fullest, without fear of consequence from a conjured-up supreme entity, which supposedly created us all in his image. What's God have, twenty images of himself?" Huxley asked rhetorically. "Because if you look throughout the world, there are many different species of *Homo sapiens* who look nothing alike, which only evolution can explain and you cannot deny! You then say this God of rationality sacrificed his only begotten son as the final sacrificial lamb to save our souls—poppycock!" Huxley exclaimed as a flash of lightning illuminated the horizon in the far background and then rolling thunder cracked in the distance, which momentarily captured everyone's attention.

"I tell you all earnestly that I cannot explain it, for I will not lie to you, but I do know that God can do any feat of wonder to boggle man's mind. Truth has been preached to you and man alike by the prophets and us. As for me and my house, we shall serve the Lord," the clergyman said to the group.

"Well, my job as a scientist is to expose the truth and remove fraud, such as these many crackpot cults you people call religion," Huxley responded.

"You have made your choice, brother," the clergyman said. "These actions will release the evil in man's heart without the moral restraints of religion. The consequences you bear for this defiance can never be repaid, for hell is an eternal fire that never quenches its thirst!" The men walked away from one another, not seeing eye-to-eye as they left the gravesite of Charles Darwin, noted scientist, who shied away from a medical career. Then he took up the study of divinity at Cambridge, but while there, his interest turned to natural history. Then he forsook religion.

Now there were only two people left at the gravesite: the workers, who would seal Darwin's casket in the grave of its final resting place.

"What was that commotion all about, I wonder?" the slender gravedigger asked his chubby coworker.

"Are you ill, man? Don't you know who this is you're laying to his final resting place?" the chubby gravedigger asked.

"No," he said with a blank expression on his face. "Should I?"

"Don't be daft, man! This here is none other than Charles Darwin the scientist, who discovered humans came from apes, and there is no heaven or hell, says I."

"Really? You mean we can do whatever we want and not get punished for it?"

"Precisely, lad. Within the confines of man-made laws, mind you."

"Well, why don't we shove off to ol' McDaniel's tavern, have some drinks, and pay a couple of lively ladies of the night for a good ol' time, if you know what I mean."

"I do for sure, me boy, but maybe first we should toast the departed?"

"Right, governor!" They pulled out a bottle of ale to celebrate Darwinism.

"Now, to the rightfully departed Mr. Darwin, we toast you with a nip," he said as he started pouring out some of the fermented drink upon Darwin's casket while saying a few words. "Here's to the man who has cleared everyone's conscience to party till you drop, without any consequences of burning in hell. Much obliged, Mr. Darwin."

"Amen!" said the slender gravedigger, who didn't know of Darwin. The chubby gravedigger slapped him on the stomach with his hat.

"Ow—what was that for?" he asked with a bewildered expression.

"Here Mr. Darwin is kind enough to get rid of our good and bad consciences. Then you try to put them right back with a hearty amen! Excuse him, Mr. Darwin, he's lacking."

"I'll show you who's lacking!" the slender gravedigger boasted.

"Now, now, your manners—not in front of the deceased. Sorry, Mr. Darwin. Now let's you and I go have that good time we were talking about."

"Right, ol' chum," the slender one said as they walked off with merry thoughts.

Years later, in 1888, at the Chapel of St. Faith in Westminster Abbey, a young priest came charging into the office of the chief minister.

"They found another one! Sir, that makes seven altogether," the young priest gasped.

"Dear God, no!" the chief priest exclaimed in agony.

"In White Chapel, I believe. I think her name was Marie Kelly."

"How?" the chief asked with his hands to his face.

"She was slashed in the same way, by this Jack the Ripper, Scotland Yard's constables believe, though they don't think she was a prostitute like the others before her. People are in sheer terror. They're calling him a madman on the loose!"

"Dear God, I knew this Darwinism would destroy the moral fibers of this society—in less than six years yet! I can only foresee it getting worse." Then all the men in the room looked around at one another while the chief priest grieved with his face down toward his desk and silence fell over the room.

"Why would someone do such a thing—to women yet?" someone in the room asked.

"Prostitution has been on the rise in London since Darwinism. Perhaps he's seeking revenge on these women, for contracting a life-threatening disease that destroyed his home and marriage—sort of taking them down with him, so to say, before he goes?" another said.

"Whatever this fiend's reasoning for losing his ethical restraint in this once morally conscious society, Darwinism is the center of it, and has cost us all greatly!" the chief priest said as everyone just stood there silently looking on. In years to come they would see much moral decline in Britain until it reached even the throne.

# HISTORY OF THE WORLD REVIVED

Now comes the clarification of the truth in detail with no holes of faith, belief, or hypothesis: the exact relationship between DNA and the many mysterious human variations we have today. Step by step, all events will be explained with the stirring emotions that altered the course of history.

Are we able to handle truth, though? Readers, beware! It is said that truth cuts like a knife, and something inside of you will bleed if you dare to continue reading. Once you know the truth, you can never go back to that lie of only evolution explains genetic mutations.

"In the beginning, God created the heavens and the earth. Now the earth was formless and empty, darkness was over the surface of the deep, and the Spirit of God was hovering over the waters. (Genesis 1:1-28)

"And God said let there be light." You see the waters of the ocean swaying tranquilly along in small ripples on the surface, reflecting the sun high above.

And God said, "Let there be an expansion between the waters to separate water from water." The sky formed, giving life to the horizon with a light cloud formation in the background that still allowed you to see the blue of the sky like a backdrop.

And God said, "Let the water under the sky be gathered into one place, and let dry ground appear." Then land formed to separate the oceans with vast mountain peaks, and valley lows that swept your breath away. The land produced vegetation: plants bearing seeds according to their own kinds and trees bearing fruit with seed in it according to their own kinds. And God saw that it was good.

And God said, "Let there be lights in the expansion of the sky to separate the day from the night, and let them serve as signs to mark the seasons and the days and the years, and let there be lights in the expanse of the sky to give light on the earth."

And God said, "Let the water teem with living creatures, and let the birds fly above the earth across the expanse of the sky." So God created the great creatures of the sea. Then you see a herd of whales swimming by with dolphins leaping out of the waters next to them in playful gestures toward the gentle giants.

And God said, "Let the land produce living creatures according to their kinds." Then you see herds of animals moving and grazing along the Great Plains.

Then God said, "Let us make man in our own image, in our likeness, and let them rule over the fish of the sea and the birds of the air, over the livestock, over all the earth, and over all the creatures that move along the ground."

So God created man in his own image, in the image of God he created him; male and female he created them. And all you see of the man is his shadow moving on the ground along some beautiful shrubs and bushes that he passes.

God blessed them and said to them, "Be fruitful and increase in number; fill the earth and subdue it. Rule over the fish of the sea, and the birds of the air, and over every living creature, that moves on the ground."

Then God said, "I give you every seed-bearing plant on the face of the whole earth and every tree that has fruit with seed in it. They will be yours for food. And to all the beasts of the earth and all the birds of the air and all the creatures that move on the ground—everything that has the breath of life in it. I give every green plant for food." And it was so. God saw all that he had made, and it was very good, and there was evening, and there was morning—the sixth day. Thus the heavens and the earth were completed in their entire vast array.

By the seventh day God had finished the work he had been doing, so on the seventh day he rested from all his work. And God blessed the seventh day and made it holy, because on it he rested from all the work of creating that he had done.

# ADAM AND EVE, 100 PERCENT HUMAN

Genesis 2:7 tells us the Lord God formed man from the dust of the ground and breathed into his nostrils the breath of life, and he became a living being. The detailed image of man is that he had pure white hair, like snowcapped mountain peaks, which included every hair on his body. He had sapphire blue eyes that reflected the beauty of great oceans, as if viewed from space by God for many centuries. Not a brown speck could be found in man's eyes, even if you had used the Hubble telescope to look into them. His skin was pale, clear as a flawless cloud in all its whiteness, not a freckle or brown spot of pigment to be found on it anywhere, and not a sickle cell in his entire body. Nor could 100% pure humans pass this sickle cell trait on to their children, because it was genetically impossible, it wasn't configured in their genome.

Men could pass on to their children only what they were made of, which in turn meant that all people were born virtually 100 percent identical—like twins, only small differences set them apart. The only practical way to distinguish people from one another in those days was by size, shape, voice, or altered marks upon the body. Imagine, if you can, having to look at a group of the first humans on earth, and trying to distinguish one from the other. It would have been like looking at a large herd of zebras, and then trying to identify a certain one from a photo just handed to you to pick out that very one. This is how much they all looked like, imaged from the likeness of the Lord, who created us. Revelation 1:14 says his head and hair were white like wool, as white as snow—freshly driven snow—and his eyes were like a flame of fire; alcohol burns a blue flame.

Then there in the Garden of Eden you see Adam counting and naming the animals as the Lord had instructed him. Adam made many friends among the animals that he named, even the larger, ferocious-looking ones. Though he made many friends of them, he still felt alone. He saw that all the animals of the garden had a mate of the opposite gender they usually associated with; this made him lonelier, not having a direct companion and suitable helper. God saw that the man was in need of a companion. So God caused the man to fall into a deep sleep. Then God took a rib bone from the man and created a woman. Man awoke and God brought the woman before him, and then Adam, upon seeing the woman, said, "This is now bone of my bone and flesh of my flesh; she shall be called woman, for she was taken out of man." She had all the pure white features of the man; they looked nearly the same except for the features of her female gender.

For this reason a man will leave his father and mother and be united to his wife, and they will become one flesh. The man and his wife were both naked, and they felt no shame. (Genesis 2:20-25)

They lived in the garden together as one, and he informed her of all the things that God had told him, especially about not eating from the Tree of Knowledge. There for a while they lived happily in the Garden of Eden and prospered.

Now in the garden there was a serpent craftier than any of the animals the Lord had made. (Geneses 3:1-13).

> He said to the woman, "Did God say, 'You must not eat from any tree in the garden'?"
>
> The woman said to the serpent, "We may eat fruit from the trees in the garden, but God did say, 'You must not eat fruit from the tree that is in the middle of the garden, and you must not touch it, or you will die.'"
>
> "You will not surely die," the serpent said to the woman. "For God knows that when you eat of it your eyes will be opened, and you will be like God, knowing good and evil."
>
> When the woman saw that the fruit of the tree was good for food and pleasing to the eye and also desirable for

gaining wisdom, she took some and ate it. She also gave some to her husband, who was with her, and he ate it. Then the mind's eyes of both of them were opened. And they realized that they were naked, so they sewed fig leaves together and made coverings for themselves.

Then the man and the woman heard the sound of the Lord God as he was walking in the garden in the cool of the day, and they hid amongst the trees of the garden from the Lord God, whose image looked just like them. But the Lord called the man, "Where are you?"

He answered, "I heard you in the garden and I was afraid because I was naked, so I hid."

And he said, "Who told you that you were naked? Have you eaten from the tree that I commanded you not to eat from?"

The man said, "The woman that you put here with me—she gave me some of the fruit from the tree and I ate it."

One can only imagine that during Adam's explanation of why he ate the fruit, Eve must have been nervously waving with hand gestures, to signal for him not to mention her name to God, but once he did, she felt mortified, and utterly betrayed, as she sought to counter him by telling her version of how the serpent influenced her in much the same way. (Genesis 3:14-24)

Then the Lord God said to the woman, "What is this that you have done?"

The woman said, "The serpent deceived me and I ate."

So the Lord said to the serpent, "Because you have done this.

"Cursed are you above all the livestock and all the wild animals! You will crawl on your belly and you will eat dust all the days of your life.

"And I will put an enmity between you and the woman, and between your offspring and hers; he will crush your head, and you will strike his heel."

To the woman he said, "I will greatly increase your pains in childbearing; with pain you will give birth to children. Your desire will be great for your husband and he will rule over you."

To Adam he said, "Because you listened to your wife and ate from the tree about which I commanded you, 'You must not eat of it,'

"Cursed is the ground because of you; through painful toil you will eat of it all the days of your life.

"It will produce thorns and thistles for you, and you will eat the plants of the field.

"By the sweat of your brow you will eat your food until you return to the ground, since from it you were taken; for dust you are and to dust you will return."

Adam named his wife Eve, because she would become the mother of all the living.

The Lord made garments of skin for Adam and his wife and clothed them. And the Lord God said, "The man has now become like one of us, knowing good and evil. He must not be allowed to reach out his hand and also take from the tree of life and eat, and live forever."

So the Lord God banished him from the Garden of Eden to work the ground from which he was taken. After he drove the man out, he placed on the east side of the Garden of Eden a cherubim and a flaming sword flashing back and forth to guard the way to the tree of life.

# CAIN AND ABEL

Adam lay with his wife, Eve, and she became pregnant and gave birth to Cain. DNA states 100% human + 100% human = 200 /2 = 100% human offspring produced. She said, "With the help of the Lord I have brought forth a man." (Genesis 4:1-7) Inside a cave next to a warm lit fire with her husband beside her, she held the child to her breast to give warmth, and nursed him. Later she gave birth to his brother Abel. She nursed and held him in much the same way. You could see Adam tending a fire and showing little Cain, a large toddler now, how to add twigs to the fire to maintain it as Adam stacks the logs on the fire to keep them all warm. Both of the boys were born with pure white hair, as white as freshly fallen snow that blankets the ground and has never been tread upon, and like their youthful parents, they would keep it for the rest of their lives.

Abel kept the flocks while Cain worked the soil. In the course of time Cain brought some of the fruits of the soil as an offering to the Lord. But Abel brought fat portions from some of the firstborn of his flock. The Lord looked with favor on Abel and his offering, but Cain and his offering he did not look at with favor. So Cain was very, very angry, and his face was downcast. (Gen. 4:1-4)

Then the Lord said to Cain, "Why are you angry? Why is your face downcast? If you do what is right, will you not be accepted? But if you do not do what is right, sin is crouching at your door; it desires to have you, but you must master it." Cain was riddled with indecision and deceit on how to handle his dilemma with pleasing God. (Gen. 4:5-7)

Now Cain said to his brother Abel, "Let's go out to the field." And while they were in the field, Cain attacked his brother Abel and killed him. (Gen 4:8) There have unfortunately been many murders since then, though none seems to have had the significance of this one, not only because it was the first one, but also because of the scene of it. The sight of Abel, a full-grown young man with pure white hair as white as a snowcapped mountain looking defiled, splattered and soaked with the redness of his blood! It was enough to send chills down most anyone's spine. Imagine the horrific sight that Adam must have beheld when he came upon Abel and saw the alarming red color that today is recognized as a danger signal, mixed within the whiteness of his son's hair.

The contrast must have been a hundred times more alarming than any red stoplight or danger cautioning sign. At first glance Adam most not have been able to tell which one of his sons was lying there before him in that stricken state without a closer view. He had to have pondered in his mind with each carefully placed step closer to his son, as though the ground might crack or break open, as though he were walking on thin ice while looking at this terrible, gut-wrenching sight. He wondered whether it was a serious injury or much worse than he perceived. But through his agonizing denial of the worst, he quickly found out the meaning of death, by means of the limp body of his son Abel, who had been cut down in his youthfulness.

Then the Lord said to Cain, "Where is your brother Abel?" (Gen 4:9)

"I don't know," he replied. "Am I my brother's keeper"?

The Lord said, "What have you done? Listen!" The Lord God allowed Cain to hear the horrific sound of terror that was made by the sound of the blood spilled onto the ground. It must have been a defining sound that immobilized Cain in his tracks, as he realized beyond all decree that he was guilty of murder, even more evident than being caught in the act by many witnesses. "Your brother's blood cries out to me from the ground," God said. "Now you are under a curse and driven from the ground, which opened its mouth to receive your brother's blood from your hand. (Gen 4:9-11)

"When you work the ground, it will no longer yield its crops to you. You will be a restless wanderer on the earth."

Cain said to the Lord, "My punishment is more than I can bear. Today you are driving me from the land, and I will be hidden from your presence; I will be a restless wanderer on the earth, and whoever finds me will kill me." (Gen 12-15)

But the Lord said to him, "If anyone kills Cain, he will suffer vengeance seven times over." For Cain had shed innocent blood and murdered because he wanted the love of the Lord as his brother Abel had received. Thus he killed for the love of the Lord, not for silver or gold, but for something far more precious. The worst, though, was not obeying instead of doing the rightful thing, as the Lord had commanded. Then the Lord put a mark on Cain so that no one who found him would kill him.

So Cain went out from the Lord's presence and lived in the land of Nod, east of Eden. Now you see Cain running with all his might. His pure white hair was dirty, from where he had fallen many times over because of fatigue, by losing his balance. He escaped from the land and the people he loved outside the Garden of Eden, where in the distance you can see the cherubim that is still guarding the entrance to the garden as well as the tree of life with the sword flashing back and forth after all these many years.

Next you see Adam walking back to the cave with Abel's body draped in his arms like limp linen cloth while Eve sits there nursing a baby girl about ten months old in her arms. She stands as they approach. She is horrified at the site of Adam bringing Abel home like this, so she falls to her knees while clutching her infant female child with pure white hair. Then she breaks down and cries out for her son. The child can sense the distress from its mother, Eve, and the child's face expresses a frightened bewildered look. She virtually has no concept of life or death to reason with, though her instinct tells her something is seriously wrong. The child begins to cry once Eve lets out a high-pitched moaning sound of remorse, pain, and pity for her slain son. Adam continues walking into the cave with Abel in his arms without saying a word, but the redness in his eyes from previously crying tells the story that he cannot as he disappears into the cave.

# CAIN BANISHED

(Genesis 4:16) Cain traveled for a many days eating of the brush, which he foraged through, while dodging vicious-looking creatures along the way. He came upon a valley that seemed like it had a vast richness of fruit. He thought that perhaps the Lord God was being forgiving toward him for a moment, and possibly he could return home someday, but this was to be his domain forever. The Lord was providing for Cain, but his punishment was to stay put, as the Lord had commanded. Soon he reached the edge of the tree line with waterfalls in the background of this huge forest of fruity, delicious nectar that would have satisfied Adam and Eve outside the Garden of Eden. *How could this be my punishment?* he must have thought. Though nothing he planted would grow from the ground for him, he thought he wouldn't even need it in this lush paradise, where he could not see the ends of the tree line from one end of the valley to the other. It seemed like the fruit trees went on into the mountains from one side to the other and deep into the valley.

He almost smiled for an instant, something he hadn't done in many days, since he had left his homeland and family behind with nothing but memories to cherish of them. But there was one memory that he did not want to remember, though it made him often think of the love that he had for his brother and the good times that they used to have as boys, though it always ended the same way with the realization of the tragic, heinous atrocity he had committed. He could never face his family ever again, to look into their eyes, for he shuddered at the thought of it the first couple of times.

The trance of his dreamlike state was interrupted only by hunger pains, which radiated from his stomach because of the natural sweet smell of nectar that dominated his nostrils with a pleasing scent. Cain proceeded to eat his fill, and he carried many varieties of fruit, filling both arms just as full as he could. The trees here grew in many small groves with different types of fruits. He had never been able to gather fruit this easily before back home. Surely this place had many more advantages than tilling the soil, and he raced from tree to tree. He settled down to eat his fruit and then napped, because he was weary from his journey.

He awoke shortly to explore the beauty of this nectar-rich garden. The brush around the trees became denser and denser, covering almost anything shorter than four feet high off the ground, as he walked deeper into the forest. There seemed to be a small opening in the trees by which brilliant sunlight showed through some of the branches. Cain figured to go there and warm himself in the sun, but as he neared a cluster of brush, it shook violently once. It startled Cain, who instantly froze, so as not to frighten whatever it was that had just frightened him. Cain nervously scanned the brush with his eyes back and forth. His eyes locked onto a pair of darker eyes that had already been peering from inside the bush at him.

All of a sudden, a huge four-hundred-plus-pound silverback bull gorilla charged at him, snarling and growling in a ferocious tone that echoed raw power. Cain fell back against the base of a huge fruit tree, where he let out a frightful high-pitched cry almost like a woman's scream.

"Ah!" Cain exclaimed as the menacing beast stood towering over him, ready to pounce and rip him limb from limb to leave him for dead, to protect its tribe. Cain looked up into the eyes of the beast, frightened, while it beat its chest to challenge as well as provoke Cain into a fight to the death. At that moment it looked like Cain was done for, but instinctively he threw his arm up to protect his head. When he did so, it swept all the long pure white hair back from his adult face. The irate beast saw the mark that God had placed upon Cain's forehead. It instantly stopped, like it had been frozen into its position, totally transfixed by the mark Cain revealed. The gorilla snorted and slowly backed up while scanning Cain's entire body. After only a few steps backward, the huge gorilla turned and quickly ran deep into the dense forest.

16

Then Cain saw at least a dozen other gorillas of various shapes and sizes run off behind the large beast deep into the thick underbrush of the woods. The only thing that had saved Cain was the mark on his forehead. Minutes later, after feeling safer, Cain got up and went to a pool near the waterfall to see what the gorilla had seen on him that had frightened it off.

Cain reached the water's edge of a huge lagoon that looked like a master craftsman had designed it. He leaned over the edge to see his reflection in the clear pool, where he made a grim discovery about the mark on his forehead that repulsed even himself. He looked at what seemed more like a growth that had developed there; it was enough to bring tears to his eyes, but he got over the shame of it as the days went by. Then he began to notice that the gorillas were becoming a more regular sight now, but he did not mingle with them, because he still had some fear of the dominant male that ran the clan. Cain was not completely sure if the gorilla was just trying to frighten him off or if the mark had indeed deterred him, but Cain was about to find out the true power of the mark on his forehead, because at that instant a large jungle cat—a tiger—came to attack the primate clan.

Cain heard the commotion of the apes yelling and screaming, and he stood to his feet. Quickly all the apes climbed up the nearby trees to safety. Cain was left alone standing on the ground when the large cat spotted him. He was cornered in a wide-open clearing in the forest with all the other apes looking on from their safe havens, while expecting that he would be shredded to pieces by the stalking tiger. It crouched low to pounce on top of Cain, but once again he threw his arm up to block the cat, exposing his forehead. The big cat growled as it went to jump, but it saw the mark on Cain's forehead and stopped in the middle of its leap, which made it look like a short lunge forward.

The big cat then turned and ran, leaving Cain standing there with his eyes closed and still anticipating the pounce. Cain opened his eyes slowly, only to discover that the big cat was running away from him. He was bewildered and started feeling the mark on his forehead once again with his hands. Soon the apes began to feel safe at the sight of Cain, who had scared the big cat out of the forest. He knew now what the Lord God had said was true: no one would kill Cain, lest he be punished seven times over.

Cain soon became accepted among the ape clan, as he ate with them and found that the younger ones would follow after him from time to time. This close to humanlike tribe became his adopted family. It would have been a lot more pleasant had they had the ability of human speech. He found that he truly missed the interaction of human intellectual conversations; it felt like he'd been deserted on a drifting distant asteroid.

Many years passed with the coming and passing of many members of this primate tribe. Cain cut the long, pure white hair from his forehead as a way to be prepared against attacks from other creatures. Predators seeking primate blood came calling into the woods less and less because of Cain, and whether he wanted it or not, some apes looked to him for leadership in the group. Cain had officially become the "Great White Ape"—*the Great Pure White Ape, in fact.*

In those years Cain noted all the habits of the gorillas, especially their mating courtships. Strangely enough, most of their interactions seemed odd to him, but he picked up on their courting rituals so instinctively that he knew when females were courting the male apes for mating. Cain had never seen Adam or Eve doing these types of acts before. They had made sure to keep it secret from their children for many reasons. He called out unto the Lord God, who could hear him but would not answer, for Cain was lonely. He began to become aroused by this primate action, while wondering why it made him feel this way. He called again unto the Lord God, but he would not answer, because Cain had to fulfill his debt of punishment the Lord God had set him up for.

# THE FAMILY TREE
# BRANCHES OUT

Once while Cain was wrestling with one of the apes he instinctively sensed that she was in her mating courtship period. Cain *felt* aroused in a sexual nature, but he soon got up and left, feeling ashamed. Some time went by, and Cain found himself more and more aroused, even when he was on his own or watching the apes mating. Cain became very depressed and lonely for human companionship. No telling what he would have done for a blond-haired woman named Jane Goodaul, who befriended the apes, but blondes could not exist until Cain had completed the shameful act that he was to commit.

Cain followed a young courting female ape into the thick brush of the forest. You could see him looking back behind himself, to see if anyone might be looking. He saw no one, but God was there; he saw Cain at his lowest point of humanity. Then the bushes started to shake while he and that ape moaned and groaned to the point of exhaustion. Cain fornicated with an animal, a practice some men still carry on today.

Now Cain sat high up in a tree upon a large branch with his head bowed low between his legs. You could see birds migrating in the background as a bright red sun set on the distant horizon of the mountains just as night began to fall on the earth once again. He felt much remorse for the actions that he had committed against God and humanity—all of them, especially the one against his brother that had put him here in the first place. He pondered the thought in his head, *Why did I not listen to the Lord God and do right in the first place, by giving the best of my first fruit offerings as required of man?* He certainly would have given all the yield of his field for the Lord God to set everything back straight now, as it was before, because with the Lord God, all things are possible.

Cain found it easier and easier to lie with the apes when he became aroused, with less and less remorse to make his conscience ache. He felt lonelier than ever, and many years went by while he sought a word with God to plead his case, but he was not heard.

One day while walking along in the forest amongst the apes, Cain literally came face to face with his own shame when he happened upon the nesting spot of one of the nursing female apes in the brush. A feeling of discontent rushed through his entire body as his face sagged with the expression of guilt. There in the arms of this docile creature was a nursing half-man, half-ape newborn. DNA states 100% human + 0 combined with 100% primate + 0 = 100 / 2 = 50 + 100 / 2 = 50 for a fused genome of 50/50% human, primate offspring produced. Cain became transfixed with ignominy in his tracks and then he bolted like before, when God had banished him from the homeland of his people. He ran to the edge of the forest, where he dropped to his knees and began to cry by calling out unto God.

"Why hast thou forsaken me so? It would have been better if thou had slain me seven times over." Cain paused for a moment to think about his dilemma, which had brought him to this sorry end, and then he rolled onto his back to lie prostrate upon the ground. He felt mentally and emotionally drained; he stayed that way for most of the day while pondering his life, which was sinking lower and lower into the epitome of disgrace.

Many years had passed by now, and Cain saw the offspring of his own creation come forth, 50 percent human 50 percent primate. They seemed much like the rest of the apes: hair covered most of their body, and to him they lacked much of the intelligence of man. Sickle cells generated in their blood as a result of the genetic mutation that had changed the nucleotide in their genome, which arranged the DNA compositions of their bodies to mark their *Homo sapiens* transformed genetics. Cain had not one sickle cell in his entire body, like Adam, Eve, Abel, and the sisters who were born as well.

That means man did not evolve from the sea, by starting out as a single-cell amoeba, but in fact man started out 100 percent human, the creation of God, and has now transformed within a century into the *Homo sapiens* that we are today.

One day as Cain sat on the branch of a tree looking out at the horizon; he called out unto the Lord God in loneliness again, hoping to hear a voice answer.

"Lord God, hear Cain now. Answer my cry."

"Cain!" he heard a strange voice call back unto him. The voice came from below him. It was not the voice of God that he had heard before, but the voice of one of his own creations. He looked down at it in astonishment as it repeated his name once again.

"Cain," it said to him. He was amazed that it had a form of speech. It was female, though she had no name. Cain recognized her as the first offspring he had seen with the nursing ape in the brush many years before, which had made him, run off in shame to the edge of the woods. There he had collapsed from fatigue, knowing he had created it.

He looked at it more closely; he could see more of her human side as he looked at her. The closer he came to her, the more she began to submissively squat into a fetal position before him, out of respect for his male dominance, as most creatures of habit do.

"What did you say?" Cain asked, but she was hesitant to speak now, mostly because she feared she had done something wrong.

"Did you call my name?" he asked once more of her. She started to loosen up with slight movements of her head as she glanced timidly into his eyes. Then she spoke again.

"Cain," she said, almost reluctantly this time.

"You did, you said my name. Yes! My name is Cain—Cain, that's right!" He was reeling with emotion while trying to get her to say more words, because he had been calling out to God in loneliness, needing someone to talk to. *Cain* was the only word she knew at that time.

As time went on, Cain taught her many more words of his language. Her entire vocabulary was a little more than a hundred words, which included the names of certain animals. Her breasts and reproductive organs were more like that of a human female, but hair covered more than 95 percent of her body. Unlikely as it was, Cain found companionship in her, even with the limited conversations that she was able to provide for him. Although a far cry from what he wanted, she was better than nothing at all.

Cain went to speak to God once again, though he knew that he would not answer him. Cain sensed that God was listening all along, and he was, so Cain said, "As thou hast taken Eve from the flesh of Adam, to create him a wife and companion. Now thou hast created from the flesh of Cain a wife, and companion." Then, as it says in (Genesis 4:17), Cain lay with his wife, and she became pregnant, giving birth to Enoch. DNA states 100% human + 50 human, combined with 50% primate + 0 = 150 / 2 + 50 / 2 = 75/25% human, primate genome offspring produced. He was born with ebony-colored skin, and curly black hair on his head with eyes as dark as black pearls. Cain held him, they looked like ebony and ivory keys side by side on a piano, in harmony. He was mostly hairless throughout his body, like Cain. When Cain held him, they looked like ebony and ivory keys side by side on a piano, in harmony.

Cain was then building a city, which he named after his son Enoch. Cain lived many years and had many children. He found that all he expected of himself, they could do if he asked it of them. He found that they were obedient and gave him much respect before he passed on. His children buried him, and they became the forefathers of many.

One day after the passing of Cain, one of his descendants named Lamech, while out hunting for food in the outer rim of his territory, was spied upon by a group of young men from the tribe of pure white humans who were the direct descendants of Adam. When the young men spotted Lamech, they were bewildered at the sight of him and said, "Look! Do you see the man creature that walks about? What can it be?" Then one of the other young men with them, who was lacking wisdom, said, "Let us kill it, so we will be heroes like our fathers. Then that man creature cannot go tell the others of its kind, where we live, and therefore may not come back to attack us with many." So they pursued Lamech, and wounded him with an arrow. Lamech tired to outrun them as he thought, *Why are they pursing me? What have I done?* though because of his wound they started to gain on him. He hid amongst some brush to save himself, as the pursuers had lost sight of him. Later one of the younger trailing pursuers unfortunately happened to stumble upon his hiding place, and before he knew it, Lamech had thrust a knife into his heart and killed him.

(Genesis 4:23) says that Lamech was disturbed because he was a young man with much life left to live. Lamech fled back to his home, where he told his two wives, Adah and Zillah, all that had happened.

In (Genesis 4:1-2) God said that Adam created Cain and Abel, but did he say he had done it in his own image? No, because it was a given fact! Then in (Genesis 4:25) Adam lay with Eve again and she gave birth to Seth, whom she said God granted to them because Cain killed Abel. But in (Genesis 5:1-3) says Adam at 130 years of age created a son in his own likeness, in his own image, and named him Seth, to distinguish between the offspring of Cain, who were of dark skin, and Seth, who had pure white hair and skin from birth until death with sapphire-blue eyes like his brothers Cain and Abel.

Cain is the missing link between men and ape, and the world would be lost until this discovery of the sickle cells that mark this event.

This is the lineage of Adam and Eve.

# ADAM AND EVE

Seth and Cain

When Adam had lived 130 years, he had a son in his own likeness named Seth. Adam lived 800 years and had other sons and daughters. Altogether Adam lived 930 years, and then he died. When Seth was 105 years, he became the father of Enosh. Seth lived 807 years and had other sons and daughters. Altogether Seth lived 912 years, and then he died. When Enosh had lived 90 years, he became the father of Kenan. Enosh lived 815 years and had other sons and daughters. Altogether, Enosh lived 905 years, and then he died. When Kenan had lived 70 years, he became the father of Mahalalel. And after he became the father of Mahalalel, Kenan lived 840 years and had other sons and daughters. Altogether Kenan lived 910 years, and then he died. When Mahalalel had lived 65 years, he became the father of Jared. And after he became the father of Jared, Mahalalel lived 830 years and had other son and daughters. Altogether Mahalalel lived 895 years, and then he died. When Jared had lived 162 years, he became the father of Enoch. Jared lived 800 years and had other sons and daughters. Altogether, Jared lived 962 years, and then he died. When Enoch had lived 65 years, he became the father of Methuselah. Enoch walked with God 300 years and had other sons and daughters. Altogether Enoch lived 365 years. Enoch walked with God; then he was no more, because God took him away. When Methuselah had lived 187 years, he became the father of Lamech. Methuselah lived 783 years and had other sons and daughters. Altogether Methuselah lived 969 years, and then he died. When Lamech had lived

182 years, he had a son: he named him Noah and said, "He will comfort us in the labor and painful toil of our hands caused by the ground the Lord has cursed." After Noah was born, Lamech lived 595 years and had other sons and daughters. Altogether Lamech lived 777 years, and then he died. After Noah was 500 years old, he became the father of Shem, Ham, and Japheth.

Adam had Cain and Abel. Abel died, and Cain was banished to Nod, where he took a wife. Cain had a son he called Enoch. Cain was then building a city named after his son Enoch. To Enoch was born Irad, and Irad was the father of Mehujael. Mehujael was the father of Methushael, and Methushael was the father of Lamech. Lamech married two women, one named Adah and the other named Zillah. Adah gave birth to Jabal; he was the father of those who lived in tents and raised livestock. His brother's name was Jubal; he was the father of all who played the harp and flute. Zillah also had a son, Tubal-Cain, who forged all kinds of tools out of bronze and iron. Tubal-Cain's sister was Naamah. Lamech said to his wives, "Adah and Zillah, listen to me; wives of Lamech, hear my words. I have killed a man for wounding me, a young man for injuring me. If Cain is avenged seven times, then Lamech seventy-seven times."

# MAN'S FALL FROM GRACE

When man began to increase in number on the earth and daughters were born to them, the sons of God saw that the daughters of men were beautiful, and they married any of them that they chose. Then the Lord said, (Genesis 6:1-5) "My Spirit will not contend with man forever, for he is mortal / his days will be a hundred and twenty years." The Nephilim were on the earth in those days—and also afterward—then the sons of God came as giants to the daughters of men, and after that they had many children by them. They were the heroes of old, men of renown as their knowledge far exceeded mere men, but no matter how pure in whiteness they were, their ways were corrupt and they so infected the people.

The Lord saw how great man's wickedness on earth had become, and that every inclination of the thoughts of his heart was only evil all the time. The Lord was grieved that he had made man on earth, and his heart was filled with pain. So the Lord said, "I will wipe mankind, whom I have created, from the face of the earth—men and animals and creatures that move along the ground, and birds of the air—for I am grieved that I have made them." But Noah found favor in the eyes of the Lord. (Gen 6:6-8)

Noah was a righteous man, blameless among the people of his time, and he walked with God. Noah had three sons: Shem, Ham and Japheth. (Gen 6:9-10)

Now the whole earth was corrupt in God's sight, and was full of violence. God saw how corrupt the earth had become, for all the people on the earth had corrupted their ways. So God said to Noah, "I am going to put an end to all the people, for the earth is full of violence because of them. I am surely going to destroy both them and the earth. So make yourself an ark of cypress wood: make rooms in it and coat it with pitch inside and out. This is how you are to build it: The ark is to be 450 feet long, 75 feet wide and 45 feet high. Make a roof for it and finish the ark to within 18 inches of the top. Put a door in the side of the ark and make lower, middle and upper decks. I am going to bring floodwaters on the earth to destroy all life under the heavens, every creature that has the breath of life in it. Everything on the earth will perish. But I will establish my covenant with you, and you will enter the ark—you and your sons and your wife, and your son's wives with you. You are to bring onto the ark two of all living creatures, male and female, to keep them alive with you. Two of every kind of bird, of every kind of animal and of every kind of creature that moves along the ground will come to you to be kept alive. You are to take ever kind of food that is to be eaten and store it away as food for you and them."

Noah did everything just as God commanded him.

The Lord said to Noah, "Go into the ark, you and your whole family, because I have found you righteous in this generation. (Genesis 7:1,2) Take with you seven of every kind of clean animal, a male and its mate, most of these were the animals of their own herds, sheep cattle and oxen, considered clean that man feed upon. *It would make sense, so man would not need to hunt the wild herds in the beginning.* (Italics are mine) *That way they would out multiply the predators,* and take two of every kind of unclean animal, a male and its mate. *These were the predators that spilt blood, the lions, tigers, and bears and such,* also seven of every kind of bird, male and female, to keep their various kinds alive throughout the earth. (Gen 7:4) Seven days from now I will send rain on the earth for forty days and forty nights, and I will wipe from the face of the earth every living creature I have created.

Noah and his family had built the ark. It was a huge undertaking, and as Noah's sons grew, they became a great help to him. Even with the ridicule that they received from the other members of the pure white race who mocked and taunted them on a consistent basis for days on end, it became the focal point of the surrounding villages at that time. The mockers came and stood before them, hurling insults like stones at glass houses. Every one of them had snow-white hair with sapphire blue eyes, and very pale skin in the image of God. They looked like a sea of whiteness that laughed with every wave of jokes that pounded the shores of Noah's sanity, but he stood firm on his position of what the Lord had told him, even though his own family often doubted his works.

Noah was six hundred years old when the floodwaters came upon the earth, which meant that Japheth, the elder son, as in Genesis 10:21, was one hundred years old now, and his brothers near to him in age. The animals started to enter the ark, male and female of every kind. Now all the hecklers, who had been laughing and doubting Noah, slowly became skeptical of their own remarks at the sight of all the animals that had come from afar to enter the ark without being led by anyone that they could see with their own eyes. God had the leash of his command on them, an unbreakable lead that humbled them with obedience. The crowd formed around the ark to watch from a considerable distance as the huge predators, lions, tigers, and other such creatures entered. They witnessed the last of the most dangerous-looking beasts going inside. Then Noah called to the crowd, saying, "My brothers, the rains will come soon—this is the last chance for you to come on board. Will you not bring your families to safety with us?" But they laughed at him once more to make a louder mockery of him.

"Noah, you have all kinds of wild animals in there. You and your family are doomed to fill the bellies of the big cats and other dangerous things you have inside," they said.

"Which of you will come before I close the door? For once it is closed, I cannot reopen it," said Noah. Silence fell over the entire crowd as they peered around at one another.

"No, you are a fool, Noah," someone shouted. Suddenly from behind the crowd, Noah noticed two figures in the distance walking toward the ark. As the two tall, dark figures got closer, Noah realized what they were, though he had never seen one in person before. The rest of the crowd noticed the intense look on Noah's face as he tried to make them out. One person turned to look, and then the rest of the crowd did the same. They also saw them approaching the ark, right through the middle of their crowd. Some were alarmed, but no one had any weapons with them, for they had come only to make fun of Noah and his family. Noah thought out loud to himself, "Can this be right?" Even his family members standing at the ark's door looked bewildered while shaking their heads no, as if to object. They thought that surely this was some kind of a mistake. But it was not, for God had called them as well.

"Look! The dark man creatures approach," an older man shouted, and the crowd parted wide while they made their way through to the ark's main door. It was the descendants of Cain, a male and female each making their way calmly through the crowd of pure white humans. Compared with Noah's relatives, it was like looking at two flies walking through a sugar bowl, and the crowd stayed their distance from them on both sides. Women grabbed up their smaller children in fright, but Noah remembered that God had said that none of the things aboard the boat would harm them. One of Noah's daughters stood at the door frightened, and then ran to tell her mother what she had just seen.

"Mother!" she cried in alarm as she ran. "It is the dark man creatures. Two of them are coming on board."

"They will kill us!" some in the crowd said in panic.

"Do not fear, for the Lord has called two of every kind, like its own," Noah shouted to the crowd. "He says no one will be hurt who climbs on board."

These strange humans walked to the top of the plank, where they stood before Noah. They were dressed in sheepskins, and neither said a word; they simply stood with silent, piercing stares on their faces. Their skin was as dark as charcoal, and the female was more shy, almost hiding behind the male. Then Noah waved them on board with a gesture of his hand.

"Ham, show them to a living space." Ham walked cautiously ahead to keep a good distance in front of them while leading the way as they followed along behind him to a place, where they would stay near the other creatures in the ark. The crowd of people outside began to speak and murmur amongst themselves. They were certain that they would not enter this ark now for any reason, especially since the creatures that they had only heard about, which had killed one of their young men, had entered the ark.

"Perhaps with the lions and tigers, but for certain now, none of us will get on there with you and those dangerous things that just came onboard," someone proclaimed. "Besides, the sun is shining brightly and there is not even a cloud in the sky, but inside I see a dark and cloudy future for you and yours, Noah. You and all your family are doomed to death." Suddenly from the background beyond the mountains, you could hear thunder. They all turned their attention to the horizon, where they saw bright flashes of lightning and dark clouds brewing over the mountains.

"I am sorry that none of you will come in, for once I have closed this door, it cannot be opened until the flood has subsided," Noah said while looking out over the crowd, which had reassembled as one group; they looked like a sea of pure whiteness once again as they stood before the ark.

"We shall see who feels sorry for whom when the rains are over," a man said. Some of the crowd turned to leave with doubtful minds and started heading back, wanting to beat the rain home, although a few others lingered on until the door of the ark would finally close while making their final smug comments. They were growing more and more doubtful, though, for with each sarcastic crack made now, God answered back with a crack of thunder and a flash of lightning that lit up the ever-darkening sky. It was like a floodgate had opened each time one of them heckled Noah and his family with malice.

"The sky has never been so dark in the middle of the day by rain clouds like this before, Father!" Japheth said worriedly, but he didn't sound as worried as the looks that overtook the faces of the remaining hecklers. Their faces were pure white, and there wasn't a freckle or brown age spot anywhere on their bodies. But somehow, after hearing those words from Japheth, they became a little whiter than they already were.

"Shem, you and Japheth seal the door tightly with pitch inside and out, exactly as I instructed you to do," Noah said, and they immediately hopped to the task of putting pitch on the edges of the huge plank door and the inside frame, which it was to seat against.

One woman outside looked to her husband and said, "It looks like the storm clouds are coming this way." They could all see dense, dark clouds coming as it started sprinkling.

"I have called unto all of you with my last breath to save you. Now you are in God's hands," Noah said as he made his final plea. Then he walked inside the ark. For it was God's will that they not be saved, because of their mockery of sin toward him they possessed. The door was prepped with pitch for an airtight seal as the floodwaters came upon the land, rising faster and faster, as though a dam had burst in the sky. It collected to run off the land in huge waves in the distant background as it headed for them.

Down below, Noah's daughter ran to tell her mother that the dark man creatures they had heard so much about before had come onto the ark.

"Mother!" she panted as she got there. "Dark man creatures have come onto the ark."

"Dark man creatures! Are you sure?" Noah's wife exclaimed, and she stopped feeding the chickens.

"Yes, I overheard Father telling Ham as he went to find them living quarters."

"But they are dangerous! They have killed one of our kind before," exclaimed the other daughter.

"I know! I remember the story of the boys who brought back the body of their young friend saying that they were attacked by a dark man creature," Noah's wife said. Just as they looked up, Ham came walking by, looking very nervous and a little wide eyed as he passed his mother and wife, who was also his sister by blood. They stood motionless as the dark pair passed by. They seemed to be as menacing as a tiger to them as Ham led them to their living quarters for this mind-blowing voyage that seemed like childbearing labor—not wanting to go through with it, but at the same time wanting to get it over and done with.

# GOD'S SEALED PROMISE

When the huge plank door of the ark slammed close and the inside became nearly void of light, as if the sun had been eclipsed, every man, animal, and creature on the ark felt chills at the confinement of incarceration, which criminals sentenced for the first time do at penitentiaries after hearing their cell doors close. Then Noah lit a single torch in the area where his family gathered as the sound of thunder could be heard louder and louder. Then rain began to beat on the roof of the ark. The animals stirred, but they quickly settled with the rhythmic beating of the rain, which calmed all of them, including the people. No man spoke, and the animals hardly made a peep.

Hours later muffled voices of panicked pleas began to penetrate the walls of the ark from outside. "Noah! Please save us. Let us in, Noah!" cried out aunts, uncles, family members, and friends as they pounded their fists on all sides. His family inside looked to him for orders, for they knew he was a kind and reasonable man. He felt their stares looming upon him and said, "We cannot open the door or the pitch seal will be broken. That seal is like a covenant between the Lord, and us—it seals only once. We must obey his commands. If it is broken, so is the covenant. It will leak, and then we will not be under his protection—we would all surely drown." Noah proved he was also a logical man as well, and sometimes logic wins out over matters of the heart.

The voices continued to cry out from all sides of the ark as well as from the distant hills while swelling waves tore against the side of the ark. The waves knocked people down who tried to scale the slippery sides of smooth, wet pitch that covered the lumber of the ark like a slick diving wet suit. But it was all in vain, because the waters hampered their efforts while laying destruction to everything outside the ark. The voices outside began to fade one by one like the freezing survivors of the *Titanic*. The cries of babies were silenced as people short of breath clung to logs and trees for their very lives. They were worse off than the ones who had already drowned, for they would drift on the logs until starvation, cold, hypothermia, and the lack of willingness to live came to consume them.

Man and beast alike struggled to stand on the last bit of space above water on the peaks of the highest mountaintops. Many of the vanquished lay floating upon the ever increasing waters of the earth as rain steadily poured down on their lifeless bodies. To see mothers and children floating side by side with their pure white hair was devastating, the children just smaller versions of their parents, as the fish of the ocean, great and small, dined on their flesh. Some people floated with chunks of flesh missing from their bodies, so it was also with the herds of the ground while the seas continually consumed the land, and within two weeks the last of them would be gone.

Genesis 7:23 says, "Every living thing on the face of the earth was wiped out; men and animals and the creatures that moved along the ground and the birds of the air were wiped from the face of the earth. Only Noah was left, and those with him in the ark."

One might think it a shame to waste the flesh of the pure white race that we all came from, but the Lord is not a prejudiced God. He dispenses life and death with equality, but through Noah they would still live.

The members of the dark-skinned race, the seed of Cain, did succumb to the same fate as the members of the pure white race outside the ark. Their bodies floated upon the rising waters as well, but their heritage would also be saved alive through these two people, who shared the ark with Noah's family and all the rest of the creatures saved.

Everyone inside clung to something or steadied themselves as the ark swayed and dipped into a large pool of water as the ground gave way beneath it, because the rushing torrent swept away the soil it rested upon. Hearts pumped with uneasiness as the ark skimmed along the bottom for a few feet, as fearful thoughts of puncturing it below the waterline were raised. Just as all inside became expectant of the nerve-racking jolts and jerks of the large craft, it started to float smoothly along, unhindered now as the rains fell.

For much of the first couple of hours now, every living thing on the ark sat quietly and didn't make a sound. Then without warning, the ark took a downhill plunge as it went over a huge overspill and down into a large overflowed river. By now the river was a virtual boundless lake that was overflowing its banks into the ever-encroaching sea, to become the new bay. Now much of the earth was under water as the rains continued to fall. Soon it would all be under water.

At the first sign of light that peered through the clouds while still pouring out its raining fury, Noah told his sons to go and open the upper hatch to fill the many water barrels they had stored for collecting rainwater. When the hatch was opened, water that was collecting on the deck would run into the hatch and down a makeshift spout, quickly filling the barrels with the precious water they and the animals needed to drink.

They often wondered why the animals stayed in their pens, but of all the creatures on the ark, they were most curious about the dark-skinned man and woman. One day while Shem and Ham were filling water barrels with rainwater from off the deck, they lagged behind in their task of carrying the water barrels, for they had a lot of labor in caring for all the animals, and all the tasks seemed just too much for the two of them. Shem, who was working by himself at the moment, was struggling to change out a full water barrel with an empty one, as it was already overflowing onto the deck, when he heard a voice from directly behind him.

"Dost thou need help?" He quickly turned to find that the dark-skinned man creature was standing within an arm's length behind him. It caught him so off guard that he stumbled backward a few steps, for neither of the dark humans had ever spoken face-to-face with any of Noah's family before. As far as they knew, these creatures were mute and had no form of speech, but the fact was, they were just as leery of Noah and his family as Noah's family was of them. Shem ran calling to tell his father and brothers about what had just happened.

"Father!" he shouted. The whole family came running to see what was wrong with Shem; perhaps the first thought that raced through Noah's mind about Shem's cry was *Lord, we can't have sprung a leak that fast.* They all came as quickly as possible.

"What is the matter, Shem?" Noah asked as he reached him with the rest of the family members closely looking on.

34

"The, the dark man creature, it spoke to me! He asked me if I needed any help," Shem said, stuttering with all of them looking onward. Noah's entire family was in disbelief over Shem's claim, but Shem was known to be honest. "He did! Honest!" Shem exclaimed to all of them.

Then Noah said, "You women stay here. Come, my sons." They made their way back to where the dark-skinned man was standing, having already changed out the full water barrel with an empty one. Noah spoke first. "Do you speak our language? My son said that you spoke to him." He waited for a response from the dark-skinned man. A second or two went by and the dark-skinned man looked over at his female companion. Then he looked back at Noah, who hunched his shoulders and said, "I don't know. Perhaps you were wrong, Shem."

"It seems to me that you speak our language." They were all amazed to hear him speak so clearly and understandably. He had a different accent, but most of the words he spoke were exactly the same as Noah's—a few were different. Noah's wife and daughters were listening from nearby.

"They can speak!" one of the daughters exclaimed, though none of the men could hear her. Noah's wife commanded her not to speak, so she could listen.

"Quiet! I want to hear." Then she instantly quieted down as her mother instructed while Noah was talking with the dark-skinned man again.

"I apologize. I did not mean to offend," Noah said humbly. "But we have heard a story of one like you who attacked a young boy and killed him while out hunting." Then there was a moment of silence.

"We heard a different story. Tubal-Cain said mildly. While our father was out hunting in the outlands, he was attack by a group of young men with arrows that wounded him. They chased after him, and he killed one of them, and then he was sad, because the one he killed was a very young man with much life left." Then he said "If Cain is to be avenged seven times, Lamech will be avenged seventy-seven times."

"Cain!" Noah exclaimed in amazement to hear him mention his name. "You know of Cain?"

"Yes, Cain is the father of all our people," he said as they all looked transfixed by the words coming out of his mouth.

"If Cain is the father of thy people, then why do you not look like us, with pure white hair?" Everyone paused at the question, and then

35

it hit each one of them like a ton of bricks. It became obvious to all of Noah's family what had happened, so they skipped to the next question, but no one could think of what to say.

Suddenly the water started to spill over from the barrel that the dark-skinned man had replaced. Japheth grabbed the overflowing barrel with the help of Shem, and they started to move it out the way. The dark-skinned man, thinking quickly, grabbed another nearby empty water barrel and put it in the place of the one Shem and Japheth had moved out of the way to catch the rainwater that was pouring in from the open hatch. Noah saw potential in this dark man, who had obvious knowledge. Then he asked him if he had a name, for Noah knew that creatures on this planet did not give themselves names; only man did that.

"What is your name?" Noah asked him.

"My name is Tubal-Cain, the son of Lemech," he said.

"They have names!" the daughter said to her mother, who quickly shushed her once again.

"Thank you, Tubal-Cain," Noah said. "We would be appreciative of any help that you could give us, for the labor is more than we can bear."

"I would be honored to serve you," he said.

"How did you know to come here?" Noah asked.

"By a great calling of the spirit. I was making tools out of brass over a fire when it told me to stop working, bring my sister, and then go west with her. It led us here," he said as Noah's wife and daughters crept closer.

"This is great, Father! The Lord knew that we would need a skilled toolmaker when the floods end, and he has provided us with one," Japheth said.

"Then it is no mistake that you are here, for the Lord God has called you also to be saved," Noah said. "My name is Noah, and these are my sons, Shem, Ham, and Japheth, and my wife and daughters, who are their wives. Like you, my father's name was Lamech."

"This is my sister as well. Her name is Naamah, and she is also my wife. You will find that she is also a good worker and obedient. She will be very helpful with the women's labor," Tubal-Cain said.

"We are glad to have you aboard, for I called many unto the ark, but none except you came," Noah said with a sad heart. "It would seem that only those the Lord has had in mind would be here. Perhaps we will be good friends." Noah reached out to shake Tubal-Cain's hand.

"Yes, let it be so," Tubal-Cain said. They all felt at ease with one another; even Noah's wife and daughters were all smiles at the friendly gesture.

"It seems that they can be quite friendly," Noah's wife said quietly to her daughters as they came forth, and from that day on, they all worked as one unit. Noah divided up the chores equally amongst them all, as they found that the extra help, which came from the two who came on board last, was just enough to keep the labor from running morning until evening with breaks in between.

# MAN PULLING TOGETHER

The men moved the large barrels and bulk amounts of food for feeding large animals, while all the women tended to the smaller animals on board, and the grinding of wheat for bread, along with the cooking and baking. Daily the men would cast a net over the side to haul in a fresh catch of fish, which they used for themselves, as well as to satisfy the appetites of the big cats, bears, and some of the other meat-eating animals on board. The big cats, though, would often play and frolic around with their fresh catch, until the lively responses from the fish were all gone. Then they would consume them.

Once after hauling in an unusually heavy netted catch of fish from over the side—they always chummed the waters with the leftover pieces from the previous day—they could feel and hear a thud against the side of the ark, like they were bobbing up against a big tree or log perhaps. Then the men went to look over the side with the aid of what light showed through the rain clouds that refused to cease their relentless pour. To their surprise they saw a great-sized, land-walking creature, which looked much like some of the smaller lizards they had seen under rocks before; it spanned the entire length of the ark. None of them had ever seen a creature as enormous as this before. They had no idea that creatures even grew so large. Fish of all kinds were eating of it, from huge sharks to the tiniest of schools of fish. The waters had indeed been chummed, but mainly by the flesh of this enormous creature, giving them their best catch ever so far. Thus the creatures of the ocean benefited from the excess of land dwellers that had perished in the floodwaters. Then the men got back to their regular chores once again.

For many days and nights, the routine was the same, like the continuous rains of forty days and forty nights. All the life forms on board were aware that the rains had come to ebb, for it meant that at some point in time, this voyage would come to an end also. It was great to open the hatch and see pure sunlight through the opening, unaltered by clouds. Days later it started raining again, and everyone inside feared that they would endure another forty days of rain, increasing the time of their confinement aboard the ark. It lasted only a day, like the normal rainstorms they had known before, just long enough to refill the barrels full of fresh drinking water for all their needs. It would rain on and off to give fresh water for the rest of the voyage to sustain their very lives.

Long after the forty days of constant rain had stopped, the springtime of the year must have come, because the animals were in their mating season, and so were the young men and their wives, for there were a lot of pregnant females on board the ark now. Life had started to renew itself before the ark had settled on dry land. Noah could tell that all on board were weary with cabin fever, especially the female species, given their conditions, so he started to send out small birds in hopes to find out if there were any signs that the land was dry again, for he knew that this would help to lift the spirits of all on board.

Genesis 8:1 says, But God remembered Noah and all the wild animals and the livestock that were with him in the ark, and he sent a wind over the earth, and the waters receded." The floodwaters covered the earth for 150 days. The water receded steadily from the earth, and by the end of the 150 days the waters, had gone down. Then on the seventh day of the seventh month, the ark came to rest on the mountains of Ararat, on the northernmost part of the African continent, between the borders of Nigeria and Egypt. The waters continued to recede until the tenth month as the tops of the mountains became visible. This brought quite a bit of cheer to all on board; even the animals sensed it with the ark now rested.

After forty days Noah opened the window he had made in the ark and sent out a raven, and it kept flying back and forth, to see if the water had dried up from the earth. Then he sent out a dove to see if the water had receded from the surface of the ground. But the dove could find no place to rest its feet because there was water over all the surface of the earth, so it returned to Noah in the ark. He reached out his hand and took the dove and brought it back to himself in the ark. He waited seven more days and again sent out the dove from the ark. When the dove returned to him in the evening, there in its beak was a freshly plucked olive leaf. He waited seven more days and sent the dove out again, but this time it did not return to him.

By the first day of the first month of Noah's 601$^{st}$ year, the waters of the earth had dried up from the earth; Noah removed the covering from the ark and saw the surface of the ground was dry. By the twenty-seventh day of the second month, the earth was completely dry, and many female creatures on the ark were pregnant or had given birth to young, as the women did also, who all helped with the births of each other's babies.

# THE NEW WORLD

Then God said to Noah, "Come out of the ark, you and your wife and your sons and their wives. Bring out every kind of living creature that is with you—the birds, the animals, and all the creatures that move along the ground—so they can multiply on the earth and be fruitful and increase in number upon it."

Genesis 8:18 says that Noah came out, together with his sons, his wife, and his sons' wives. All the animals and all the creatures that move along the ground and all the birds—everything that moves on the earth—came out of the ark, one kind after another. He released the herds first to give them a chance to survive against the big cats, and then all the predators. Then the predators, who once out on their own found that there were many shallow lakes and pools created by the receding floodwaters, teeming with many types of fish that had been trapped. At that time, it was still easy for riverbanks to overflow with each new rain, to refill the shallow pools with more fish; then as the waters receded, the big cats and other predators feasted on the trapped fish, exactly the way the sea creatures feasted on the many land animals that perished in the consuming floodwaters day by day, until all the land dwellers outside the ark were gone.

One need only envision some tiger cubs trying to chase a dolphin trapped in a shallow pool next to a flowing river that led to a large bay, which opened into the sea. The cubs tried to tackle it, but the dolphin managed to elude them by skimming and lunging along in mere inches of water. The cubs frightened it into the direction of the running stream, where it plunged in. Thanks to these two cubs, which inadvertently saved it from being beached on dry land, it would now live to see another day back out in the ocean.

Other fish were not so lucky, such as the four-foot shark trapped by the big cats in another nearby shallow pool of water; clawing at it, they ripped its flesh to pieces until it no longer fought back, to provide them with a tasty meal. The bears, wolves, and all other meat-eating creatures did the same thing in the first days of release as God allowed the herds to multiply.

It is often said, "What goes around, comes around." Once the sea creatures feasted on the land dwellers, who perished in the floodwaters; now the land dwellers feasted upon the sea creatures trapped in the receding shallow pools.

After they had released all the animals back into the wilds, to flourish as they had before this voyage, there remained only Noah, his wife, their family, and the dark-skinned people with a few select animals used for farming. No one said much of a word to the other as they stood at the huge opening in the ark's doorway with inquiring looks in their eyes of "What next?" wondering what the next move was or what to do. Then Tubal-Cain said to his wife, Naamah, with discernment and heavyheartedness, "Let us go and find a place in the world that the Lord God has provided for us." Naamah breathed in a sigh of worry as she looked at him, but not wanting to debate her husband before the others, out of respect for him, she said nothing. He also had enjoyed the companionship of Noah and his family, but he would not impose by asking to stay. Naamah was worried, because she carried a newborn in her arms, and they would have to face the elements with no ready-made shelters or skins to cover the baby properly in good weather, never mind the often-rainy atmosphere they were in.

After coming to know them so well, their leaving had saddened Noah and his family. They were so different from what they had first thought they would be like. They had formed a bonding friendship with them, and it almost seemed like saying goodbye to a loving family member.

"Thank you all, for what you have done for us," Tubal-Cain said. "We will go now." Naamah just closed her eyes and nodded to them as she followed behind her husband. While she clutched her newborn child, who was wrapped in a single skin, to her breast to keep it as warn as possible, they headed for the long plank to walk out of the ark. Noah's wife turned to Noah and grabbed him by the arm while looking into his eyes; it said all that she could not say to him. Before Tubal-Cain and his family reached the huge opening in the side of the ark to walk out, Noah spoke up.

"Brother! Where shall thy go?" Both Tubal-Cain and his wife stopped to look at each other and then at Noah and his family, but they had no response. "Your skins are tattered like ours, and your child is nearly bare. How wilt thou survive the exposure to the weather? Please, if only for the sake of the child, stay with us, even if just for a little while?"

"You have saved our lives once already. I do not wish to be a burden to you or your family," Tubal-Cain said earnestly to all of them.

"If that is thine only concern, then ye need not worry, for all are glad to have you here," Noah said with everyone nodding in agreement. "Besides, with most of the animals gone, there is much room for many families now."

Naamah gave a pleading look of concern to her husband, urging him to say yes, and he looked back at her, realizing that this was the only obvious choice, so he walked forward to Noah and knelt before him to say, "This is the second time that you have saved me and my family. I will stay under one condition only." Noah seemed surprised that he would be making demands, as did all.

"And what is that?" Noah asked.

"That I and my family be servants in your house, to repay our debts for you saving us twice." Noah was surprised and touched by the gesture.

"Oh, no, my friend, thou need not be a slave in my house!" Noah said.

"It is the way of our people if someone saves your life. You owe them a debt that can never be repaid except by saving another's life." Noah looked at him with heavy eyes and accepted the terms with a response by nodding. Tubal-Cain and his family became good servants in the house of Noah, but more like dedicated children, and he referred to Noah that day after as Master Noah.

Noah was a good master himself, for he never gave Tubal-Cain more labor than he gave his own sons to do. Besides, Tubal-Cain had a special skill: he worked with brass metals and made tools, which they desperately needed in this new world to ease their chores of farming, hunting, and just about every other kind of laboring task. Noah seemed more like a fair foreman on a job site than a taskmaster, and his wife as well, for she never gave Naamah more instructions than she gave her own daughters. They all shared the harvest like one single family unit under the leadership of Noah, who built an altar to offer the first of all they harvested, clean animals and clean birds; he sacrificed burnt offerings on it like Abel did unto the Lord.

"The Lord smelled the pleasing aroma and said in his heart: "Never again will I curse the ground because of man, even though every inclination of his heart is evil from childhood. And never again will I destroy all living creatures, as I have done. As long as the earth endures, seed time and harvest, cold and heat, summer and winter, day and night will never cease" (Genesis 8:21).

"Then God blessed Noah and his sons, saying to them, 'Be fruitful and increase in number and—fill the earth'" (Genesis 9:1).

"'I now establish my covenant with you and with your descendants after you and with every living creature that was with you—the birds, the livestock and all the wild animals, *all those that came out of the ark with you*—every living creature on the earth'" (Genesis 9:9, italics are mine).

"And God said, 'This is the sign of the covenant I am making between me and you and every living creature with you, a covenant for all generations to come: I have set a rainbow in the clouds, and it will be the sign of the covenant between me and the earth'" (Genesis 9:12).

"So God said to Noah, 'This is the sign of the covenant I have established between me and all life in the earth.' The sons of Noah who came out of the ark were Shem, Ham, and Japheth. (Ham was the father of Canaan.) These were the three sons of Noah and from them came the people, *who were scattered over the earth*" (Genesis 9:17-19, italics mine).

Noah blessed the marriages in the name of the Lord God. Children were born to all who were on the ark.

The ark had provided many years of shelter from the weather for the small community that had grown within it, but soon its upkeep became more than it was worth, as it sagged in every direction, springing a newly discovered leak during every rainstorm. Noah, after a while, ordered that they all pitch tents to live outside for safety, because the ark might collapse onto their heads. They used whatever dry wood from inside the ark that they could find as fuel, for keeping the campfires burning. The wood from the sides and the roof of the ark was useless, for he and his sons had done their jobs well in coating the ark with pitch. But this was also part of God's plan: it meant the remains of the ark could be found many years later, because the pitch preserved the wood of the ark, as if it had sunk beneath the La Brea tar pits, for man to find in the twentieth century in the northern part of Africa.

> Noah, a man of the soil, proceeded to plant a vineyard. When he drank some of its wine he became drunk and lay uncovered inside his tent. Ham, the father of Canaan, saw his father's nakedness and told his brothers outside. But Shem and Japheth took a garment and lay it across their shoulders: then they walked in backwards and covered their father's nakedness. *With their faces turned the opposite way, so they would not see his body.* (Italics are mine).
>
> When Noah awoke from his wine and found out what his youngest son had done to him, he said,
>
> "Cursed be Canaan! The lowest of slaves will he be to his brothers."
>
> He also said,
>
> "Blessed be the Lord, the God of Shem! May Canaan be the slave of Shem.
>
> "May God extend the territory of Japheth; may Japheth live in the tents of Shem, and may Canaan be his slave" (Genesis 9:20-27)
>
> He had to serve alongside Tubal-Cain's family.

Noah must have wondered, *Why are my children so disobedient when the seed of Cain gives their father such respect?* scolding them for one's mistake. Canaan must have thought, *This is so unfair* of his grandfather's judgment, to make him a slave—even lower than that of the dark-skinned man—Tubal-Cain's family. Perhaps even Noah's wife thought it a bit harsh, too. Noah's mind was set, though, as he figured that this harsh example would prevent any such further disobedience, which conflicted with the ways of the Lord, from ever happening again.

But Tubal-Cain came to Noah in private later, asking, "Master Noah, may I speak with you about today?"

"Yes, Tubal-Cain. You may speak, my friend," Noah said.

"About your son, and his son. I am hoping that you did not give a hard punishment because you think my children are much more disciplined or to show that you will deal with your children more harshly, to make us feel accepted among you. For your kindness to us has been more than one could ask for."

"No, Tubal-Cain. I did not make the punishment harder because of you for any reason, but because the Lord God requires us all to be clean in his sight, and sexual immorality is the worst sin, other than willfully disobeying or dishonoring him. I did this to cut off any sexual fornication at all, for God accepted me over all my brothers, because my heart and mind were pure in thought, and not because of sexual immorality. There is a greater punishment from the Lord God for this sin. I did what I did not to hurt my children, but to save them, and on this matter I will deal with them all the same way, even yours."

"I understand," Tubal-Cain said as he hesitated to get up and leave.

"My friend, is there something else on your mind that I can help you with?" Noah inquired.

He sat back down before Noah, saying, "I should have known that you would sense something. I have a matter somewhat like you dealt with today, but on a different level."

"Yes, go on," Noah said.

"As you know, my oldest child—a daughter—has come of age. Her oldest male sibling—my son—is many years away from being ready for the responsibilities of manhood, and my wife and I thought that before she does something disappointing, perhaps—"

"Perhaps one of my sons would take her as a second wife?" Noah said calmly.

"Well, yes. She understands that the first wife has privileges of being first in marital matters."

"Which of my sons did you have in mind?" Noah asked.

"Since Ham is closest in age, and he just lost a son, perhaps him," Tubal-Cain suggested.

"No!" Noah said, and paused. Tubal-Cain wondered if his proposal had been indecent. "She deserves better. Ham has proven be unfit to raise the son that he had taken. I will ask Japheth first, my eldest; he will be offered first. I will let you know if he will have her," Noah said.

"Thank you. I will await your answer," he said as he got up to leave.

"I thank you, my friend, that you would consider one of my sons a good enough husband for your daughter," Noah said. "It means that I must have done something right as a father in raising them, and I needed that after today."

Then Tubal-Cain shook hands with Noah, saying, "It is no mistake that the Lord God saved you alive to repopulate the earth, for you are more than a good father: you are also God's good friend." And he left with those words of encouragement for Noah to ponder.

# THE FIRST BIRACIAL CHILD

Later Noah went and spoke to his sons, offering up the proposal that Tubal-Cain had made concerning the hand of his daughter to his son Japheth, who at the time was uncertain of what to say. After speaking to his wife and family, he agreed to accept the hand of Tubal-Cain's daughter as a second wife. Noah wed them, and she became pregnant. It was a good union, as she honored his first wife and her rights to her husband.

When the time came for her to birth the first child of this interracial marriage, everyone became mystified by one of Noah's pure white granddaughters asking a simple question.

"What's the baby going to look like?" Everyone was struck with awe! No one had even considered what the child might look like. They came up with all kinds of different speculations of how the new child might look—pure white hair like his, but dark skin like hers, white skin like his, but short, curly, dark hair like hers. Each offered up countless different black-and-white combined scenarios that would have made the child look like a zebra. Then his same little granddaughter offered up a simple explanation.

"Perhaps if it's a boy, it will look 100 percent pure white like him, but if it's a girl it will look 100 percent black like her," she said, and everyone agreed that this must be the obvious result as the mother's labor pains increased. Later that day inside a tent converted for birthing, where the first interracial child was being birthed through its mother's birth canal, a bewildered look overtook all of the women's faces present at the delivery as the child was born. To everyone's surprise it looked nothing like what any of them had predicted. Instead of 100 percent mixed images of black-and-white traits like a zebra, it was something of a blend of them all. The child's skin color was tan to light brown, like freshly cut wood, and had wavy, dark brown hair, neither straight nor curly. It was somehow unique, with its own features.

All present thought at first that perhaps something was wrong with the baby. Would it live? Had God done this to show his opposition to the marriage? Many illicit thoughts were lingering about in everyone's heads, and each person in the tent kept them concealed inside the vault of their own mind, like top-secret holdings at the Pentagon in Washington, D.C. Finally one of Noah's daughters broke her silence to ask, "Is it all right? It is stillborn or is it not?" Noah's wife cleaned the last of the waste out of its mouth, and then Naamah spanked the child's butt and it started to cry. It seemed healthy enough, by all normal standards. Then she handed it back to its mother, laying it across her bare breast to nurse.

"It seems to be fine healthwise. I think it's just a mix between our two people, but we'd better keep an eye on the child for the next couple of days, I suppose," Noah's wife said. She did not sound sure of herself, but none of them were as they passed on the news to the rest of the family members that a child had been born to unite the two families forever. Japheth already had sons in his image by his first wife; now he was informed that he had another son not in his image, and all seemed well. Noah's other son Shem came to bring him word of the child's birth in his tent. He announced himself first, which was now customary, since the incident with Ham.

"Father Noah, may I enter?" Shem said.

"Yes, my son."

"Father, the first mixed child of this world was born this day."

"A boy or a girl?" Noah asked.

"A strong healthy boy . . . I think," Shem said hesitantly.

"You could not tell whether it was a boy or a girl?"

"Well, I'm sure that it was a boy; it is the health of the child I'm not so sure about."

"Why? What's wrong with the child?" Noah asked as Shem stuttered around the specifics.

"He uh, um."

"Well, say it, for heaven's sake," Noah urged.

"The child came out looking like wood."

"The child was born a real live wooden boy!" Noah exclaimed, nearly horrified. "Oh, God, forgive me, for the union of our peoples is cursed by the devil! I should have never done this thing." Noah covered his face with both his hands in anguish.

"No, Father, I did not mean that the child is like wood from a tree. I merely meant that the child is the color of wood."

"Oh, praises be to God! The child's color of flesh does not matter, so long as this union is not cursed and produces fruitful souls for the Lord," Noah said while breathing a sigh of relief as he sat there on his mat. "Bring the child to me that I may bless it in the name of the Lord God as is customary." They brought the child to Noah around the campfire that evening, where he blessed the child in the name of our ever-living God, the creator of heaven and earth, with everyone watching.

"I offer this child up unto the Lord, which is good, to honor God with his life's work. Let this first mixed child be a symbol of our people serving the Lord as one tribe, to heal the wound of brother against brother started by Cain against Abel, to bring peace forth this day." And it was as he said for many years to come; no warring violence was upon the entire earth. No murder or rape was committed for more than a thousand years.

Noah handed the child to his father, Japheth, who hoisted him high into the air, saying, "I name him Tubal in honor of his grandfather Tubal-Cain, who is a friend to my father and helped to heal the wound of brother against brother before the flood came."

Then all came to touch and hold the baby, while passing him around and finally back to his mother. They all danced and ate around the campfire to celebrate not only the birth of a child, but the birth of a new family as well. The child grew and came to know one family. He had many other brothers and sisters after himself, like his full brother Javan. Many today would look and say they were mixed 50/50 of the 100 percent pure white human blood of Japheth and Tubal-Cain's daughter. Actually these children were made up of the 75 percent human blood, 25 percent primate—considered pure black blood of Tubal-Cain's daughter, plus the 100 percent of human blood from Japheth, which actually calculated out to approximately 87.5 percent human and 12.5 percent primate interracial children. The process of Kendihuchrodnamixgenesis caused him to become darker as he grew, to make him look like a form of Egyptian with fewer sickle cells in his blood than his mother, but far more than his 100 percent pure white father, Japheth, who had no sickle cells in his blood. Then Japheth had Javan, his second interracial son.

Noah grew older while the children kept coming forth—pure human or mixed. He continued blessing them in marriage and birth in the name of the Lord. The interracial children of Japheth who married pure white humans in descent produced children closer to white descent as they came forth, whereas ones who married blacker humans produced children closer to black in descent who came out with more sickle cells in their blood. The only other choice was to marry their full-blooded interracial sibling, because they were the first interracial family on the earth, after the flood.

Javan chose to marry a granddaughter of Noah's who was genetically 100 percent pure white. Javan and his pure white wife brought forth the next different species of interracial mix. When his wife lay there moaning with labor pain, about to give birth, they all started guessing again what the child might emerge looking like.

"Oh, they will all come out looking light brown like the first interracial children did," someone said. They all agreed with that theory of interracial conception, believing that they could produce only tan to light brown-skinned children with wavy hair no matter the parental mixture. But to their surprise, the child was not light brown skinned with wavy hair, and they all gasped at the sight of it.

"Oh, my Lord!" someone said as they blocked the view of its mother from the newborn baby, which made her nervous.

"My baby! What's wrong with my baby? Give me my baby!" she urged while still panting heavily. Her long, pure white hair was in a frizzle that draped onto the ground like Rapunzel as she struggled to her elbows upon the birthing mat to see the child. After tying off the umbilical cord, they lifted it for the mother to see. She was as amazed as everyone else present to see that the child had bright, fire-red hair. It's funny, knowing how superstitions can get started by something as simple as this, so Noah's wife, very elderly now, quickly said, "Oh, it's a beautiful little girl!" She said it to get everyone to agree before someone's imagination started entertaining the thought that this might somehow be the work of the devil, by cursing the child with fire-colored hair. The child cried as they laid her on her mother's pale, white bare breast with its pink nipple, for warmth from her mother's body, and they covered both mother and baby with a blanket. Everyone started nodding their heads yes, to acknowledge the comment that Noah's wife had made, and they added to her previous remark.

"Oh, how beautiful. She looks so adorable—with red hair like I have never seen before." Once babies become the center of attention in a room, all else seems to fade away. A man can't help but feel that all this comes from the sympathy of other women feeling the pain that the laboring mother just bore by delivering this precious gift of life into the world. Most men, however, unless they're the fathers of the child, would look and say. "Okay, it's healthy—job well done, Dad." The usual differences of "You're from this planet and I'm from that one" is the reasoning one would guess; besides, women naturally bond better with children. The child was 93.75 percent human and 7.25 percent primate with fewer sickle cells than its interracial father, Javan, but still much more than its 100 percent pure white mother, but growing through the Kendihuchrodnamixgenesis DNA tug-of-war process to reach adulthood changed her eye color from blue to a bluish green—her hair from red to a darker brownish color.

Shem came calling to Noah at his tent again, to tell him about the child. Noah was getting older now, and his hearing was not as accurate as before.

"Father," Shem called.

"What is it, Shem?" he asked.

"Another mixed child was born today, a girl this time."

"Was it born healthy like the others?" Noah asked.

"Well, the child was born with hair like fire," he explained with uncertainty in his voice, but what Noah heard was slightly different.

"The child was born with fire for hair, you say?" Noah exclaimed with alarm in his voice, and his mouth gaped open slightly like he was in pain.

"No, Father! What I was saying is that the color of the child's hair is red—like fire," Shem said more loudly for his father to hear.

"What, what did you say?" Noah asked him once again.

"Father, I said that the child has red hair. That is the color of fire," Shem explained carefully.

"Oh, the child has red hair! How interesting indeed, but like I said, hair and skin color doesn't matter as long as the two parents produce good fruit for God," Noah said. "Prepare things, then, so that I may bless the child in the name of our Lord." Then Shem went out and had things prepared for him.

That evening, just like the ones before, Noah blessed the child and offered it in the name of the Lord. Then the child's father held it up to the heavens and named it. They partied and celebrated again. Many children were born to Javan, and to his brothers and sisters also. By the time they had gone through the DNA tug-of-war to reach adulthood, the children of Javan and his wife resembled people of Hispanic descent.

They also married 100 percent pure white humans, pure black, and other interracial children as well, bringing forth even more different types of interracial children. When this generation was about to give birth, everyone started to guess again what the conception might look like. The mixed children's numbers, and variety of mixtures, began to increase rapidly with every generation. Still at this present time, though, the number of 100 percent pure white humans outnumbered all the other peoples on the planet.

One of Javan's Hispanic-looking children—a son—married a 100 percent pure white woman, who was about to give birth. The eyes of every woman in the tent were on her to see what the child might look like this time; all the guesses were widely ranged as usual, but when the child came out, they were all wrong again, to their surprise. It was another little girl; she was born with golden yellow hair like no one had ever seen before. The gossip amongst the women of the tent flew into high gear as all put in their opinion, and Noah's wife shushed them all, saying, "That will be enough now. I have seen enough different children to know that God can do anything." Then everyone started to congratulate the mother, who was pure white and adored the young child. There were many types of mixed women assisting in the deliveries of the children now, though most were 100 percent pure white. They all got along together like real full-blooded brothers and sisters with a good father like Noah to lead them.

Shem came to tell Noah once again that a new child of difference had been born that day.

"Father!" Shem said. "Another mixed child was born again to us today to one of your grandsons through the blood of Tubal-Cain and Japheth."

"What does the child look like?" Noah asked.

"Father, the child is a girl, and she was born with golden hair." Noah peered at him with a puzzled look.

"You mean the child was born with hair as strong as shiny metal?" he asked, sounding surprised. Then Shem spoke more clearly for his father to hear.

"No, Father, not metal hair. Yellow hair that looks the color of golden rays of sunshine."

"Oh! Are you sure the child was born with yellow hair?" Noah asked, to be sure of what he was hearing.

"Yes, Father."

"Yellow hair!" Noah said once again, as if speaking to himself. "Surely, I will never be surprised ever again at what the Lord can do."

"Shall I go and prepare the ceremonial offering to the Lord for the child's birth father?"

"Oh, yes. Go, Shem," Noah said. They blessed the children again in the name of the Lord while offering praise and sacrifice, and the father held the child up to name it. The child had many other brothers and sisters like herself. They grew to adulthood while losing their yellow hair through the DNA tug-of-war process of Kendihuchrodnamixgenesis, as they still do to this very day; these children, after finally reaching adulthood, resembled the redheaded members of the Caucasian people that we know today.

These redheaded adults married some of the 100 percent pure white humans, so when the time came for this interracial mix to bear children, all the women in the child birthing tents looked on, and to their surprise, the mixture of the redheads and 100 percent pure white humans produced children with pure white hair.

Something seemed amiss. Its color was no different from the 100 percent pure white human parent; not a trace of the red-haired parent could be found. Questions arose from within the minds of all attending this birth. Did this pure white human female cheat with one of her 100 percent pure white human brothers? In their minds this was the only way this could have happened. None of them had ever seen mixed children born with pure white hair before this birth, unless both parents were 100 percent pure human. What kind of punishment would Noah inflict on her for this, if he took away Ham's son Canaan and made him a slave to his uncles—Shem and Japheth—to make all mindful of obedience to

God? *Surely Noah would give her a more horrific punishment than Ham received,* the others thought.

They lay the baby on the bare breast of its mother, and Noah's wife had everyone leave except Naamah and herself. They then proceeded to question the mother of the child.

"Now tell me the truth!" Noah's wife insisted. "Has thou lain with any other brother besides thy husband?" The girl was insulted and offended by the questioning, but she answered the two most elderly women alive on the earth.

"No, I tell you this day before God and man that I have been faithful unto my husband." Noah's wife looked at Naamah and hunched her shoulders.

"And you are sure that this child is a part of Tubal-Cain's and Naamah's blood through your interracial husband, who has red hair?"

"Yes, I swear that it is true, Great-Grandmother." Noah's wife sighed, as if to say, "I have no more questions." She looked to Naamah, and they questioned her no more.

In Noah's tent now the child lay before him and his son Shem, who looked at it with Noah's wife standing silently at the tent's opening.

"She says that she has been faithful unto her husband, Father," Shem said.

"It does seem odd indeed that the child would come out looking so much like us, although no mixed child has done so before." Noah pondered to himself with his pointing finger to his mouth. "She is your granddaughter, Shem, married to Japheth's grandson. What dost thou think?"

"I have no reason to doubt her, and her husband stands behind her with belief as well that she is telling the truth." Noah breathed in deeply. "She has a full pure white brother who is married to a girl with fire-red hair, does she not?" Noah asked.

"Yes, also due shortly with child," Shem said.

"Then nothing more is to be said by anyone on the matter until we see what the others like them produce. Prepare the offering unto the Lord, Shem." The baby was blessed like the others before, and everyone carried on as usual.

Soon her pure white brother and his redheaded wife gave birth to a male child, and it too was born with white hair on its head like the 100 percent pure white human race. The mother of the first child was exonerated of the gossip within the village. It seemed true that this closer-to-white interracial mix of Caucasian children naturally had white-looking hair at birth, but as they got older, their hair color started getting darker. Indeed the blood of Tubal-Cain and Naamah were in them, and when they were adults, their hair changed to a blondish color or darker, which surprised them. None of them knew about the genetic effects of Kendihuchrodnamixgenesis from that DNA tug-of-war, which seems to be less effective the closer you are to the pure white race genetically in composition. The primate genetics races to lay its cell building block pattern faster than the human genetic building block pattern that constructs people's bodies in cellular arrangement. Now these white-haired interracial children grew to become natural blonds, 96.875 percent pure human and 3.125 percent primate with even fewer sickle cells than their redheaded parents who were married to 100 percent pure white humans—Noah's direct descendants.

# VINDICATED

Ten years later outside Noah's tent, while most of the young men were preparing to gather the supplies for dinner, Noah, Tubal-Cain, and their wives were examining the hair of the first interracial child born with white hair while commenting on how it had changed.

"See, Tubal-Cain, my friend, how the hair changes from white to the darker color of golden rays of sunshine? Indeed, at least some of your blood is also in the child," Noah said.

"It would appear so," he said calmly to Noah, as the pure white mother of the child who was in question at birth stood in the background with her husband looking on happily. They held each other, having been cleared of all insinuated wrongdoing. She bore many other children by her husband. One of the girl's little sisters, about five years old, whose hair was still white, was standing next to her big sister of ten, to whom Noah had taken a particular liking, as they examined their hair color difference with their parents looking on proudly.

"See, Grandfather Tubal-Cain, my hair was like my little sister's when I was little, and now it is like sunshine, right, Grandfather Noah?"

"Yes, my grandchild, it seems so." Noah said. Then one of the little girl's cousins, who was pure human, standing nearby, spoke up, saying, "I want my hair to be like golden rays of sunshine too."

Noah's wife just smiled, as she said to her, "Oh, I'm sorry, my dear, that's just not possible. You would have to be of interracially mixed blood, and you're not. You're going to have all pure white hair like most of us for the rest of your life. Besides, it's always best to be satisfied with what you have."

"I liked it when I had white hair for a while, and I was happy with it—wasn't I, Grandmother?" she asked as she stood between her grandmothers of ebony and ivory.

"Yes, you were, dear!" Noah's wife said, and she gave her a kiss on the cheek.

"Grandmother?" the little girl turned to ask Naamah.

"What, dear?"

"Will I ever have all white hair again?"

"Yes! If you live long enough," Naamah said.

"When?" she asked inquisitively.

"When you're very, very old like your grandparents. No matter what mixture you are, if you live long enough, you will have white hair again. Just look at your grandfather Tubal-Cain: his hair used to be black."

"Wow! He must really be old—all his hair is white now." It made everyone around started laughing at her innocence, which made them all feel good.

"Well, there is someone here much older than I am—perhaps as old as the mountains," Tubal-Cain said, and they all laughed louder, because Noah was very old then. The laughing toned down until it ceased. There were many types of interracial children now—different shades of black, brown, yellow, and nearly white skinned with dark specks, and just as many types of hair and color.

Soon interracial children were born with white hair that stayed almost white all of their lives. These were in fact 98.4375 percent or higher nearly pure white humans genetically with 1.5625 percent or lower primate genetics. Each had fewer sickle cells than their closest blond-haired interracial relatives, but even though it was a small amount, they still had more than Noah and the other pure white humans left on the earth, who at this point still outnumbered all the other mixes of people.

"Okay, everyone!" Noah said to get everyone's attention as the laughter died down. "Let's get the supplies for dinner." His words were heeded like law when he spoke—everyone listened. The young men went to gather up the needed supplies for dinner. The many different types of young men were as different as the supplies they needed to gather: wood, game, vegetables, water, spices, and so on. The list went on, but it was organized very well, with the elder men leading the way while teaching the skills of hunting—real on-the-job training.

Suddenly a shout was heard, for Naamah had cried out.

"Tubal-Cain!" He lay facedown, passed out on the ground. Shem was the first to his aid, and Naamah held his hand. His gray head was covered with dust. Shem hoisted Tubal-Cain's head to his lap as he knelt before him while calling out.

"Tubal-Cain!" Shem shouted in a panic-stricken voice. "Can you hear me?"

"My sons, come give help quickly!" Noah called out to all the young men standing nearby. Naamah was wailing quietly, and Noah's wife held her for comfort. Quickly some of the young men standing near came to help. "Carry him inside my tent," Noah said, and about six young men lifted him carefully to carry him inside, where an unconscious Tubal-Cain did not make a movement on his own, as though he were paralyzed. Noah's wife held Naamah's head close to her bosom, to comfort her as she tried to control her sighing while all the little girls and women stood by, watching in fear, after Tubal-Cain was whisked off into the tent.

Hours passed by without a word, and Noah leaned over his friend, who was covered with a blanket, while he checked for vital signs. He sat back up slowly with a sad look on his face as the elder male members inside looked for an answer. Noah shook his head no, and instantly all the men in the tent dropped their heads simultaneously toward the ground.

Shem came out of the tent with a distant look on his face as he peered over at the group, specifically at his mother, who was still holding on to Naamah. Then he just closed his eyes and shook his head no to indicate that Tubal-Cain had not survived.

"Ahhhh! No!" Naamah cried out mournfully, ending in sudden silence. Noah's wife clutched on even tighter to hold Naamah up as she started to collapse upon the ground. Then the other women around quickly took hold of Naamah also.

"Let's take her inside her tent!" Noah's wife ordered, and other weeping young women helped her hold Naamah up until they could get her seated inside to give her moral support. Their eyes were tearful and mourning as well, but none were like Naamah's. They hugged and comforted one another like one big family, because they were. Every grown person knew every other person living on the earth at this time.

A day later they prepared a burial for Tubal-Cain, and all passed by for one more look or just to say goodbye in their own way of respect. One in particular, the little blond-haired girl whose hair Noah and the others were examining before Tubal-Cain passed on, stood with her mother, who had pure white hair, and her red-haired father. They nodded their heads to her as a signal, and she turned to lay freshly picked flowers on her grandfather Tubal-Cain. Her long blond hair covered some of his face as she said, "Goodbye, Great-Great-Grandfather Tubal-Cain." She stood up straight and walked off, crying silently to herself. Her mother carried her little sister, who still had white hair on her head like her mother, for the time being.

The little girl looked on as her mother touched his hand saying, "Goodbye, Tubal-Cain." She was related to him only by marriage, but her husband with red hair was a great-grandson. He just stood there looking on silently, and then he sighed deeply yet quietly.

"Goodbye, Great-Grandfather," he said in a slow, calm voice. Then they went and stood behind Naamah, and he rested his left hand on her right shoulder, saying, "It will be okay, Great-Grandmother." She shook her head full of white hair to signal yes in response to his comforting words as Noah's wife, who was sitting next to her, placed her hands into Naamah's hands, making their hands look like piano keys as she consoled her. Naamah wiped away the tears that ran down her face with her other hand. It was hard for all, because it was the first human death after the great flood had ended. No one had really even thought about death before now. It reminded the elders of all the mass deaths in the flooding of the earth. Even the ones who had only heard about it were mournful in their own way, for they would miss him, as Noah stood to eulogize the last remarks for Tubal-Cain.

"Our brother Tubal-Cain has gone on in flesh, which is but dust from the ground. The Lord God has said that from the earth we came and back to the earth our bodies must return. Chase not after the flesh, but the spirit! The flesh is not to be considered in matters of marriage, birth, or death. I witnessed unto you, as I performed the first union to create many mixed people between our two peoples who came off of the ark, which is good and righteous as long as it produces good fruit for the Lord God. Our spirit belongs to him forever, as Tubal-Cain, the maker of tools out of bronze and iron, will be a part of us forever. He was a good friend who willing gave service unto me like one of my own sons. Thus he is loved like a son, so his children will also be my children, for we are one people now, and he will be missed." *This author considers evidence that suggests the ark landed in northern Africa, as both New International and King James reference eastward travel one to, and one fro. Where Maritime people is used, an original word may have referenced mixed people, who developed language and dialect from both the 100% pure white race and the Dark skinned race.* (Italics are mine) Because (Genesis 10:31) These are the sons of Shem, after their families, after their tongues, in their lands, after their nations. Next the Tower of Babel (Genesis 11:1) And the whole earth was of one language, and of one speech. *Noah's direct family all spoke the same language before the ark there was no need to change.* (Genesis 11:5-7) And the Lord came down and confounded their language.

Then Shem, with a gesture of his hand, ordered the appointed young men to come carry the body of Tubal-Cain to its final resting place near the ark, where they could visit.

Then as time went on, Naamah passed as well in her old age—some might think from the loneliness of missing Tubal-Cain. They cried for her also, and she was buried next to Tubal-Cain.

# THE GREATEST WAIL OF ALL

Sometime years later after that, Noah's wife died at a very old age, and the whole village mourned her soulfully also. She was the mother of many, and they buried her near the ark as well.

The rainfall brought fewer and fewer floods near the mountain of Ararat, so the increasing herds moved farther away to the greener pastures of the plains. This made the gathering of meat from the hunt a longer and longer journey. It was to the point of taking nearly a full day of sunlight to complete some hunts, depending on what they were searching for that particular day, because they still had to regulate the hunting of certain herds so that their numbers would continue to thrive. Noah's sons along with some of their sons sat down with him in his tent, which was almost the size of a large hut, to discuss how to feed this small village now.

"Father, the herds are moving farther and farther away from the ark out into the plains," Ham said. "It is taking the hunters longer and longer trips to bring back meat for our people."

"Yes, Father, Ham is right!" Japheth said. "We may have to think about moving closer to the herds with the way our numbers are increasing—particularly the numbers of the mixed children (Maritime) are growing rapidly amongst us. In just a few short generations they will equal the numbers of us who are made in the image of Adam and Eve, created by the hands of God in his likeness thereof." He agreed with his brother as Noah barely moved his head, batting his eyes only once.

"And what do you think, Shem?" Noah asked. Shem was slow to answer, for he knew that his father wanted to stay near the ark, where his wife and good friends were buried.

"I feel that they may be right, Father. Soon we may have to leave Mount Ararat. Bad weather could interrupt the flow of meat on the tables for days at a time or cause rationing," Shem said.

"I see," Noah said softly. "Tell the scouting leaders of the hunt to start mapping out prime locations that might be suitable for a new village from now on, Shem, and when they have found four places, I want you and your brothers to go on a hunt with them to choose the best one near fresh water for us. Also plow no more fields around here. If you find a good spot, the plowing must be started there for the next season; that way we won't have to climb all the way back up here to harvest. Now everyone leave me, for I must rest." Noah was getting old; he had lived more than three hundred years now, since the ark had landed on this mountain. He really did not want to leave it. It's funny how God will sometimes grant those little wishes, because they found the new village. Noah, years later, was also carried back to the ark, where he was laid to rest next to his wife.

Genesis 9:28 says that after the flood, Noah lived 350 years. Altogether, Noah lived 950 years, and then he died like the others before him. There was never before heard such a wailing of sorrow for one person, by the fewest numbers that were on the earth. They mourned for days while a lot of the regular chores were not performed, because of much grief in their village. It seemed like the telephone connection between God and man was disconnected when Noah passed. Who could interact with the Lord God almighty for man's sake now?

Noah was buried near the ark on that mountain in the graveyard of black and white skulls. It is called that because everyone in it was either 100 percent pure human of white descent directly from Adam and Eve or 100 percent pure black directly descended of the seed of Cain. No children of interracial mixed blood—blond to near dark black skin—were buried in this graveyard; that is why it is called the Graveyard of Black and White Skulls, because God left it as a marker for man to find the ark's remains one day, so man might come to know the truth of his existence. Of all the countless graveyards on this entire earth, there is only one graveyard of Black and White Skulls, and it is near Noah's ark.

After Noah had passed, his sons Shem, Ham, and Japheth called all the people together and told them they would soon be leaving this place. The mountain would not sustain them much longer without more than doubling or even tripling everyone's daily chores, especially the hunting parties for the meat.

The Table of Nations:

(Genesis 10:1-4) says, "This is the account of Shem, Ham, and Japheth, Noah's sons, who themselves had sons after the flood.
The Japhethites
The sons of Japheth:
Gomer, Magog, Madai, Javan, Tubal, Meshech, and Tiras."
(Genesis 10:4-5) tells us that Javan had four mixed-race sons, Elishah, Tarshish, Kittim, and Dodanim, who married different types of women not alike, and from these the Maritime peoples spread out into their territories by their clans within their nations, each with its own language.

(Genesis 10:6-20)
The Hamites
The sons of Ham:
Cush, Mizraim, Put and Cannaan.
Cush was the father of King Nimrod.

(Genesis 10:21-32)
*The Sheites*
Sons were also born to Shem, whose older brother was Japheth; Shem was the ancestor of all the sons of Eber.
Elam, Asshur, Arphaxad, Lud, and Aram.
"These are the clans of Noah's sons, according to their lines of descent within their nations. From these the nations spread out over the earth after the flood" (Genesis 10:32).
Men moved eastward, and as they did, some of the interracial children became old and died along the way. Now the graveyards were becoming more and more filled with the skulls of interracial children each time they moved eastward from what today is called Nigeria. They found a plain in Shinar, which today is called Egypt, and they settled

there. God did this so that man could have a map, to trace the graveyards back to the ark like a trail of breadcrumbs. The fewer interracial skulls that are found in the graveyards, the closer man will get to the ark, which the Lord ordered Noah to build.

# ONE WORLD GOVERNMENT

The number of the people on the earth began to increase dramatically, but all men still called each other brother when they met, even though they spread out upon the earth in different villages. They all still knew of Noah and where they had come from even though their history was being passed on only by word of mouth from one generation to the next, because they all spoke the same language. But they had no purpose or direction.

The world was beginning to need a leader to guide their direction instead of just village leaders overseeing their daily progress. Two brothers came, one of pure white descent and the other of black descent, for the world was going to elect itself a king.

Then man called out unto the Lord God for a sign of who was going to be king. They waited for many hours of the day, looking toward the sky for signs, but it seemed as though the Lord God would not give them a sign. All of a sudden out over the forest edge, soaring over the top of the pure black leader, a flock of about a dozen Canada geese honked as they flew directly overhead.

All the people cheered, taking this as a sign that God wanted him to be the leader of the entire world, since the flock flew over him, but before they could take the time to congratulate him, a larger flock of about two dozen Canada geese flew over the other leader's head, and they made him king. His name was Nimrod.

King Nimrod, who was known as a great hunter and a mighty warrior, became the first ruler of the world, and he made the other brother who would be king second in charge as head adviser to him from the people. The rule of this first dynasty worked for everyone, because there were no prejudiced groups at this time in the world. Men respected each other as they did themselves, and not one murder had been committed since the flooding of the earth. Men lived in harmony with one another by calling each other brother.

Genesis 11:1-3 tells us that the world now had one common language and a common speech. Men moved eastward, found a plain in Shinar, and settled there. They said, "Come, let us make bricks and bake them thoroughly." They did this to make a name and a history for themselves, so that they would know who they were and where they came from. They used brick instead of stone; that way they could build the huge bricks only inches away from their position and with tar for mortar they could more easily slide the huge bricks right into place where they needed to be placed. Then King Nimrod gave the order for men to build the first pyramid—the holy temple of Shinar. Everyone in the world now had purpose, for it was a huge undertaking, but the people had pride as one people, and they built on and on with joy and happiness. They had crews who would leave their village homes and work for months at a time and then go back to their villages to rest the remainder of the year.

Soon the relationship between men and women and God began to change. Man started to depend on the strength of his own arm, and they lacked for nothing, as their gathering parties brought back fresh food to meet everyone's needs.

On the hot nights men and women away from their villages who were building the great tower would gather at the shallow pools of water for unwed sex. Men would gather nightly, fulfilling their needs with the women who came, but women would not come as often as men, though a woman could experience as many love partners in one night as she desired, and not return until she was in the mood to desire pleasure again. Some still followed the practices of marriages, but soon marriage was not that big an issue to many suitors, because one's needs could be satisfied without personally obligating oneself to one person.

But many came to realize that all the sex in the world couldn't replace true love. True love takes a long time to build, and the hurdles of others interfering makes it a longer journey sometimes. Quite often men and women found true love after this venture of fornication, which was a sort of trying the shoes on first, to see how they fit. But this is how man started to fall from the grace of God during this period.

The elderly men and women—the grandmothers and grandfathers—often took charge of raising the children after they reached the toddler age back at the villages, when the young men and women of working age went off to build the first pyramid on their tour of duty, which usually lasted one month. The pregnant young women were ordered back to their villages when they showed signs of being too far along with child to handle the workload of carrying water. The whole village raised the children, and often no one knew who their real fathers were, but to the grandparents who raised them, it did not matter, because the children's strength supported them, and their knowledge guided the child.

There was no rape, no murder, and no homosexuality (for father Noah had nipped it in the bud with Ham). There were no disputes of any real measure, as everything seemed to systematically take care of itself. Then foolishly man began to believe that he was in control of his own destiny.

Many years later the pyramid was nearly half completed when the news rang throughout the land that their beloved leader, King Nimrod, had died. All had loved him, as he had ruled fairly amongst all the people by making them all feel the same in stature.

The building of the pyramid stopped as people mourned for many days because of his death. This also presented a problem for the builders, who had designed the pyramid with a burial place inside for the first king of the earth in mind, so that the world would forever know where we came from. The pyramid was also to be part museum inside—a time capsule with statues of human figures to represent all of the different types of people on the earth at that time, from the lightest to the darkest. It would tell a detailed history about the beginning of the world and show the exact location of the ark that lay westward from there in the mountains then named Ararat in northern Africa.

What to do with King Nimrod until the pyramid was completed? He was the first king since the flood, and a bold hunter with the heart of a lion, as songs were made of his heroic life to honor his feats of heroism. The song chanted such verses as "Who can bend the mighty bow of King Nimrod? King Nimrod! Who is so bold with a lion's heart? King Nimrod! King Nimrod!" Yes, a song was written to honor him for his fair leadership of all in his kingdom: short hair, long hair, white hair, black hair, and everything in between, he treated them all the same when he ruled the one world government that centered on the first pyramid ever built.

Then someone came up with an idea of what to do with King Nimrod until the pyramid was completed. They said, "We are already making bricks. Let us build a huge stone lion, since King Nimrod had the heart of a lion. Then we will lay him inside a specially designed sarcophagus that will fit perfectly inside the king's chamber of the pyramid." Today this huge lion is known as the Sphinx, which watches over the Nile River. Once the holy temple of Shinar was nearly completed, they would take the specially designed sarcophagus with King Nimrod's body in it out of the huge stone lion. Then they would build the pyramid around the specially designed sarcophagus, which would not be able to be removed from that section of the pyramid. There they figured it would stay forever, for the entire world to see generation after generation and remember where we all came from, to establish the one world government as long as the earth remained.

They gave special instructions to one man named Reu, the only one given permission to open the stone lion when the time came to move King Nimrod's body. But the construction took much longer than anyone had anticipated. They kept building and building upon the holy temple of Shinar.

All of a sudden, they visualized the completion of this huge pyramid, and it was near time to move the body of King Nimrod out of the huge lion and place it inside the pyramid once the final top section of the temple had been completed. The time came when they were nearly finished with the holy temple of Shinar. The pure excitement of finishing outweighed the thought of moving King Nimrod's body. They started questioning who was responsible for the task of removing the king's body into the pyramid. Someone said, "Reu was the one in charge of remembering when to remove the king's body." They called for Reu, but he did not come, for he had died. No one had figured that the building of the holy temple would take as long as it had.

Luke 20:17 says, "The stone the builders rejected has become the capstone." It was all destined by God anyway that King Nimrod would not be buried high above the earth. Jesus is the chief cornerstone, according to Ephesians 2:20, and no one is to be exalted above him. Thus God made man to forget, and King Nimrod did not become the capstone over the earth. Soon man would forget all, and not remember where we came from when God made his next move.

They still cheered and celebrated in the completion of the tower, for it was a phenomenal undertaking that they had finally completed. The world was at peace, man respected one another as he respected himself, and there still had not been one murder from the time of the great floodwaters to this point of the completion of the great tower. That was a tribute to man—not honoring God, because man was trusting in the strength of his own arms to build a perfect society.

The interracial children now outnumbered even the pure white humans on the planet, but the original genetic black race was all absorbed into the mixing bowl, and they were extinct, although there still remained a lot of dark-skinned people, who were nearly pure black.

In much the same way, as the number of whitish blond-haired people began to increase the number of people with pure white hair dwindled. The more the number of redheads increases, the more the natural blond-haired adults will be absorbed by decreasing into extinction, because of the effects of Kendihuchrodnamixgenesis.

Even adult redheads will have blond hair during their youth at one time. The only way to keep the natural blond-haired people on the planet today from extinction, besides selective breeding, will be to find a 100 percent pure white human and breed them to immense numbers to absorb all the other interracial people, including most of the Caucasian people with darker traits, or take the eggs and sperm of the remaining blond-haired people and overproduce them to absorb the other races. Otherwise all our descendants are going to look Egyptian. The people back then were happy with the completion of the tower, and they kept building the city. They continued to gather at the shallow pools for their promiscuous pleasure, and though man did not know it, they were in jeopardy of falling right into the hands of sin and being lost forever.

# SCATTERED HISTORY

"But the Lord came down to see the city and the tower that men were building. The Lord said, 'If as one people speaking the same language they have begun to do this, then nothing they plan to do will be impossible for them. Come let us go down and confuse their language so they will not understand each other'" (Genesis 11:5).

The Lord God came down to hover high above the pyramid that marked the four corners of the earth, but the people of the land could not see him, nor did they sense he was there. Men were working and talking as usual when God gave the command to confuse them. It was as if the angels went around, instantly counted all the sickle cells in everyone's body, and changed their languages accordingly within certain genetic groups, depending on the number of the cell count, so that people of certain groups would huddle together. What this did was cause the people to signify identification with groups of self-likeness, which made them feel accepted by ones who looked or spoke like themselves, and alienated by others who appeared or spoke differently. Though each group wanted to mingle with the other as much as the other wanted to mingle with them, self-induced fear took over by starting what we know now as the beginning of prejudice in this new world after the great flood. The Lord did as he said by scattering all of Noah's descendants all over the earth, and they stopped building the city. That's why it is called the City of Babel, which is now called Egypt, because the Lord confused the language there of the whole world.

For you see, God did not make us sin; he only made us aware of the difference and isolated our ability to reason it out, but even without those things man should be able to get along. The people would have been able to handle it better. If God had done us a worse favor by making us all mute, we would have all felt equal. For example, if we were dropped off at night from a malfunctioning plane to save our life into the middle of a jungle tribe we had never seen before, who were totally different in appearance from us, and we were not able to communicate with them in our language, would it be the fault of the person who dropped us out of the plane if we took a biased stance against this tribe, because we had no way to communicate with them? No! It would be up to each of us to show that we have brotherly love and are willing to get along.

Thus the one world government started to fall because of misunderstanding after misunderstanding, as if God had dropped them off in a strange jungle in the middle of the night.

The first dispute came from the nursery, where oftentimes women nursed one another's babies. When one mother with blond hair came back from her turn of gathering fruit to find her baby crying, she could not figure out why it would not stop crying, so she imagined the worst. She took the position of accusation by thinking that since people were gathering in certain groups, no one had nursed her child, and that's why it was crying aloud.

"Did anyone feed my baby?" she asked a woman of what we today consider to be Spanish descent, who was caring for the child. The lady hunched her shoulder and turned her palms up to indicate that she did not understand what her nearly white sister had asked of her, but no one around could understand her, and she became more infuriated.

Each of the women's husbands arrived upon the scene, but they could not understand each other either and became riled to a point of high tension. A bloody fistfight ensued between the two husbands, who could no longer understand each other either.

This caused much reaction throughout the villages, like when the *Titanic* shot its first emergency signal flares, warning all of a real, imminent danger. After all was said and done, some other men rushed in to break up the incident while trying to figure out what had happened. It was as useless an effort for them as it had been for the women who had been trying to talk to one another in the first place.

The natural blond-haired mother of the child went to nurse it, but it would not suck its mother's milk. The child's crying continued to get louder with even more frustration, which soon after brought the frustrated mother to her wits' end and to the point of giving up. She soon found out what the problem was with her baby, as it gave out a loud belch and then hurled a glob of milk onto the lap of its father, who was nursing his eye now.

"What the—?" the surprised father exclaimed.

"Oh, my goodness!" the mother reacted. "The baby was just too full of milk."

"What happened?" the father asked. To their own surprise they discovered that the child had been nursed, but was too full of milk. Once it spit up the excess, it was smiling happily with a slobbery grin of milky drool on its face while making cooing sounds. The child only needed to be burped, to relieve the excess gas on its stomach.

The mother and father of the baby wanted to apologize to their brother and sister of a different genetic makeup, but when they got back there, the other husband had a black eye that was still growing, much like his anger. They could no more communicate to them their apology than she had been able to communicate her original grievance about her child's welfare.

"My brothers and sisters, we want to offer an apology," the man said in vain, but they could not understand him. "We are sorry! The baby was just too full of milk."

"What are they talking about?" the brother with the black eye asked harshly.

"They are probably just trying to complain some more. She can just take care of her own children for now on," said the woman in Spanish, who had nursed the child for her; it was a bad time of misunderstanding for all. They left feeling bad about what had happened while leaving a gaping hole torn in the fabric of this dwindling society that needed to be filled in the worst way with love because they could not understand each other anymore.

A light-brown-skinned man with an Afro hairstyle and his 100 percent pure white wife were trying to communicate with each other as best they could while their children stood around, watching their useless attempts.

"My husband, I do not understand you! What are you trying to tell me?" she asked again and again.

"My wife, why can't you understand what I'm telling you?" he asked of her. Just then one of the 100 percent pure white brothers from another village walked up. She stopped him, to ask if he could understand her husband for her, so he tried to speak with him.

"Brother!" he said. "Thy wife is trying to ask you something. Do you understand?"

"What are you two talking about?" he asked. "You're not making sense!" They all realized that it was useless.

"My sister, it seems that this has happened all over the world. Only people who mostly appear alike can understand each other, just as you and I, my sister, who look like father Noah, can understand each other. God has done this to us for forgetting him and not honoring him as we should." They all gave up trying to talk and just looked at one another.

"What shall we do?" she asked sorrowfully.

"It is causing everyone to gather into groups of likeness. I'd advise you to do the same. Come join us on our journey to the north," he said.

"But I am of a mixed marriage, and our children are also different from both of us, and neither of us can talk to them—we just can't leave them," she said.

"Truly thou art in an awful position of making a difficult decision. I shall pray for you, my sister," he said, "if God will even hear it now, since he has done all of this to us." He left as people started to gather in racial groups, which made things really worse, for out of the gathering of these groups with like traits, the prejudiced mind awakened. God did not cause the prejudiced mind; we accepted it freely and willfully ourselves. We could have worked the problems out, but instead we chose not to. The human race will sometimes choose to work out our problems today, but back then, we didn't, because it was easier to get up and leave. What about this present world we live in today? Maybe we can learn from back then, to benefit us now that we have interpreters of different languages.

# CIVILIZATION IN TURMOIL

The one world government, which had held peace for so many years, was quickly unraveling as its elders and leaders tried their best to make sense of this thing that was threatening to engulf their future of peace together.

Disorganization really started to tear apart the seams of this once great society when the gathering parties that brought back the food for thousands were unable to communicate with one another. They could not tactically surround the herds and make them run toward the archers, who would shoot down at least fifteen to twenty bison as they went running by. Because they could not speak to one another anymore, they often wound up shouting to communicate now, sending the herds fleeing for safety in the opposite direction—and coming up empty-handed.

The women gathering the fruits could not speak to one another anymore, so they would wind up getting nearly all the same types of fruit instead of the nice variety everyone was used to selecting from.

The fishermen in the boats had the worst catches ever, because they could not communicate about when and where to move the boats on the rivers or lakes to cast their nets in sequence, so the nets would not get tangled. They tried to cover a school of fish nearby, which basically resulted in just scaring off the fish—thus decreasing the supply of fish needed to feed everyone at the required mealtimes. All these gathering parties started by Noah centuries ago with just a handful of people were falling apart now.

Until this point no one owned any land. Your household and the possessions in it were yours, just like how the American Indians lived in teepees amongst their tribe. Outside of that, king and elders ruled by assigning daily tasks to villages. Village elders designated the assigned work according to your skills, strength, and youthfulness—all other unwanted chores trickled down, to serve as adolescent punishment. People ate when the food was prepared around the village campfires or wherever it was served.

Everyone knows that hungry bellies can intensify a bad situation, and it did in this once peaceful world. When some people came in from their hard labor of gathering supplies or building the city to eat at the dinner lines, which were normally full with plentiful food to fill every stomach, they were surprised to find that the serving tables were empty, because no one had experienced this situation before; even after second helpings, there had always been plenty of leftovers for domestic animals. It didn't help by asking the women serving the food where the rest of it was, because they could not communicate to you anymore to tell you that it was all gone, unless they happened to speak the same transformed language as you.

Soon more fights and disagreement broke out as people started confiscating things for themselves. Men began hoarding sheep in the pens, chickens in the henhouses, cattle in the fields, grain in the storehouses, and every other food that they could get their hands on. It was now complete chaos, and no one could settle it, for there were no armies, no police, no National Guard, no lawyers. There had been no other government to war against, so no enforcers of the law existed, except the elders of the people, who judged for themselves the good and right thing to do. Men were fair with their brothers and sisters in the reconciliation of all matters. Before this, theirs had been a simplistic world of sorts. There had been no murders, no property disputes, no lawsuits for collecting large punitive rewards or for accidental damages caused by another. This was in essence a perfect society of oneness that settled most things with an apology.

God recognized this, but man's sins were still growing in number, so to save at least some of them from the second death that was meant only for the fallen angel, which is a far greater suffering than anyone could imagine, he dismantled their perfect society by taking away their abilities of communication, in hopes that man would repent and seek him out once again.

Then it happened! The most terrible thing that one could think about while a group of men had been fighting over food for their immediate families: one of our brothers was struck over the head and killed. He lay there bleeding from the head like Abel with his own blood soaking into his pure white hair also, just as Abel had suffered. Everyone stopped to look, as all the men, women, and children seemed to be paralyzed by the sight. In the hundreds of years since the great flood, nothing remotely like this had happened. His sister with her pure white hair rushed over to hold him as she called out his name, "Sven! Sven!" But he did not answer as she picked up his limp, bloody head in her arms. The mood was that of sheer shock to everyone's system. Nobody wanted this! How could all of this have come to happen? His brothers came to pick up his lifeless body as the dark-skinned brother who had hit him over the head tried to apologize, but it was as useless as the women who tried to apologize for her accusation that no one had fed her baby.

This was the beginning that ignited the prejudiced mind—within all types of man, not just the Caucasian race, as is the conclusion thought by most races today, since they have dominated most of the world in the past few centuries.

King Nimrod's body, made of 100 percent human genetics and entombed inside the special sarcophagus built for the pyramid, is sealed inside the Sphinx to this very day. The day will come when scientists will want DNA samples from his corpse to try to clone a 100 percent human being back to life, but is that in the Lord God's plan?

Every type of man on the earth today had a descendant from his so-called race to help build the pyramid—for surely all of us left alive on this earth today are just a mixture of black and white blood, but many races don't perceive themselves as interracial. God has done some things to us that we don't like, but we realize after all that they are good disciplinary measures and respect him anyway like a good parent who guides us.

The fighting intensified as the supplies became shorter and shorter. Thefts became a problem now as well; the respect and caring for the elderly all but disappeared. Total communication broke down within this one world society, along with its governing authority.

Most of the 100 percent pure white humans who still existed went north, headed into what we call Europe now; they spread out into the northernmost part of that land, being followed closely by the Caucasian people from lightest to darkest in this order: blonds, redheads, brown haired, and brunettes. The pure white human race became irritated by the presence of these Caucasian people spreading out behind them.

They would always settle in a valley away from the Caucasian people, but once the Caucasian people's population spread out into the pure white people's territory, their attitudes flared just like during the 1960s in America when an Afro-American family moved into a white neighborhood. The Caucasian people would rebel and then slowly start moving out, which is how the 100 percent pure white race felt in Europe whenever the Caucasian race spread into their territories. You can imagine what they must have said.

"Hey, Sven, some more yellow-haired people have moved into our valley again."

"No way. Thou art kidding, right?"

"No, I jest thou not."

"Well, we need to run them out of our valley." One can imagine, I'm sure, the many heated discussions and vulgar name-calling. Quite often the 100 percent white humans afterward just decided to pack up from that valley and move farther north, like the American Indians out west.

"Pack up, everyone, we are moving from this valley, because we don't want our children mixing with those half-breed, yellow-haired people."

"Yeah, you're right about that, so let's go." Soon, though, they found themselves in what's known today as Norway, backed against the frozen north, like the American Indians forced out west into the desert plains onto reservations. Like the Indians they changed their fleeting responses to being more brutal in response to the Caucasian followers, who really only sought a place to live and settle. A literary masterpiece was written called *How the West Was Won*, but this is an account that could be called *How Europe and Africa Were Won*.

The 100 percent pure white race gave themselves a name, and by being led by a barbarian king, they became the Vikings. They alienated themselves from the rest of the world just as we all did. One could say that they became the ultimate rednecks, considering themselves the one and only true supreme race, for they even looked at blonds, redheads, brunettes, and whatever else type of Caucasian mix that emerged as half-breed black dogs. They took the same disposition toward them as the Caucasian clan members took toward the Negro race brought to America many centuries later. The 100 percent pure white humans gave themselves the elite positions above all the *Homo sapiens*. They considered all the other people on the earth as like the animals or livestock that the Lord God told Noah and his sons they would rule over. Not all the Vikings were 100 percent pure white, for some of them were actually about 99 percent human, but that was white enough to have white-looking hair. Even if you examined them under a microscope, you could not find mixed traits.

Back at the holy temple of Shinar—the great pyramid—the darkest members left of the black race moved southwestward, deep into the African continent. Instead of heading back toward the northern part of the continent where the ark landed on what was called Mount Ararat, they headed toward the equator for the best hunting grounds. They also had their qualms about the lighter-complexioned black people, especially the ones with whiter-looking features, like the Arabic-looking people who followed them to the regional area of west Africa. The lighter-complexioned people became mostly nomads in this desert region; they fought with the dark-skinned African man over certain territories in this area past the desert land around Libya and Egypt. The people with more Asian looks traveled to the Far East, settling in China, India, and so on.

The parents children created from interracial marriages outnumbered all the other races totals and possessed the area around the holy city of Shinar, the great temple (pyramid), the sphinx, and all the lands around it, for themselves along with their spouses, which included some members from the pure white race, black race, yellow race, and others who toughed it out to stay for the sake of peace. They were dedicated to staying together, even as most of the others of their kind left. They blended together and became the modern light-brown-skinned Egyptians that Abraham's descendants would come to know as heavily burdening taskmasters. They would build more pyramids, although the Egyptians claimed many centuries later that their ancient ancestors in the day of Khufu's rule built the first pyramid—the holy temple of Shinar, which was actually designed mostly by the 100 percent pure white race under King Nimrod's rule, who were the direct descendants of Noah and would later become known as the original Vikings.

# DYNASTY FROM THE ASHES

Egypt, the residue of the one world government, still had one huge problem in the very beginning of trying to rebuild as a nation. They were still many different so-called races that were unable to communicate with each other the way they needed to. The gathering parties still needed to be organized, along with all the other tasks that had to be completed. How would they get everyone to understand what their responsibilities were during the tasks of fishing, hunting, harvesting, collecting firewood, and all the other chores that were needed? All the other nations that had split up into groups with the same language, after God made this change, could talk to one another, so they could easily organize tasks and begin as a new nation, settling in areas they claimed as their own to build another city upon.

The king of these left-behind people of Shinar may have been Khufu's grandfather, who was hoping that the leaders and elders could still hold the remaining members of the one world kingdom together, but to the king's dismay he saw many stragglers leaving in droves daily to catch up with the others who were able to speak the same new language they did.

One day the king who was in charge of this falling-down, crumbling kingdom looked down upon the city with almost certain doom as he sat outside the throne room. He peered down toward the ground as the elders who could barely figure out what one another were saying just happened to focus on two small boys about seven years of age. One was light brown with a large Afro, and the other was Caucasian with brown hair. They were trying to talk to each other by relating certain words in their new different languages. The king watched them, sort of transfixed, as they tried to sort out the problem.

"Bird," the Caucasian boy said, but the other boy did not understand the word.

"What are you saying?" the brown-skinned boy with an Afro asked in an African tongue, though he could not understand his friend. The king, however, could understand the Caucasian boy, who spoke the same language he did.

Finally the Caucasian boy said. "Let me draw you a picture," although the other boy still could not understand a word he was saying. The king watched intensely as the boy grabbed a nearby scroll and began to draw a picture on it. He drew an amateur image of a large bird with its wings spread out wide, as though it was in flight.

"See? This is a bird," he said. It certainly was not the best picture ever drawn, but the obvious distinction of it being a bird had clarity beyond a doubt.

"Fowl!" the other boy said while flapping his arms as though he had wings. "Foul," he said once more, and they both flapped their arms like wings while saying *bird* and *foul* over and over to each other. They had succeeded through the fogginess of this dilemma to communicate where many adults had failed, but it had the most amount of clarity to the king about what to do with his kingdom that was in danger of collapsing. They would create a new language of drawings and symbols to communicate with the people in order to get the gathering party tasks done. If he could just organize the hunting parties to get food and supplies, then all the rest would come in due time.

"I have it!" the king exclaimed, even though most could not understand him. He took a large number of scrolls in his arms to a nearby table while eagerly waving with his arm. He signaled for the rest of the elders to come near, and they all meandered over toward him to see what he was devising. There he completed several drawings in no time at all, it seemed. The first was that of a man casting a net off the edge of a fishing boat to catch fish. The next drawing was of an archer shooting an arrow at some birds in the sky, the next was of archers shooting at a herd of animals stampeding by, and yet another was of women picking fruit from a tree, with the type of fruit in the bottom corner of the scroll, and a woman carrying a pitcher of water on her head. He did many other drawings as well, and then he showed them all to the elders.

"To those of you who can understand me, listen," he said. "We will be communicating from this day forward with all the people through drawings, signs, and symbols." It was the birth of Egyptian hieroglyphics. "Show these pictures to all who gather so that they will know what their task is for that day." All the elders looked at the pictures and understood just like the two small boys the king had watched. They showed these pictures to the gatherers to have them collect the provisions they were shown. It was still rough going in the beginning for this new nation, but soon things came to be organized. The king ordered stonecutters to carve huge detailed tablets; others had the task of explaining what the pictures and symbols meant, and they soon took words from every language to create the Egyptian language. Then they named their kings Pharaoh.

Out of the potential ruins of the holy city of Shinar rose Egypt; it would become the most powerful kingdom of its time. Many would flock back and forth to its marketplaces for selling and trading of all kinds, but this time as foreigners instead of brothers and sisters. God would soon call a man named Abraham here to this place with his wife, Sarah. After that his descendants would become slaves here, to build more temples and cities to the sky, and soon gold would be used as a form of currency. When it was the one world government, there was no form of currency; everyone just did as they were instructed and shared in the wealth of the gathering parties' reaping. They were all still family oriented, having been originally influenced by Noah, who had started them out. Now, every new kingdom needed some form of money for trade with different kingdoms while some men still roamed over the earth. Some small clans decide to embark on their own, but this was still a dark time for everyone not part of a large group or kingdom, for you see, two of the things that became of considerable value were women and slaves, in that order.

You see, all kingdoms and large groups of men realized they needed to build armies to defend what land they had grabbed for themselves; therefore they needed to create larger defending army's than anyone else. They had to have more women for producing young boys to be trained as soldiers, and Egypt brought, captured, shanghaied, and traded for as many young women and child slaves as they could get for their possessions.

Often those small clans of nomads that would later decide to leave and go where the ones who spoke their language had gone, to see if life was any better there, only fell prey to desert marauders, rape gangs, or worse. They would kill off the strong men that resisted them to enslave the women and children, whom they exploited mentally, physically, and sexually. This is what Abram feared most about God telling him go to Egypt.

The family ties started by Noah that they all once knew disappeared more and more with every family generation that died off on the earth. It usually takes only three generation for most people to forget their great-grandparents, thereby making strangers of close relatives beyond three generation. Even though we all come from Adam and Eve, most of us don't look at each other as brothers or sisters in that way, unless we look alike—meaning some women were raped by close cousins and uncles they didn't know.

Even today, sex is the largest-selling single item next to food, of course. Yes, the captured women, children, and even occasionally men too would be sold into bondage in Egypt or some other neighboring kingdom. All the seller had to claim was that the slaves were the spoils from an aggressive warring village that had attacked them first, and they by fighting back had conquered them over. Then it was their choice to either kill or sell them off to whoever would pay their price in gold, but of course only after the capturers sexually satisfied their immoral desires.

There was almost never a captured female left to be sold who still possessed her virginity no matter her age, unless these capturers knew a wealthy purchaser who would pay the extremely high price for the right to be first to defile her. Sometimes the seller would watch the buyer perform intercourse with the young maiden on a clean white cloth to confirm that she did indeed bleed. That way no one was cheated out of the deal (except for the captured maiden, of course) for there is no honor among thieves, they say, and the Geneva Conventions didn't exist. More than 95 percent those captured were from innocent nomad families trying to find a place far away from any turmoil to settle in this world that had not already been claimed by larger groups.

> Now there was a famine in the land, and Abram went down to Egypt to live there for a while, because the famine was severe. As he was about to enter Egypt, he said to his wife Sarai, "I know what a beautiful woman you are. When the Egyptians see you, they will say, 'This is his wife.' Then

they will kill me but will let you live. Say you are my sister, so that I will be treated well for your sake and my life will be spared because of you."

When Abram came to Egypt, the Egyptians saw that she was a very beautiful woman. And when Pharaoh's officials saw her, they praised her to Pharaoh, and she was taken into his palace. He treated Abram well for her sake, and Abram acquired sheep and cattle, male and female donkeys, menservants and maidservants, and camels. (Genesis 12:10-16)

Abram's wife, Sarai, most likely had natural whitish blond hair, which more than a century later was a rarity in this territory, after the 100 percent pure human race left to become Vikings. She had the beauty of Eve on her face. Abram, though sandy blond, possessed slightly darker features compared with his wife, Sarai.

"But the Lord made clear that he inflicted serious diseases on Pharaoh and his household because of Abram's wife Sarai. So Pharaoh summoned Abram. 'What have you done to me?' he said. 'Why didn't you tell me she was your wife? Why did you say, "She is my sister," so that I took her to be my wife?'" (Genesis 12:17-19)

"I told you the truth. We have the same father, but not the same mother," Abram said.

"Now then, here is your wife," Pharaoh said. "Take her and go!" Then Pharaoh gave orders about Abram to his men, and they sent him on his way with his wife and every possession he had obtained from Pharaoh. One can imagine that Pharaoh gave orders to his men to make sure that no one stole his wife or death would befall him from Pharaoh's hand, and to get Abram out of Egypt safely, as quickly as possible, before more tragedy befell them.

Man now warred by waging battles for years, because of miscommunication. From the northern part of Europe to the southern tip of Africa, most descendants of men have still been carrying on the battles of their forefathers. Since this time the Lord God came down and changed most of the languages—only the 100 percent pure white humans kept their original language. Others from so-called ethnic groups have been trying to blame one another for prejudice dividing the world. The truth be known, we are all at fault, if you sit back and think about it. Because men have often failed to follow the Lord's commands, just like Adam and Eve failed to, are they to blame for all this? Truth says we're all guilty, not just the ones who seem to be in power over us at that time in history, as in American's rise to power, when the Caucasian's dominated rule. You will see that all so-called races had a time at the top in power and misused it for self-gain.

Egypt like so many other kingdoms in the beginning became a beautiful place on the outside, but on the inside it festered like a sore, oozing with the pungent pus of slavery along with all the other improvisations that demoralized others, to reap the monetary benefits of wealth for one's own benefit.

# WE NO LONGER KNOW YOU

Far to the north now, some interesting events were shaping up, because the Vikings had cornered themselves against the frozen north by moving out of valley, after valley in northern Europe to be segregated from the interracial Caucasian people, to keep their pure white-haired children from mixing with them to preserve the pureness of their people. Charlemagne, one of the leaders of that time when the Vikings were purer in human form as compared with today, but not quite 100 percent, died and his son Louis the Pious ascended the throne; unfortunately the empire was too large for one man to rule alone. Wars broke out between the emperor and his three sons (Charles the Bald, Lothair, and Louis the German). The empire later split into three parts. Two sections then became the countries of France and Germany. In those days Europeans feared attacks from the Viking invaders, who were also called Norsemen and worshiped several different gods. There was Odin, the one-eyed god of war. Another god was Thor, the giant-killing god. A third god was Frey, who had a twin sister, Freya; they were the god and goddess of love. They began to war against the English, Irish, and Scottish, who were the mostly redheads, brunettes, and everything else mixed between. The original Vikings expressed pure hatred for all other humans, whom they considered half-breeds or worse, and wanted them extinguished from the face of the earth.

Once long ago a severely cold winter forced the Vikings to abandon their northern territory in Norway, because they were facing starvation in the frozen tundra. The Viking king made a choice to head back to the southern part of Europe to wait for the unexpected winter to pass.

"We will be leaving this land until the spring has come," he ordered.

He gathered up his people to move, but as they traveled to what they considered their homelands and valleys below, across the icy ridges between them and central Europe, it took its toll on some of them. Most of the travel left was virtually all downhill, so he pushed on to get them off the icy summit. A woman was carrying her sleeping baby in a bundled swaddling cloth clutched in her arms. Happily the child slept for this part of the journey, and they were unaware that an angel of the Lord came down and touched the baby, causing it to wake. The loud outcry could be heard echoing through the rugged snow capped valley summit, and it was just enough to cause an avalanche that swept away five members of their tribe's party.

The women who was carrying the child was swept off the ridge and scraped the side of the mountain as she went down, receiving a large gouge on her back as a chunk of flesh was ripped out, along with other injuries. But she never let go of her baby the whole way down. She was 100 percent pure white, but her baby was not, because her husband was only about 98 percent pure human. Two older men, one about thirty five, and the other about forty, were swept away as well, but the most significant loss was the prince. He was about sixteen years of age, and he too was 100 percent pure human, buried with snow and ice in the crag of a rock on the mountainside.

The Viking king was upset with the loss of his son and blamed the ill fortune on the mixed people, for in his mind, if they had never entered the Viking valleys, he would not have moved his Viking clan farther north to this frozen land in northern Norway. Therefore he would never have lost his young son to this fate by trying to cross these mountain passages in winter. More than ever now, he was intent on extinguishing the rest of the people from the earth, so that they would be the only ones populating the world. The truth be known, these people lay buried in the snow many centuries for man to find when his biotechnology is advanced enough to check their DNA and bloodstream, to see that they are in fact 100 percent pure white humans who have no sickle cells in their bodies. Being in ice more than five thousand years allows them to prove that they were the first people on the earth, so modern man in the twentieth century could ask himself, "Where did we come from, and how did we get sickle cells in our blood?" According to Darwin's theory of evolution, we should not be evolved into 100 percent pure white humans with pure white hair from birth until death for approximately another 100 million years from now; how then can the natural blond be an endangered species, if we're evolving into 100 percent pure white humans? The natural blond's numbers should be increasing as we evolve toward 100 percent pure whiteness. It's only obvious by man's mixing with an ape that we are interracially mixing and transforming into *Homo sapiens* from our original 100 percent pure white form. Which essentially means that Darwinism is dead!

The Vikings conquered most of Europe for the longest time by sending warriors into battle. The most fearless fighter would earn the title of Berserker for his courageousness in the sieges that they waged against Englishmen and others in nearby territories. In their minds they were the only people now on the earth who had the right to exist. All others were to be pillaged and vanquished from the face of the earth.

Once a Viking group met some people soon to be known as Englishmen on a battlefield covered in snow, to destroy them for crossing into their land. These men only wanted to resolve the problem and bring understanding for their coming into Viking land, because their number of settlers were increasing, much like the people who made the land rush onto Indian lands out west in the United States, but the Vikings would not have it.

The first Viking king early on, after the fall of the one world government, was like Conan the barbarian; he ruled ruthlessly by taking no prisoners for many decades. He and his troops came within shouting distance of the soon-to-be Englishmen. There was a great distinction of contrast between the two traits of people ready to fight to the death. The contrast of these pure white humans standing next to darker-complexioned Caucasian people was like standing a Mexican person next to an Afro-American person of light complexion.

"Why have you come to our lands?" the Viking king asked loudly for them all to hear. A foggy mist rolled off his breath, and his long, pure white hair flowed from time to time in the north winds.

"We have come in peace," the leader of the Caucasian people said with his sandy yellow hair that flowed in the wind also.

"You were not invited, yet you are here, so how can you say that you come in peace?"

"Our numbers are increasing and we need to spread out. Besides, there is plenty of room for all of us, if we just work together."

"You mean like everyone did a century ago, when our people, the direct descendants of Noah designed and built the great temple, only to have it stolen from us by the black dog races, which you are a part of?" the Viking king asked.

"From the way we remember it, everyone built it and just about all were losers," the Caucasian leader said. "But we hope that we can live in peace together."

"That will never happen, for we will not ever again mix the pure white blood of our children with the mixed blood of the half-breed black dogs that you are," the Viking king said sternly. This enraged the Caucasian men, and they whispered amongst themselves.

"You are making things difficult for all of us by thinking that you are pure and high above everyone else."

"We are pure," the Viking king said while reaching under his garment to pull out his penis. Then he urinated on the snow in front of him, staining it yellow. Once he finished, he picked up a handful of fresh snow off to his side with his other hand, saying, "See this freshly fallen, pure white snow in my hand? It represents us and our pure white hair. See the yellow snow on the ground? It represents you and your yellow hair . . . Which one would you eat?" The Viking king said as he took a mouthful of the pure white fresh snow in his hand and ate it. Immediately thereafter all the Viking clans with him started to laugh aloud. This stirred even more heated emotion within the future Englishmen, as they consorted amongst themselves with dislike toward their pure white brothers, who had seemingly separated themselves from them and the rest of the world. "And if we mixed our pure blood with yours," he said as he dumped the rest of the fresh white snow from his hand on top of the urinated snow upon the ground, "it would still not be worth eating; thus the children created between you and me are not worthy either."

Instantly the Englishmen held their swords high in the air. The Vikings did likewise, beginning a century or longer of fighting between them as they charged each other.

Back on the African continent near the northernmost part of it, the Arab and Mandingo tribes were at odds and lining up to fight as the Vikings and English were.

"This is our land, and you are not welcome here," the Mandingo king said.

"How can you claim all of this land for yourselves? We know that it goes on for many moons of walking by foot day and night, yet you are claiming all of this earth for yourselves," the Arab leader said.

"Yes, this is our land."

"What about that behind you? You can't even fill this corner part of the northern territory that you are in now. We only want to cross over into the lands behind you that are not used. What about that land?"

"When we birth enough people, we are going to possess it too."

"That is greed. What about us?"

"You have the desert territory—that is yours."

"Living in the desert is hard on crops and livestock. It will be nearly impossible. Can't our people get along?"

"No, you are partly half-breed, like the white maggots who want to devour everything for themselves. There can be no peace between us." All of a sudden they went at each other with swords clanging and shields banging.

The same clashing happened in the Far East, which provoked the Chinese emperor to build the Great Wall of China against their enemies the Huns from the north while man was land grabbing all over the world now, it seemed. Some got into boats at the risk of death on the high seas, to find new lands or beyond. Often getting lost in storms, some of them even wound up on the North American continent and other places around the world. There was no more share and share alike as Grandfather Noah had ordered all to do before the one world government; it became everyone for them selves.

# VIKING PRIDE

Back up in the Northern Hemisphere many centuries later, some of the Caucasian people settled on a large landmass and eventually called it England. The Vikings, who before this time would gather their own supplies, were now pitted up against the frozen north. They started to raid the harvest of the Englishmen and all others south of them, since they felt that they lived on their lands. Viking raids along with the wars waged by them began to take their toll on their numbers of Viking warriors from casualties. They needed to replace their fighting men they had lost, so they started capturing the settlers' women as plunder that moved into these proclaimed Viking European valleys while putting the men and boys to death by the sword.

It was written in the English prayers, "Lord save us from the north men." They would pray when these ultimate rednecks raided the castles of England, Scotland, and Ireland, which the Vikings considered their hallowed grounds. They raped the women while degrading them with vulgar names, and brought back as many young maidens as they could to increase their fighting numbers by treating these women like bed wenches—like an individual being passed around in a state penitentiary for a pack of cigarettes or a cold alcoholic beverage. When these young women were brought back to the Viking camp, they were usually orphaned by the raids, with no one to return too. They saw no hope of getting home, since England had no navy and virtually no ships to perform a rescue. Only the Vikings knew how to navigate by the stars and the sun in longboats, to make the long journeys up and down the coastline of the oceans.

Once back at the Viking village, the men shared the captured women. It did not matter who got the women pregnant, as long as he was a Viking warrior who participated in the raids. The Viking women, however, were not thrilled by how the Viking men decided to handle the problem of increasing the numbers of their warriors. They were at first appalled at the presence of the young captured English maidens and quite often made their disgruntled feelings known to their Viking husbands as they divided up the spoils from the raids.

"Hey, Jon!" Sven said. "I'll trade you this keg of fine English wine for the first night with the young English maiden you have captured and brought back, yah?" Sven was a slender built kind of a guy

"Nay," he said. "You will have to do much better that that, Sven, to get her virginity."

Jon was no fool and knew he could command a higher yield than that as they stood outside his house with three English maidens huddled together on the cold ground, a blonde, a redhead, and a brunette. All of them were afraid of what the Viking men might do to them, but they had an idea, and they dreaded to think of the inevitable conclusion of being raped by a longboat full of warriors a short time from now.

"Me thinks you might have a problem with the fair Helga. Yah?" Sven said.

"Nonsense!" Jon insisted.

"I'm just trying to be a friend is all."

"Well, you leave the worrying about my wife to me," Jon said. Just then Helga popped her head out the door and came stomping her feet as she approached the two men. She was not skinny but on the lean side with long white braids down past both sides of her hips with a pale complexion, deep blue eyes, and carrying a hot attitude.

"What are you doing with more of those English bed wenches? You're not bringing them into our house for sure!" she demanded.

"I warned thou," Sven said, smirking a barely visible crooked grin.

"Now, Helga, be reasonable. I did it for you so you won't have to do any cleaning around the house," Jon tried to explain.

"Ha!" she exclaimed. "In a pig's eye. You did it to satisfy thy own loins with them."

"Ah! Be nice and fair, Helga," Jon said.

"Nice my foot!" she grumbled. "And I can do my own cooking and cleaning. You'd better not bring one more of those half-breed black bitches into our home," she demanded in anger. "And trade them for some food to your brothers." Then she stormed off toward the house, as the ever-insulted English maiden with blond hair spoke out in reply to Helga's jeers at them.

"Who does she think her high-and-mighty jackass is to be hurling insults? I will surely thrash her white ass with my foot if she comes near me," she said as the other two captured women just sat still with fear.

"Well, at least my ass is white!" Helga said, standing in the doorway fit to be tied. Then Sven spoke up.

"Now Helga, you know that's not right to call them half-breed black wenches . . . because they're only about a tenth of a percent of black wenches."

"Ha, ha, ha!" Jon laughed aloud with his crew like they all had tummy aches. Helga took one sterner look at all of them, and vehemently slammed the door closed.

"Ah! Brother Sven, upon further consideration of your offer, I have decided that perhaps it might not be the wisest of choices to bring this English maiden into yonder house. So I will except your generous offer of fine wine in exchange, for the English wench," Jon said.

"Methinks you have made a wise decision after all. Beside you will need the wine to calm down the fair Helga, yes?"

"Me believes that you are right twice! She is yours," Jon said as he picked up the keg of wine.

"Come with me, my lady-in-waiting," Sven said to the young blond-haired maiden.

"No!" She responded by refusing to be handled and pulled back against his hold on her hand. He merely laughed as he gathered a better grip of her as she kicked and squirmed in an attempt to get away from him.

"Ah! A spunky one thou art," Sven said. "I like that fieriness in a maiden. It makes it more fun." He hoisted her to his shoulders while all the Viking clan members standing around started laughing. Sven took off with her straddled across his shoulders while barely paying a bit off attention to her resistance as she pounded on his back while he walked onward to his home. Maybe he had a Helga of sorts there too, because back then, men were men and women were women.

"Men, for all your brave fighting, these two maidens are community property—have at them as you like," Jon said to his Viking longboat crew. Immediately eleven or twelve Viking warriors surrounded the two young teenage virgin maidens. They were obviously frightened, as they interlocked their arms together to hold on to each other tightly. The group of long-white-haired men towering above just encircled around them, to draw lots to see who would be first to break in the two maidens. Soon these young girls of about sixteen would learn a harsh lesson in the reality of men's desires for women; especially for the flesh of young, fresh, untouched women. Jon strolled into his house with his keg of wine. Once he closed the door behind him, he fixed his eyes on his beautiful wife.

"Ah, fair Helga!" he said, trying to clear the air. "I have brought fermented drink for us to share." But the fair Helga stormed off into the bedroom without even looking back, and locked the door behind her by bracing a chair up against it. Jon set the keg down to breathe deeply as he sighed with disappointment. Then he glanced at his Viking children, who were looking on but not saying a word. That lasted a few seconds, and then he hunched his shoulders and put a normal look on his face, as if to say "Oh well." He then went to a nearby room and opened the door, where he looked inside to see a woman with blue eyes and brunette hair. She held a small child next to her who had white hair with blue eyes.

"Ah! There you are," Jon said lustfully. He drooled a bit and then wiped his lips off like he had just taken a shot of hard liquor. The woman looked up at him, revealing a blackened eye that was healing like it had happened a while ago. Then she closed her eyes for a second, because she had come to know oh so well what that penetrating stare of his meant.

Jon latched onto her arm and then pulled her to her feet. The little girl grabbed onto the woman's leg, saying, "Please don't hurt Mother, Daddy, please don't hurt her!" The little girl spoke with more of an English accent than a Viking one, though she was a mixture of the two.

"Don't you worry, my little princess," he said. "Just as long as she learns to obey me, nothing will happen to her."

"I'm not some common slave, for you to degrade whenever you drunken please," She said in rebuttal.

"You are what I tell you, you are, you black-haired wench," he said as he pressed her against the wall while breathing heavily upon her flesh like he wanted to kiss her, as though her rejection was turning him on. It always had, with his long white hair draped in between them. She squinted her eyes, as though she were in more pain than usual. He looked down from sensing that her discomfort was coming from her stomach.

"No, Dad no, please don't hurt Mommy," the little girl said, as he slowly released the hold on her to observe her figure. Then he saw it as he backed away, looking as the little girl scooted between them to protect her mother.

"I see that thou art with child again," he said with a grin on his face, which caused the major part of Helga's frustration more than anything else—knowing that she was carrying another one of her husband's children. Make no mistake about it, even though she performed all the house duties around the place, it didn't make Helga any happier that she was having a child by her husband. "This time you make sure that it's a boy. We need more warriors to fight for us," Jon said. She realized that these children were going to be used against her own immediate family perhaps back on English soil. They would not know that some men raiding and fighting against them might be their own blood relatives. They would be bent on killing them or vice versa, but we are all brothers and sisters, whether we like it or not.

"If I could help it, I wouldn't have any for you." She spoke her mind without caring at this point whether she got another black eye to match the other one she already had. "I would rather be home, far, far away from here."

"Well, you're barefooted and pregnant, and it's a week's journey through some of the highest freezing mountain passages thou can imagine," Jon said. "I think you'd just better get used to being here for a long while, and put some herbs on that black eye. It should have healed by now, for Valhalla's sake. I didn't hit you that hard, you're just trying to make me look bad." He placed his hand to her face softly, as though he were concerned for her well-being, but she just turned her head away to the side, to show that she didn't enjoy his touching her. He was not an ugly man on the outside, but she couldn't stand the ugliness of his personality or dominating ways, which she couldn't do anything about, because most women prefer freedom of choice in sexual relationships. Then he just looked at her lustfully for a second again.

"Barbara, honey. Thou needs to go out into the living quarters of the house with the rest of the children for a while," Jon said.

"Is Mother going to be all right?" Barbara asked with concern for her mother.

"Yes, she is, dear," Jon said.

"Mother?" Barbara's inquiring tone waited for her to confirm what her father had just said as Jon leaned in closer to speak in a low tone of voice into her mother's ear.

"Tell her you're going to be all right," he ordered as she sensed that it would be the best thing for her to do, instead of resisting.

"I'm going to be all right, honey. You just go on out and play with the other children," she insisted to her daughter.

"Okay . . . Bye, Mother," Barbara said as she walked slowly out of the room. Her mother headed toward the bed and sat down on it with her head held high and her hands neatly folded in her lap, peering straight ahead. Jon shut the door behind Barbara as she exited the room into the living quarters reluctantly. There she saw her half brothers and sisters sitting at a table eating, and she moved ever so closer to them with caution.

They saw her coming, but the older ones pretended not to notice as they sat on each side of the table; it was four of them all together with pure white hair like their mother and father. The oldest was a girl of about eleven years old named Arija; then there was Nick, a boy of about nine, Hon, another boy of about six, and another girl, Tina, about three. Barbara was about five. They were eating bread by dipping the end of it into a hearty beef stew, and then ripping off a chunk of it in their mouths after each dunking. Barbara stood at the end of the table looking on for a second.

They knew she had smelled the delicious stew by the flaring of her nostrils, but none of them acknowledged her presence at the table except for three-year-old Tina, who looked on with a blank stare that neither invited nor discouraged as she absorbed Barbara's image like the bread her full brothers and sister dipped into their bowls to sop up the succulent juices of the tasty, seasoned beef stew.

"Hi!" Barbara said mildly in hopes of seeking a friendly response that deep inside she knew she might not get. The three-year-old little girl grinned politely, but the others only momentarily cut their eyes toward her direction and then to one another and back to their bowls again. They were all caught up in the middle of a dispute between the two women that their father had initiated in the home. Since Helga, their mother, was upset because of their father's lustful desires toward the other captive women, the children sided with their mother's emotions, which in turn transcended to Barbara in the form of alienation by her half brothers and sisters through any meaningful associations.

Barbara was just the innocent victim in the middle like her mother. Still, Jon dominated the household by laying claim to being the master of the home, which he lorded over with profound dictatorship.

"Look, it's the half-breed English girl," Nick said, obviously repeating what he had often heard his mother say in a fit of rage perhaps or off by themselves without Barbara and her mother around.

"I'm not a half-breed," Barbara said in a sorrowful voice as her eyes started to well up.

"Yes, you are!" Hon insisted spitefully. "Mother says that your hair is going to turn yellow when you get older—she did." He was assured, as if his mother were an all-knowing sorceress that he got the information from firsthand.

"Huh-uh! That's not true—my hair is just like yours," Barbara insisted, and she started to cry, bawling her little eyes out.

"Yes, it is true!" Nick said scornfully as Barbara continued to cry. Arija began to feel sorry for her. After all, she was old enough to realize that her half sister wasn't to blame for what their father had caused in the home.

"You guys just leave her alone—she didn't do anything. After all, she is our little sister too," Arija said.

"Oh yeah! Only our half, half-breed sister, like, duh!" Nick remarked.

"Oh, why doesn't thou just "shut up"? Arija insisted.

"Why don't thou just shut up too?" Nick said as his younger brother joined in on his side.

"Yeah, you girls need to shut up," Hon concurred as Arija ignored them.

"Would you like some soup?" Arija asked Barbara, who was just seeking any form of kindness from the four at the table.

"Yes," she said, sniffing while trying to hold back her tears.

"Okay, here you go," Arija said while grabbing a bowl off the handcrafted mantel over the fireplace. Then she dipped a large ladle into a black cauldron that brewed over the fire. After pouring it into the bowl, she felt compelled to caution Barbara as she set the dish in front of her and tore a chunk off the large mound of bread in the center of the table.

Helga was walking out of her bedroom as Arija was helping Barbara get seated at the table.

"Now, this is hot, Barbara, so you be . . . careful . . . now," Arija said as she slowly stopped assisting Barbara, because her mother had entered the room. Then all the children paused as a teary, red-eyed Helga looked upon them. Barbara felt just as afraid as the rest of them, for they thought Helga might become upset by them taking acceptance of little Barbara. Only the three-year-old was unafraid, because she didn't know any better, as she revealed.

"Arija is getting Barbara some soup. It's good too. Do you want some, Mommy?" Arija just cringed some more, which she thought was not possible until she did it. Helga just looked at them all sternly for a second and then headed for the front door of the small four-room dwelling. Before she got out the front door, she heard the moaning and groaning sound coming from the bedroom, where Jon was with the captive English woman. "Ah! Ah! Oh!" It turned like a knife in Helga's heart to hear them having intercourse. She opened and slammed the front door and then sat on the front porch soaking in the cold air to brood over the event, but it was the Viking way, and the man had all the advantages.

Time soon passed and Jon came out of the bedroom, where through the open door you could see the dark-haired English woman resting under the covers of the bed. He shut the door behind him as he came out into the living space to eat with his children—all of them. He poured himself a bowl of stew and then yanked off a chunk of bread nearly half the size of the entire loaf in the center of the table. He was good to all his children, even Barbara, whose hair was still white like the rest of them. All the children crowded around him. He was barbaric only to the emotional concerns of women, just like most of the other Viking men.

"Father, how did you do in battle this time against the English?" Nick asked as Helga came back in the door. Her tears had dried up, but she was still feeling downhearted while harboring a solitary mood.

"By Valhalla, I did slay six Englishmen, and brought back plenty of spoils," Jon boasted as Helga walked across the living quarters to their bedroom.

"What did you bring back, Father?" Hon asked. Jon hesitated to answer.

"Well, food, and plunder enough for all of our Viking clan to share," he elucidated.

"Yes, tell your sons of the glorious rich treasure that you brought back, just like the ones before, which are going to make all of our lives easier," Helga said. "I just bet you're going to adorn me with precious crown jewels from England, huh, Jon?" Helga dashed off into the bedroom while shaking her head from side to side, which made her long white braids dangle, while thinking, *I don't believe this mess.* The children picked up on their mother's uneasiness. Certainly Barbara felt that some of the resentment was directed toward her indirectly, but she was too young to understand just yet.

It didn't faze Jon that much, because in his mind the man had the right to have more than one wife or bed wench if he chose. To him he was just exercising his manly right to preserve himself and his kind, but to Helga it was a slap right in the face, by exercising extreme rule as master over his domain. If she disagreed, then he had as much right to slap her as he did the English wench. Having an English woman in her home to share her man was like sporting a black eye around the community before her friends, even though a few of them were experiencing the same thing. She may have been more receptive to it had it been the wife of a fallen Viking brother in her house.

Helga had been taught to hate the English, as well as other Europeans, since her childhood was like being raised as a redneck, and now her husband had moved a black bed-wench slave, as beautiful as a famous black Oscar-winning actress, into the bedroom across the hall. Her husband was sleeping around with his slave basically right under her nose, but indirectly of her in the presence of their house, which happened in the old South when Dixie shined like a brand new penny. Helga was living in turmoil, feeling cast down like a beautiful, discarded porcelain doll years ago by Jon, who appeared on the very same blessed threshold of their own front door that he carried Helga over on their wedding day while toting the black-haired, blue-eyed English woman in restraints behind him to live in their home as a bed-wench servant, to increase the numbers of their fighting Viking warriors, as so proclaimed throughout their Viking land.

Soon the Viking men would take many more of the young, dark-haired English maidens captured in their raids for bed wenches. Over a period of time they produced an abundance of children; most had blond hair at adult age, although some had red, brown, and, rarely, brunette hair, with pale skin that had splotched brown specks now referred to as freckles. The specks increased in size with age, and become referred to as age spots—not brown skin through Kendihuchrodnamixgenesis.

They fought well alongside the rest of the pure white Viking clan, but these half-breed warriors did one thing that the original Vikings who took these women for breeding did not expect and overlooked. They started marrying the pure white Viking daughters, as the original Vikings started accepting them as sons and brothers when they fought valiantly side by side with them against the English, French, Irish, and Scottish.

Over time it caused the Vikings to lose their pure white hair completely, by devolving into mostly blonds, redheads, and or light-brown-haired humans who were later accepted by the decreasing numbers of pure white-haired Viking brothers who adopted them. In just a few short centuries they became like the last of the Mohicans. The last of the 100 percent pure humans (Vikings) were being edited into final *Homo sapiens* form, as each partially English child, became accepted into their formerly isolated society that rejected so many before. Of all the races that we must learn about, the Vikings are the most important. They were the last direct descendants of the original people on the earth—Adam and Eve—handcrafted by God in his image as he breathed the breath of life into Adam's nostrils.

It should be noted that the last of the 100 percent pure white humans (the Vikings) as white as snow died just over two thousand years ago, just before the word was made flesh, as it says in John 1:1. Now it seems destined that it is time for man to dig up the 100 percent pure white humans buried by an avalanche nearly five thousand years ago and prove God's existence through their existence in this century of 2000, when cloning became an issue.

Extreme caution is given here: Men will seek out these Viking remains to harvest eggs and milk the sperm from these children brought back to life for huge monetary gain by whiting man's blood, like a dentist does our teeth through those who are the direct descendants of Adam and Eve. Basically for their reproductive traits, greedy men will violate their natural human rights of selection, to breed the whiteness of the "genetic norm" back into people through artificial insemination, because man will soon come to realize that natural blonds are an endangered species in the mixing bowl of life all around the world.

# RARE FIND

If there were only one existing vial of 100 percent pure white human sperm and two 100 percent pure white human eggs in the world today, they would be worth more than $1 billion cash in American currency to whoever is the possessor of them. These items will be sought by a queen in this modern century 2000, to put true blue blood on her throne to outrival even the ersatz blue blood on the throne of England hands down.

The specific area of the country will not be mentioned so as not to give possible clues to the greedy profiteers who would exploit them like exotic animals. I do caution all the European national leaders north of Italy to have stringent rules regarding the removal of the frozen dead from a time passed, to help prevent the exploitation of the 100 percent pure white humans from your borders. If you don't heed this warning, it will be like the drunk driving law conception. Why wait until you have numerous drunk driving fatalities to institute a drunk driving law that is clearly needed? This accident should be prevented before the removal of any 100 percent pure white original Viking descendants from the frozen north of Europe; the law should be enacted first, before exploration begins.

Just look at the possible mistakes made with the frozen mummy known as Oetzi the Iceman. Doctors, scientists, and researchers at the University of Camerino have no idea of the possible prospect that they have before them. It has been since 1991 that he was found, and yet not one of the top scientific minds in the entire world has thought to collect his sperm or do a genetic "norm" DNA mapping of him to see if he is

100 percent human, or a sickle cell test. That means they have no clue into this man's real past. Heck, they collected the sperm of the woolly mammoth, considered highly valuable, that they found frozen in ice. So are they saying that man is less important than an animal? God said that man is the most important creature and he will rule over all other living creatures on the earth. Man's thinking is backward and these words seek to change it.

Let's give Oetzi a plausible past in which to track his life. Oetzi, like Jon was a Viking warrior, who went on a raid years before Jon was born. He went down into Europe by longboat to raid, pillage, plunder, and rid the land of what they considered a Caucasian infestation upon the earth, even though at the time they weren't called Caucasian people. They were identified by either their colorful genetic traits, which sometimes linked them to the lands, or territory that they occupied such as the redheads, who were mainly found in the territory today known as Ireland. Oetzi and his pure white Viking brothers for the most part had many successful raids, raping and carrying off much plunder, which included many of the Caucasian women.

This time, however, it was not so fortunate for Oetzi, because the Caucasian men had anticipated a raid just after the harvest time of the year again. They surprised the Vikings by how fast they could assemble their organized fighting men in the middle of the night, like Paul Revere and the Minutemen during the American Revolution, to thwart their menacing raiders. The Vikings had pillaged and plundered as usual while hurling insults of half-breed-ness at the European Caucasian settlers to burn an impression in their minds that would cause them to have a complex about their genetic makeup. The European sect would soon create a fashion trend of wearing white wigs, which was like a soothing ointment applied to the burned impressions left in their minds by the original Vikings, especially in the courts of London, where all lords of high nobility wore them. You were looked down upon as a peasant if you didn't, and this trend lasted well into the American colonial era of George Washington and longer. European men pursued Oetzi and his Viking brothers back to their longboats this time, and more of them fell than usual. An arrow in his shoulder blade, which caused him to drop mostly all that he had carried as plunder, and also to miss the boat, as they say, struck Oetzi. He knew as the boats sailed out of sight into the night that they would not come back for at least another year, for that is what had happened to his fallen comrades who did not make it back to boats that he sailed off on back to the Viking lands, but he was able to escape on foot.

Oetzi's only hope of getting home was to make a long, treacherous hike through the freezing mountain passes to his Viking homelands that were known to consume the life of most healthy men if crossed at the wrong time of year. It was at the end of the harvest season, basically nearing winter, and the first snow was likely to start falling within a week or two. He had to cross now if he was going to do it at all. Though he was wounded with an arrow piercing his back, he had no choice but to try. The Europeans would most certainly kill him if they found him, so he started the long journey back toward home with a quiver of arrows and a copper ax, with which he was able to get large game to survive on and use the hides like extra clothing as he made the trek up the mountain summit.

The weather at the peak of the mountain started to get colder and colder the higher he climbed, and the wound he had received to his back from the arrow made the climb all the more difficult. He was virtually unable to use one arm, which made him realize that perhaps this was the wrong decision to make, but he journeyed on to his last stride, where he fell from utter and complete exhaustion. He just waited now, to succumb to the fate that would freeze him for the preservation of study by modern man many centuries later, and as he lay there, the first snow of the season started to fall on him. Perhaps the last thoughts on his mind were of his homeland, as he envisioned his family members, especially his young, beautiful wife who would be looking for his face to greet hers once the longboats returned. Oh, God, how he loved her. The last image of her long, beautiful, flowing white hair, which easily blew in the slightest wind like strands of silk, appeared in his mind.

God had planned for all these things to come by his will. It was not by accident that the pure white race chose to go the frozen north of Norway instead of south to the continent of Africa to settle on the Ivory Coast. How else would the pure white race have been preserved for man to find and study centuries later, so we'd know where we came from or that God created us? Obviously some men have been lost, not having much of a clue as to where we came from unless God feels it necessary for us to learn a lesson that he is our creator, and we should not have so many different ideas of where we come from!

# MAN'S INHUMANITY TO MAN

The world was now totally divided, and man knew not his brothers as he had when they got off the ark. God now found someone to call on who would bring his people back into his glory as he had intended for man in the beginning. Now came the calling of Abram.

> The Lord had said unto Abram, "Leave your country, your people and your father's household and go to the land I will show you.
> "I will make you a great nation and I will bless you;
> "I will make your name great, and you will be a blessing.
> "I will bless those who bless you, and whoever curses you I will curse; and all the people on earth will be blessed through you." (Genesis 12:1-3)

These words are written so that the mystery of man's past would be made clear. We all know much of man's history from the point of Abraham, but it was the previous story of Abram that mystified us all. Blessed be the name of the Lord God that is allowing the past to be cleared up. I feel humbly unworthy of, yet enthralled by, having such an honor as this bestowed on me, to bring forth the truth to my fellow man.

History tells us about how Abram and Sarai had their trials by trying to have Isaac, and Ishmael. It tells us about the trials Isaac had with his wells, and the trials of Jacob and Esau. Then came the trials of Joseph sold into Egypt by his brothers and all that he endured, but what we need here is for all to understand the details of what took place.

Joseph saw his brothers who had sold him into slavery when they came into Egypt to buy grain to feed their livestock, because the famine was so severe, but after putting them through a trial, he reviled himself unto them, and they all had a tearful reunion.

Genesis 41:55-57 says that when all of Egypt began to feel the famine, they cried to Pharaoh for food. Then Pharaoh told all the Egyptians, "Go to Joseph and do what he tells you."

When the famine had spread over the whole country, Joseph opened the storehouses and sold grain to the Egyptians, for the famine was severe throughout Egypt. And people from all the countries near and far came to Egypt to buy grain from Joseph, because the famine became severe in other parts of the world also. At one point Pharaoh must have come to Joseph to say, "Your predictions have come true, Zaphenath-Paneah. Your God is with you, and now perhaps he will bring everyone here to Egypt, to make us a one world government to end all fighting among men." Pharaoh may have remembered something about the world being one and had his hopes set high on this dream that all men would be brothers in this land. Genesis 41:54-57 Perhaps he had heard ancient rumors about it from centuries earlier, after God came down above the triangle-shaped holy temple and changed everyone's language.

"If it is his will, then it will be so," Joseph must have said in confidence says that when Pharaoh and his officials heard that Joseph's family was there, they were pleased. Pharaoh asked Joseph to bring his entire family to Egypt to live in the best land.

Jacob and his family came to Egypt to live; he was very happy to be reunited with his son Joseph once again. The beginning years of their time together in Egypt were great, as Joseph provided well for all his family. It was as the Lord God had predicted to Abram: "Your descendants will go down into Egypt and be slaves for 400 years." Most of Jacobs's family had Caucasian features and still had blondish to brown-colored hair, but some of them were of darker mix through the darker servants that Abraham received from Pharaoh after he took Sarah from Abraham to be his wife. Ishmael was born by one of the former Egyptian servants of medium-brown skin with wavy hair, because all the races that had remained there after the one world government broke up had blended together like a melting pot. Their appearance was mostly like that of the interracial children born of Afro-American and Caucasian descent here in America, with very light brown skin and, for a lot of them, curly to wavy hair. The famine was so bad that many people sold themselves into slavery for food, including Jacob's family.

Exodus 1:8 says that a new Pharaoh came to power in Egypt after many generations had gone by, and that this one did not know Joseph or his descendants or all that Joseph had done to save Egypt, as well as most of the surrounding kingdoms. This Pharaoh became a hard taskmaster to the descendants of Abraham; soon they came to his courts to appeal their position. Now with the Hebrews' elder members standing in Pharaoh's presence before his throne, they pleaded for their freedom.

"Great Pharaoh, for many centuries we have given service unto you for the food that our forefathers purchased from your fathers with their lives. Surely after all these years we have more than repaid our debt for the food that was given to our fathers for us to stay alive, have we not?"

Pharaoh looked on at them for a moment while an adviser spoke into his ear. "Now let Pharaoh speak for all to hear. When your father Abram came to Egypt and his wife, Sarai, was taken by Pharaoh, who then gave her back with many slaves, cattle, livestock, and other possessions, did he let any of these Egyptian people go?"

"Yes. Hagar and her son Ishmael, Abraham did release."

"Then you may release one woman and one child amongst you, but the rest of you must remain slaves to build my cities."

"Please, Pharaoh, be reasonable. Our numbers are so many, and we have served you for so long. If not for our brother Joseph, would Pharaoh have a kingdom to rule over?"

"Who is this Joseph that you speak of? I know of no Joseph who saved all of Egypt! Our gods alone have saved us and brought you to serve us," Pharaoh said sharply.

"It is written that our God has brought us into this land to be slaves," the head designated elder said humbly.

"Then if I were you, I would quickly change gods, for who needs a god that would make him a slave?" Pharaoh said, and he along with his entire court assembly laughed aloud in the faces of the Hebrew men.

"This is unjust!" one of the Hebrew men exclaimed out loud, angering Pharaoh.

"And do you accuse Pharaoh of being unfair?" Instantly Pharaoh's guards withdrew their swords from the sheaths in their belts. Then one of the other Hebrew elders put his hand on the arm of the one who was speaking, to caution him to be very selective of his next words before Pharaoh.

"No, we would never do that, Great Pharaoh, but the servants in our father Abraham's house were treated as brothers and given tasks equal to ours." Then the guards placed their swords back into their sheaths.

"That is not my concern. You sold yourselves as slaves, and now you whine like women that it is too hard for you. Be gone! I will hear no more of this," he said, turning his head to the side and placing his nose high in the air while he held the palm of his hand out toward them to signal for them not to speak anymore. The Hebrew leaders left with a downhearted feeling clamping down on their souls, because they knew that the people were waiting for them back at the villages with hopes that their freedom was at hand. They were made to feel insulted by these darker-skinned Egyptian people with smirks and grins on their faces as the elders left the courtroom, while some just downright laughed with ignorance. There might have been one Egyptian who felt remorse for the Israelite people, but if he were a wise man, he wouldn't show it before Pharaoh.

In a few centuries of Egyptian rule more of the world's history was lost, because if they couldn't remember the history of Joseph and all that he did for them, there was no way that man would remember where the world's first one world government took place or the holy tower of Shinar, King Nimrod's resting place within the Sphinx, or where the ark landed on Mount Ararat. Who would the Lord God call on to remember every day?

Out in the hot sun of the Egyptian desert cities, you could see the Hebrews—still mostly Caucasian at this time—laboring, while the raping of their women started to produce more and more curly-haired people amongst them with more tan shades of skin. Slaves were usually taken to punishment houses for more severe attitude-adjustment procedures. These were usually made up of open columns in the sun with chains linked to pillars to hold the slaves while they were being whipped for all the other slaves to see as they walked by, laboring. This punishment of their brothers was a reminder tool to thwart any inclinations toward defiance, as they beat the hide nearly off some of them. You could see a row of about twelve guards, all brown skinned, beating the Caucasian men tied to the pillars as their Caucasian women—mothers and sisters—cried and begged that they be shown mercy with tears streaming down their faces while the long lines of Caucasian men in the background worked like ants, hauling bags of sand to build the new cities and pyramids.

Off in another part of the surrounding Egyptian cities, Pharaoh was watching a certain maiden from his bedroom balcony carrying water for her Caucasian men, who labored in the sun daily. She had beautiful, blondish-red hair with pretty blue eyes with hardly a brown speck to be found anywhere. With just a gesture of his hand, he signaled to his guards to go and bring the maiden to him. Quickly they confronted the beautiful young woman, which surprised her as she clutched the water jar.

"You! Come with us." These brown-skinned men with curly Afros ordered her with direct authority from Pharaoh while wielding swords and spears and surrounding her.

"What! What have I done?" she asked, almost frightened for her life as one guard grabbed hold of her arm. Another took the jar out of her hand and set it down on the ground. She looked for help as she pulled away from the guards, who were ready to whisk her away to Pharaoh's bedroom, where he would rape her, if she didn't willing accept his offer. Her brother was summoned by someone who said, "Pharaoh's guards have come for your sister." None of the other men standing around would intervene on the girl's behalf, mostly out of fear of the sword-wielding guards.

"Help me, please!" she shouted for someone to be brave enough to come to her aid, but all the others just stood their ground, looking on. The other Caucasian women looked at their men to see if someone would move to help her. But they all just looked down at the ground as the dark-skinned guards laughed at having their way. Then they started to haul her off carefully, because they knew she'd better not get one scratch before they got her into Pharaoh's chambers and tied her to the four corners of the bedposts if necessary.

Her brother with reddish-colored hair emerged through the crowd of fellow men and women Hebrew slaves as the guards hoisted the girl above their shoulders and then proceeded to walk off with her. He saw what was going on with his sister and ran over to the guards. He knocked the last one in line down to the ground and then picked up the guard's sword to protect his sister. The other guards quickly put the girl down to deal with what they considered a menace that was preventing them from carrying out Pharaoh's orders—thus bringing harm upon themselves from Pharaoh.

"Leave my sister alone!" he shouted while facing them all alone with a single sword. He glanced back momentarily to see if perhaps one other brave soul among his fellow Hebrew brothers would come to his aid, but none would move to help him, so he went it alone. The guards realized that he was on his own by the expressions of the other Israelite men, so they surrounded him.

"You have made a grave mistake, slave." The guard gave the signal for all of them to attack. Her brother fought back valiantly and fatally wounded one of the guards first with the sword that he had taken, but in the end they struck him down from behind with a superficial wound, whereupon they continued to encircle him like vultures. Then they struck him down before the eyes of his sister as the other men, women, and children slaves just stood there looking on with heavy hearts, and the guards hacked the rest of his body into small, bloody, mutilated pieces. *Why didn't we help? We should have done something,* they thought afterward.

But it would have all ended in the same way as before, even if ten or so men had jumped in to help him save his sister from the clutches of Pharaoh. The guards would have regrouped to come back only minutes later with more troops to attack, which would have resulted in more deaths of the much-needed forces they were secretly amassing by having their women produce excessive amounts of children. They wanted to fight their way to freedom in a few short years from these harsh taskmasters. Somewhat like the Vikings, they even claimed the children their women conceived by rape from the Egyptian men as their own for the purpose of this fight.

The girl was finally taken to Pharaoh's chambers while still thrashing about and then tied to the four bedposts by each limb with tearful eyes as the guards left her there in the quiet for a moment. She struggled to free herself so she could run back to her people or into the desert—just run far away from this place that was beautifully decorated with the images of the people that she hated with every ounce of her soul now, because she had witnessed her brother being mutilated right before her very eyes. But she couldn't break free of the ties that held her body steadfast to the bed.

Suddenly she froze to listen to the sound of someone closing a door. Whether they came in or went out she could not tell, but then from around a pillar he appeared like someone delivering bad news when you are already down and out, with a knife in his hand. She was frightened enough without the weapon, by knowing what he intended to do in the first place. He stood there looking on at her without blushing, and she felt his eyes lustfully viewed her entire body as he came nearer, which caused her disgust of these people to heighten, because she saw how well pleased his perverted eyes were with her feminine features.

"We can do this with joy for both of us or just me—it's up to you," he said as he stroked his hands across her firm breast, before cutting the bondage straps loose that held her in position on the bed. She fought back by twisting her body away from his touch as much as she could. "Well, I guess it's going to be the hard way then." He proceeded to cut her ragged clothing away from her body with the sharp knife, which seemed to peel the cloth apart like slicing tissue paper as it flowed easily through the thick sackcloth material.

"Don't touch me!" she exclaimed.

"Don't worry. I'll reward you with some new clothes worthy of even an Egyptian girl."

All you could see were the shadowed images of them both against the wall so clearly as her breast flopped back and forth between the hands of the painted images of Egyptian gods on the wall while he cut the remaining portions of her lower garment off. Then after tossing the rest of her clothes and the knife to the floor, he removed his headdress along with his garments and climbed atop her. He went straight to intercourse with her as she started to moan and groan, because he had total advantage over her in every way and did as he pleased with her.

These Caucasian women were used daily at the will of the darker-skinned Egyptian men, who would marry them if Pharaoh allowed it to happen. He owned everyone in Egypt and gave many of the Caucasian Israelite women in marriage to his most faithfully dedicated guards and soldiers as rewards for their services to his throne and iron-handed rule. Soon the mixing of the blood lightened some of the Egyptians' skin and darkened the skin of the Israelite people; they were in a sense being forced to mix with the darker-skinned Egyptian people, as the dark-skinned people would soon have to in America.

The realization of Pharaoh's advantages over them is why the other Hebrew men did not get into the fight in the first place when the guards came for the young girl; they had no swords and nearly starved, so they'd have no strength to fight back now. Besides, their elders had given them orders not to interfere in order to multiply their number of fighting men by not resisting the Egyptians violating their own Israelite women. Certainly this made some of their victimized women think of them as weak, as is the case of every bonded race, but they knew the day the deliverer God promised was coming soon. Maybe someone who could slay a thousand men with the jawbone of a donkey to make jackasses out of the Egyptians would make all of them brave enough to stand and follow behind him. He would be the sign of the deliverer, so they continued to increase their numbers, to have many fighting men ready when he came to fight with them. But this was not God's plan, it was man's.

The slave boy's mother came over with her grayish-blond hair and eyes full of tears to look at her son who had just been butchered like a livestock animal for choice cuts of steak. Then others came to her aid by lifting her sobbing, limp body as the men gathered up his severed body pieces to bury him.

The elders reminded them that they were to play passive toward the arrogant Egyptians until their numbers became large enough to overrun them and take their freedom, but as much as it hurt their pride, they would just have to let the Egyptians have their way with their Hebrew women for now, so that they would increase like the grains of sand as the Lord God had promised Abraham.

# GROWING PROBLEM

Centuries later, another Pharaoh was overlooking the slaves building the city. "'Look,' he said to his people, 'the Israelites have become much too numerous for us. Come, we must deal shrewdly with them or they will become even more numerous and, if war breaks out, will join our enemies, fight against us and leave the country'" (Exodus 1:9-10).

The Israelites had more than enough fighting men to conquer the Egyptians by now, but not enough heart just like the Negros in the South who spoke of rebellion, but the more the Egyptians oppressed them, the more they multiplied and spread as they were ruthlessly forced to build cities like Pithom and Rameses as store cities for Pharaoh.

> The king said to the Hebrew midwives, whose names were Shiphrah and Puah, "When you help the Hebrew women in childbirth and observe them on the delivery stool, if it is a boy, kill him; but if it is a girl, let her live."
>
> The midwives, however, feared God and did not do what the king of Egypt had told them to do; they let the boys live.
>
> Then the king of Egypt summoned the midwives and asked, "Why have you done this? Why have you let the boys live?"
>
> The midwives answered Pharaoh, "Hebrew women are not like the Egyptian women; they are vigorous and give birth before the midwives arrive."

> So God was kind to the midwives and the people increased and became even more numerous. And because the midwives feared God, he gave them families of their own.

Pharaoh at this point must have begun to panic as he pondered drastic methods of controlling the Hebrew men's numbers in his mind.

Then Pharaoh gave this order to all his people: "Every Hebrew boy that is born, you must throw it into the Nile, but let every girl live."

Most of the Hebrew children to this point were transformed so that they had dark-brown—or brunette-haired Caucasian traits, though some were darker—tan in complexion—because of the darker-skinned Egyptian men who were forcing themselves upon the Hebrew women. That soon caused a lot of children in the Israelite tribes to have wavy, almost curly, hair instead of straight blond, red, or brown hair, but just like the Viking methodology against the English. They planned to use these darker traits Egyptian father offspring by Israelite women against the Egyptian people themselves.

Egyptian people began to believe and fear that this delivery of mighty strength would come to lead the children of Abraham to freedom, so they cast the Hebrew children into the Nile as Pharaoh had instructed them. Even if the child looked like it may have been fathered by one of the Egyptian men, they cast it into the river. This atrocity burned in God's heart, but what goes around comes around, they say. A couple of centuries later, these dark-skinned people around the northern part of Africa who said there was nothing wrong with enslaving the Caucasian Hebrews came to find themselves enslaved by the Caucasian race of Europe, who told the Vikings that it was wrong that they were prejudiced against them, because of their darker Caucasian traits—the Viking reasoning for putting them to death. Different clan of Caucasian people from Europe, and different dark-skinned people from deeper southern parts of Africa to a place called America, thus God's purpose for doing this is to even the scales on Judgment Day. All you accusers of wrongful doing over slavery, beware, for Judgment Day is coming, and all have done wrong.

The Egyptian people became even more indignant toward the Israelite people, often cracking jokes at their expense as regularly as they cracked the taskmaster's whip upon the flesh of the Hebrews' backs.

Once while two Egyptian overseers idly stood by watching the Israelites stonecutters repairing a temple stone carving, which they had made an error in, these overseers made jest of them about their intellect and appearance caused by the raping of their women.

"Look at those dumb, mixed-up Israelite dogs working, would you?" the one with hair like a short curly Afro said. "Now they have to repair that temple stone carving!"

"Yeah, what a dumb, mixed-up waste of flesh!" the other added.

"Talk about being mixed up. I remember when they looked white. Now their skin color is just Israelite. Ha! Ha! Ha!" Both men laughed at the top of their lungs. "Get it? Their skin color used to be white, but now it's just Israelite!"

"You slay me sometimes. Their skin color is just Israelite." The other man repeated what he heard once more while all the Israelite men standing around who could hear them just looked at one another without saying a word. They continued working like nothing bothered them, but it did, and they waited for their chance to pay them back in full.

Exodus 2 tells us that a man of the house of Levi married a Levite woman, and she became pregnant. Soon Moses came, and we should all know the stories of how God used him as the great deliverer to free the Israelite people from bondage in Egypt, who were awaiting a Samson figure. God paid the Egyptians back tenfold in suffering; too their pride and egos by releasing their control of God's people, for them claiming that their Pharaohs were gods.

But God called Moses to be his deliverer of the Israelite people, just to let Pharaoh's arrogance know that he could use someone as small, humble, and harmless looking as Moses to topple the great cities of mighty Egypt. Moses performed many miraculous miracles in the name of the Lord God, who lives forever. This was the second time he had done great works at the holy temple of Shinar, because its name was changed to the Great Pyramids of Egypt, when man had to use combinations of pictures and symbols called hieroglyphics to communicate, which is how it became known as the city of babble by travelers. Genesis 11:9 says all the people babbled to understand one another until the hieroglyphic writings became perfected, to create one Egyptian language.

From here we know the accounts recorded in the passages of the Bible to be true! How the Israelites crossed the Red Sea on dry land to be saved from the hands of the Egyptians, who seemingly still hold a grudge toward Israelites to this day—like rednecks hold toward Afro-Americans. After they freely crossed the River Jordan, they went prosperously into the promised land by taking it over with the help of the Lord, but because they did not follow his strict instructions to purge the land of perverted sinners and not mix with anyone who did not follow the ways of the Lord God—not because of their skin color, for everyone is mixed—the Israelites found themselves in peril over it centuries later.

# The Dynasty Falls

We know about the prophets, whom he called from the past of long ago to help the seed of Abraham come into his presence and obey till he sent his only begotten son to call them back, but the builders rejected the most precious stone needed to build up their kingdom. He is a light for all the world to follow by making a way for all men who believe in the son of God, and follow his fathers will be invited to the wedding of the bridegroom.

Some centuries later, man turned to trusting in the strength of his own arm to reunite the world as a one world government again through conquest by armed forces using ethnic cleansing to bring the world back into balance. Cleopatra and Julius Caesar through a love affair would try to bring two of the greatest world forces together to make the world one government once again, but Cleopatra had an ulterior motive behind uniting her forces with Rome. She figured that she would be able to take over where her fore fathers of Pharaoh's left off by trying to conquer the world and make it a one world government again. Then she could finally get rid of the Jews, who had been a thorn as well as an embarrassment for Egyptians by the way they left and became such a powerful nation.

Cleopatra felt as though Jews were an eyesore to her country, showing the rest of the world that the Egyptian Pharaohs were not powerful enough gods to hold the Israelites in bondage as they had claimed. She decided to put her son on the throne of Rome's governing power, which held authority over the Jewish rulers, who took Jesus from Caiaphas's hand, to the palace of the Roman governor to be judged and sentenced. Then she'd have total control over the Roman army already present in

Jewish settlements, which, if combined with the Egyptian army, would destroy the Jewish people forever who lived in Rome and the rest of the world. God thwarted that plan, though, when he allowed Julius Caesar's most faithful supporters to turn against him, which resulted in Rome destroying the Egyptian queen.

A lot transpired during that remarkable piece of history, after Cleopatra brought her soldiers to the Roman Colosseum to compete in the gladiator games. Rome became a melting pot with many different darker races brought there for the games, which created the Italian race from the once Caucasian people who had dominated the Rome territories centuries earlier. Acts 10:1 tells us that at Caesarea there was a man named Cornelius, a centurion in what was known as the Italian Regiment. They were isolated like the black Buffalo Soldiers; it was like the separation of the Negro and Caucasian armed forces in the United States during World War I and II.

In her visits to Rome, Cleopatra would lay wagers on her fighters. She was sitting in the emperor's—Julius Caesar's—reserved box for all the high delegates of honor to see that he personally invited her to the Colosseum, for an up-close look at death, which was the real thing that drew the attention of the spectators.

"My dear Cleopatra, your Egyptian fighters are showing to be worthy opponents for the gladiators, even against my own Roman forces," Julius Caesar said to compliment her.

"Well, yes, Emperor, there are a lot of things that come from Egypt that may be worthy of a Roman emperor, especially jewels from the throne," Cleopatra said referring to herself, for she was young, smart, and beautiful, with straight black hair that hung down to her waistline and was trimmed straight across.

Obviously her beauty was the result of many Pharaohs, who generation after generation took the Caucasian women of Abraham's descendants who were blessed with the beauty of Sarah passed on from Eve for their pleasure, to marry, and or to use as concubine while they were enslaved in Egypt. But no matter what the actual formulation of events were that formed her appearance, Cleopatra was a beautiful woman, whose face was touted as being so gorgeous that she commanded the most import men of that time period. She had a permanent tan that she kept all year long, but during the hotter months, her complexion was a little more copper toned.

"Indeed there are some truly beautiful jewels in Egypt," he said, admiring her physical beauty, which was accented by the best perfumes and jewelry offered on the Nile. She was many years his junior, which made him feel even more attracted to her. He could have nearly any woman in Rome, slave, married, or not: his word was law. Yet he had no control over her like most of the world he held in his power. She desired him freely, making it known with her subtle female gestures. Most any Egyptian man would have given a body part or two to be married to her, yet she chose him. She saw him as a handsome Caucasian man having sandy blond hair, but well into his prime with some youthful life still left in him.

He had one thing that she found as alluring as everything else he possessed. He was a very powerful man in stature, which was very intoxicating to her. It is almost as attractive to a lot of women as powerful, rippling muscles bulging out of a man's shirt. Each parallels the list of desires by most women, but few women find the two packaged together, and even fewer find one with all the desires united. Most women as well as men learn to settle with spouses they have found, before someone else takes them. Others take the chance of waiting for much better to come along, risking the loss of suitors with decent eligibility, but Cleopatra would seize her chance the very moment the opportunity presented itself.

"I wager three of my beautiful virgin handmaidens, three young men servants, all within their twenties, and three pounds of gold that my Egyptian warrior, Tutacaum, will be the victor. Will there be any takers?" Cleopatra asked confidently. "Will there?" The high rollers around her were nervous to take her bet, for this was a heavy wager for the average rich person in Rome, although it was a mere drop in the bucket for her. They knew their champion had never been defeated, but of course that was usually the only way you made it to the next fight, but none knew of her champion, and she didn't know of theirs.

"I don't know that many could cover your wager," Caesar said. "That's pretty high for most of these here." Others in the background talked about two or more of them covering her bet, one for the maidens, one for the men servants, and one for the gold. Yes, combined they could all do it. They nodded to the recorder, signaling that they all accepted her wager; the recorder of the bets then came to her, saying, "Oh, queen of the Nile, three of our highly honored statesmen have come forth to take up your wager. Would you please sign here?" Cleopatra looked at him as though she were insulted. She clapped her hands together twice, and her entire entourage of more than a dozen young healthy strong men and female Egyptian servants surrounded Caesar's special booth. She pointed to one of the men servants, who instantly poured out a bag of gold and jewels onto a dazzling silver tray, far exceeding the three pounds in gold—not even counting the endless sea of sparkling jewels that filled the tray like the many stars in the sky on a clear night.

"My word is good enough—all they see before them are the wages they may select from . . . *if they win?*" The recorder looked up to the three statesmen, who carefully looked over her entourage. Then they did a quick conference on the matter after seeing the youthful male and female servants that they might be able to choose from. They agreed with a nodding of their heads to signify that they accepted the bet without her signature; then the recorder bowed to her respectfully as he left.

The gladiators were about to come out of the preparation rooms to battle to the death, each with their eyes on the prize of money and slaves to make their lives easier. These gladiators did not risk their lives for just nothing; it was for the slaves brought in as prizes by the slave traders from the squashed resistant forces captured by the Roman armies, for opposing Rome's rule. The sweet prize this time was two young beautiful slave maidens in their late teens and five pounds of gold. One maid was Caucasian with blond hair, and the other seemed to have Hispanic features.

They were a tempting prize to many of the young men, and to newly recruited soldiers in these armies of Rome and Egypt. Only two of the strongest volunteer contestants remained. One each was left from Egypt and Rome to battle to the death for the grand prizes, but the maidens alone would have been enough to encourage these gladiators to battle on to destiny. They were waiting in the wings of the arena now. Each fighter had already seen the prizes, which made each man even more eager to risk it all for the chance of possessing them.

Most of the Roman army was Caucasian at this time, whereas most of the Egypt army had light brown complexions. Each of the two warriors was being aided by their troops as they headed off for the arena. Both of them were considered strong and brave for putting their lives on the line, but a wiser man would deem it foolish. The Roman was about six feet four inches in height and very stout with brown hair and weighed nearly three hundred pounds. The Egyptian was nearly seven feet tall, of medium build, with dark hair, weighing nearly the same amount. They came to the center of the arena facing Caesar and Cleopatra, lifting their swords in tribute to them.

Caesar lifted his hands, and the fighters faced each other. Then with a drop of his hand the battle was on, and the crowd went into a cheering frenzy with each person shouting for their fighter. Even from the dressing room sidelines, the supporters rooted for their fellow countrymen. The clanging of their swords was nearly nullified by the audible tones from the crowds, except the slaves who did not want to be sold off into some foreign country away from their friends, family, and loved ones. Odd how freedom or disparity lay in the hands of these two men fighting for their lives; a lot of people's lives were tied in with them, and the death of one meant life for some others.

The fighting had lasted for a half an hour so far, and both fighters were weakening after every attack and defensive move of the other opponent. Suddenly they were locked in a hand-to-hand battle with daggers in their hands pointing toward the other's face. Surely one would succumb to the other's persistent attacks. They both fell, toppling to the side, and a piece of earth gave way from under their feet by the force of tugging on each other, so to catch their balance, each flung the knife out of his hand. Quickly scrambling to their knees, they looked for where their knives had fallen. Looking in the dust that was clearing, each gladiator spotted the other man's weapon. Quickness and agility counted here, and both grabbed a knife and then turned and thrust it toward the other.

Both men let out a loud groan as each man pierced the other with his own dagger. It looked like both men had successfully delivered a fatal blow as both men fell away from each other and then lay on their backs, struggling to get onto their feet. This was going to be the deciding factor for sure; whoever got to his feet first would be able to finish the other man off. The Roman gladiator rose to his feet first, and the crowd roared to its feet along with him, thereby seeing a chance finish the other opponent off, but first he had to pull his own dagger out of his abdomen. When he did, his bodily fluids spewed out because of the jagged edges of the knife, which had been designed to rip flesh apart as it was pulled out.

This was only intended as a pitfall for his opponent, but it came as a cruel irony, and he fell back down to his knees while the other man got up to pull his own narrow blade out of his abdomen. His wound was not as damaging, because the narrow, straight design of the blade did not do any more damage coming out. He staggered over to the Roman, who had doubled over facedown on his knees, but before he could finish him off, the Roman gladiator fell forward and died. The Egyptian staggered to victory over his Roman opponent by a narrow margin, for it was not the Egyptian who finished off the Roman gladiator in battle, but the jagged design of his own dagger. The crowd fell silent like their champion, who breathed his last. You could see that the three statesmen were thrown for a loop, because they had accepted the bet from Cleopatra and were now showing emotional disgust at their loss of the bet to the queen of the Nile.

"Very well done. You have shown that your fighters are skillful and fierce—my congratulations," Caesar said happily to the queen as his comrades came to escort him home. "If the Roman and Egyptian armies fought side by side, world conquest would be achieved."

"I think you give me too much credit, Emperor, because the Romans have been masters at the gladiator games for decades, but perhaps a merger would be a great thing."

"You don't miss much, do you, my queen?"

"Not at all, Emperor," she said as the recorder came over to award her the voucher for her winnings.

"You may now go to claim your winnings, Queen of the Nile," he said as he bowed to her in the presence of Caesar.

"Thank you," she said with a smile, as she handed him a single gold coin for his service.

"Thank you for your generosity," he said. For the most part she had risked very little, and Caesar stood to proclaim the games a victory.

"Now bring out the traitors to Rome and release the lions," he said. This was usually the dessert, after the grand finale of the day's events, with their bellies full of food and wine. It was done to make the spectators happy. Those who had just lost fortunes felt somewhat better after seeing others in the arena worse off than themselves by seeing their lives hanging in the balance or on carts that carried their lifeless bodies away.

Back in the gladiators' dressing area, the friends of the warriors awaited their returns. The victor of the challenge was assisted to a cot where his physician attended to him to help stop the bleeding. A large cloth was pressed against the side of his abdomen for first aid in an attempt to stop the bleeding that was threatening his life.

"Lay him right here on the table so that I can work on him," the Egyptian physician ordered.

"Ahhhh!" the wounded gladiator grunted out in agony as they lay him on the table while he panted in short, hurried, deep breaths, to try to replenish his exhausted body with badly needed oxygen. It hurt with every breath he drew.

"This is deep, but I can't tell what to make of it yet." He didn't see any other colored fluids seeping out besides blood. "If we can stop the bleeding, he might make it," the physician said as the other gladiator was brought in under a blanket that exposed his limbs.

His friends were silent as his body was placed on the table before them. Then one of them came over and placed his hand on him with his eyes closed. "Give him a soldier's burial after his family comes to claim him." He crumpled up the blanket, and then his hand slid away from his fallen partner as the rest lowered their heads. Even though the Egyptian fighter was no longer flinging around his sword in the heat of battle, he was still fighting another battle—one for his life.

Then at that moment one of his fellow Egyptian soldiers who was standing by leaned over and asked, "Look, I know this is a bad time, but if you don't make it . . . can I claim your slave girls?" The fighter only grunted out loud as the other soldiers looked at him in disgust.

"What?" he asked with all of them looking at him out of the corners of their eyes, but only time would tell if this fighter would survive this test of his will to live.

Things were a lot better for others, because later that night in Caesar's bedroom he lay with Cleopatra making love. She conceived a child and sought to place him on the throne of Rome to unify Egypt and Rome forever and make her dream of carrying out her father's dream of world conquest a reality. Her influence over Caesar grew stronger over time as noted in Acts 18:1-4, which says that Paul, charged by the gospel of Jesus Christ, left Athens and went to Corinth. There he met a Jew named Aquila, a native of Pontus, who had recently come from Italy with his wife, Priscilla, because Claudius had ordered all the Jews to leave Rome—because Caesar was putty in Cleopatra's hand. Paul would soon find himself appealing and sent before Caesar, because the Jews were accusing him of treason against their laws, as well as Caesar's.

By this union Cleopatra would seek to conquer Israel and place them back under the rule of Egypt forevermore. Then she would continue with her father's dream of world conquest even though she was part Jew from the Pharaohs taking Israelite slave women into their bedrooms. But the Lord knew her plans and began to work things out through a turn of events to prevent it from happening. When she brought the child back to Rome to see his father, it caused the members of the Roman senate to have their own ideas. Seeing how in love Caesar was with the boy and knowing that his being son of the emperor would give him the seat upon the throne sent fear through them. They could see the will of Cleopatra influencing the boy in whatever direction she chose while she brought back with her even more servants and gifts for Caesar's comfort to win him over.

Some members of the senate gathered amongst a select few to discuss a possible solution for the problem they foresaw in the near future. They devised a plan but needed more individuals to help carry it out, so they propositioned another member of the senate.

"Brutus, come here that we may speak with you on a matter of urgency," they said.

"What is it, my fellow senators?" he asked.

"Well, we were wondering if perhaps you noticed a certain occurrence of events that have been brought to our attention."

"What matter is this that you speak of?" Brutus asked them.

"Well, to put it bluntly, Caesar being emperor and having a son by the Egyptian queen."

"Well, it is Caesar's business who Caesar lies with, just as many others in the senate have taken foreign slaves to warm their beds. Perhaps even some of you, I would gather?"

"Well, yes, but the slaves here are not the issue—it's the throne."

"What about the throne? Caesar has an heir," Brutus pointed out.

"That is just the point. You see, Brutus, we believe a web is being spun as we speak, and in the end Rome will be used to bring the flies to the spider."

"You speak treason!" Brutus said.

"Oh, no, Brutus, our intentions are only for what's in the best interest of Rome."

"It is, is it"?

"Oh yes! Perhaps we'd better shed some light on the subject for you."

"You'd better," Brutus said, not wanting to be caught up in any treasonous matters.

"Well, you see, with the possible addition of Caesar's predecessor, we've tried to envision what the next Rome might look like, for the sake of all Romans, you understand, and one startling vision has come to mind."

"Yes. Go on," Brutus said.

"Well, imagine a possible future with perhaps Caesar's newly arrived son next in line for the throne, and because of old age, Caesar tragically passes. Well, this new emperor comes to the throne, but who is he more loyal to? Rome or Egypt? He is a part of both dynasties, you know. He'll have complete control, because he is the son of Caesar with the power of dominion over everyone. Then he could choose to have certain members of the senate replaced with like-minded Egyptian people, so to will the senate's influence in favor of an Egyptian queen of the Nile. Perhaps nailing some innocent Romans to the cross with the Jews that have been ordered out—like this Jesus who's been talked about as being the king of the Jews."

"I see. Go ahead," Brutus said.

"Then the Roman way of life would just be to do the bidding of the Egyptian way of life, once this young darker complexioned lad becomes Emperor. He will certainly chose only the most beautiful senate member's daughter to be his wife, and you, Brutus, have the most beautiful daughter of us all—does he not, gentlemen?"

"Yes, surely by far his daughter is the most beautiful," they all agreed.

"Then her children shall have Egyptian black blood running deep in your family's veins."

Brutus thought, and the group of men knew they had won over their last needed member, to ensure that Rome would stay under Caucasian rule the way it had for centuries. Now they only needed to have Caesar come into their web, which they had spun for him. It was all set with the deed upon hand, and then they had Caesar summoned to them in their chambers.

Caesar came in feeling carefree of the world as he walked in to greet the men. The first dagger hit him in the back and he fell, not knowing at first what had actually struck him. By the time he was hit with the second knife, he apprehended a plot of sabotage. Though he was powerless to yell or fight off the attackers upon Rome's most victorious military leader ever, who had made them the greatest conquers of that time period. Soon word came that the mighty emperor had died, and that a new emperor would soon succeed him, upsetting Cleopatra's plans for world domination by surprise.

She looked toward some of Julius Caesar's trusted allies to help her place her child on the throne of the Roman Empire. She persuaded such as Mark Anthony and a host of others to take up the cause for her honor, love, and high positions to the throne, should she be successful to rule from behind the scenes. She was not successful though in her campaign to regain Rome, and her gamble this time unlike the one on the gladiators was unsuccessful. Her life was lost as her limp body dangled on a table like the dead gladiator had. All her dark-skinned people who were left in Rome now had no power or position, which left them to survive off whatever means they could. The Roman guards came to the small number of Egyptian troops who were left there to give them an ultimatum as they stood before the Egyptian soldier who had won the prize money and was living with his two slave women as the troops confronted them.

"By orders of the emperor, all soldiers have to swear new allegiance to the new Roman order or perish at the sword immediately," he said with his sword drawn. That did not leave much room for choice, and also knowing that Egypt had been conquered made the choice a lot easier for him.

"I pledge alliance to the new emperor," he said in a move considered smart by almost any man.

"You will report for duty first thing in the morning. Don't be late." This happened all over Rome, wherever the Egyptian people were. They made them submit or be put to death by the sword or used them to serve their purpose in the arena as lion food.

Years went by, and the Egyptian people there started to marry and be a part of Roman society. The result of this intermixing between the Egyptian and Caucasian Romans created even more Italian-like people.

Like the Negros in America, in the beginning these Italian families were subjected to bias and segregated social scheming until they later came here to America and started off with a nationality and much better life. Because as time passed, no one knew exactly where they came from, plus they had more white traits than blacks in American society. They became accepted over the black race cast into America by way of bondage, who started off in a near worthless state compared with today's social status that they have earned through the same struggle that the Jews had to endure from the Egyptians in a form of disrespect unworthy of good men. They were like the Caucasian Americans who lorded over the Negro—which some thought stands for "the mind will never grow"—race as named by arrogant others.

All people have suffered in slavery; none of us are innocent of the bloodshed if we associate ourselves with our so-called races only, which are nothing more than lighter or darker versions of interracial men who committed these atrocities. Even the Jews, who were slaves in Egypt, had slaves from different regions after they conquered the world.

It's odd how when someone lords and masters over you, they teach their descendants you are worthless in their view. This stereotype view of stigmatism can stay with them for centuries; it never truly seems to go away until prejudice does or you can prove hands down that you are equal or better in all aspects of life. Like in Egypt, but in a role reversal as in Egypt, the Israelite Caucasian race was dominated and transformed into a darker form of Caucasian-descendant people. The dark-skinned race in America would also be transformed through sexual conception by Caucasian descendants while bound in slavery into a lighter race of Negro people, which resulted in some of them looking much like Cleopatra's people—light-complexion Egyptians.

# ENEMY OF HUMANITY

The scene changes as we see the saga of the interracial dark-skinned African man's journey to America while in bondage, as *possibly seen* through the eyes of one man named John Newton, who came to write an *amazing song* about this troubled culture's role reversal and his conversion from a wretch to a Saint.

At the docks a ship was set for sail in the early morning's light. The crew was in a hustle on the deck, making final preparations for the voyage to pick up another profitable cargo of bonded men, women, and children for exploitation. There came a young man walking up the pier with a few other men, who were filling him in on the great benefits of this job. Usually this was the type of ship that rarely exchanged crews under the present captain, but this time there was an opening for a young man because someone had died for some unfortunate reason—maybe of alcoholism on this ship, with its merriment that lured strong, healthy young men to their doom. The ship needed a replacement, so a friend of a friend had let him in on what he considered an opportunity of a lifetime. You could hear the men talking as they reached the gangplank of the ship.

John was one of these gangly men, raised in a good home where his mother introduced him to catechism and many verses, hymns, and poems. However, he deserted his spiritual teachings. When he was a teenager, he was kidnapped and forced to work in the British navy. John was often punished for his laziness and hot temper. He deserted ranks to flee, and after being caught, he was publicly punished, which only escalated his hot temperament.

Finally, he was released from duty and then joined up with a slave trader. After being accused of stealing, he became an indentured servant to repay the debt to that slave master, who often abused him for amusement, until some friends of his father located him and brought him home. Afterward he continued to go to sea aboard slave ships.

"Believe me, John, this is going to be the sailing voyage of a lifetime. Do you know how many young men here in Charleston, South Carolina, want to make this trip, even if it's just once in their lifetime?" Bob said. "And I got you hired on with me. Isn't that great?"

"It's swell," John said. "I've worked aboard British navy ships, but never a slave ship before."

"And the fun is just beginning, John . . . just beginning," Bob said as he showed John a surprise he had hidden in his duffel bag that he was toting along. "And see this, my boy. This is going to get you initiated on the trip home."

"Initiated?" John asked, curious about what he meant.

"You have a lot to learn about the benefits of transporting slaves, but just stick with me and I'll show you all the ropes." Bob chuckled while sporting the grin of a weasel as the captain of the ship stood at the entrance of the ship where the gangplank connected to it.

"We be off, and if any of you land lovers be serving aboard this ship, then ye best be getting aboard now, says I," the captain called out onto the docks at them. "Cast off!" He bellowed in a louder voice this time. The captain was a stout man of about five feet eight inches tall with a disposition that echoed he was in charge, and don't bother to question or second guess his decision of command, but understand that he ran the ship the way he felt it should be run. His blood ran as deep and dark as the hair on the top of his head.

Then the men ran hurriedly up the gangplank, and as the last man made it on board, the crew came to pull up the gangplank from the dock as the vessel got under way for a distant Africa port to collect a load of slaves, which they would drop off in two different ports, one in Cuba off the coast of Havana, and the other back in America at this Charleston, South Carolina, port.

John figured he knew what happened on board slave ships, because he knew much about sailing and the chores needed to keep the ship going, but he was really a fish out of water and unaware of the events that would change his life forever.

"Who is this new land lover coming aboard my ship?" the captain asked young Bob.

"This is my friend John, Captain, John Newton," Bob said. The captain looked him over well by scanning him up and down.

"How many ships have you worked on before?" he asked John slowly.

"I've worked on many navy ships for the Crown before," he said.

"Well, we haul cargo—live cargo, in fact, that might try to slit your throat. You have no problems with that, do ya?" the captain asked, to see if he could shake John.

"No, not at all, sir, I mean, Captain," he said nervously, not really understanding.

"I see," the Captain said softly as he continued to look at the two of them standing there waiting for a response from him. "Well! What are you standing around for? Get to work, you bunch of jellyfish." The two gangly men bumped into each other while trying to get started looking busy. "Swab the morning dew off the deck before somebody breaks their fool neck," the captain said. Then he turned and went back to his cabin to relax for the beginning of the journey as the ship headed out to sea with the barely noticeable rising sun on the horizon of the rippling water's surface as they left the bay.

Days later the ship was sitting off the coast of northern Africa, where a line of half-naked slaves in chains was being loaded onto their ship. John was on deck towing the mark by pulling rope to tie down the sails; the ship was halfway loaded with its nearly five hundred slaves that would come aboard. He watched inquisitively as the sailors unchained the youngest-looking, best-figured petite girls who came aboard and stripped them of what little clothing they had on. Then they placed them on a separate chain to stow them in a different holding compartment of the ship while all the other slaves—men, women, and children—were stuffed and crammed packed into the lower third-level hull of the ship like sardines packed in a factory for shipment. John started to get the idea more clearly of why this was being done with these young girls when he saw the smirking look on his friend Bob's face as he and some of the other sailors played music while dancing with a few young naked women who were set aside out of the chains before they put them into special holding place. John felt somewhat sorry for the people who were being herded on board like cattle for the long journey to a new homeland that would offer them less than a bitter existence.

The ship was loaded and set sail at nightfall for Cuba as John watched from a distance inside their cabin bunk hold, where the men drew straws to be first. They usually unchained several different virgin slave girls at a three-to-one ratio. This way three men could wrestle the slave girl down, and then while the other two held her pinned fast to the bunk, the other could rape her and bust her virginity. They gang-raped the first half dozen virgin girls, some of whom their ages were very young—ten, eleven or less—but none of them cared, just as long as the evening merriment began and everyone got their fill of the probably 120 or so virgins on board. Bob saw John watching from the distant background out of the corner of his eyes, so he staggered over to John while trying to keep his balance in his nearly drunken state as the ship slowly rocked to the rhythm of the ocean.

"John, what's the matter with you? Come join in the fun," Bob said, tugging at him with the arm that carried the bottle of wine. John just hunched his shoulders because of the emotion he was feeling over this alarming event.

"I kind of don't feel this is right—treating these girls like this," John explained, but even good-hearted people are subjected to pressure from temptation, which John was feeling an overwhelming amount of right now as he pondered his loyalties toward his friends or his devotions to God. At times like these, man wishes that God would come and personally offer us advice, but God only wants those who are willing to be good on their own recognizance.

"Ah, come on now!" Bob said, trying to justify the acts of the other sailors as one came over to get a drink of wine from him. "It's all in good sport. Nothing's really hurt, you know; a little romping around in the sheets never hurt anyone, says I. Isn't that right, mate?" Bob said to the sailor tugging on his bottle for another drink.

"That's exactly right. Hell! We won't have done something right if we get back to port and there is one virgin Negro woman left on this ship," the wobbly, drunk sailor said with a slur in his voice as he fell flat on the floor. Bob cringed at the thought of the pain he might have felt if he were not passed out drunk when his face hit the floor. No one attempted to pick him up; they just figured that he was done for the night, and soon many other sailors would be joining him there on the floor in much the same way. The drunken sailor instantly started making a snoring sound; he didn't even move an inch after hitting the floor as the large ship continued its swaying motion.

"Here. Have a drink," Bob said, nearly shoving the bottle into John Newton's face. John was reluctant at first, but moments later he took a swig of the spirited liquor that influenced a lot of the men into making bad decisions before the night was over.

The wine was sweet with an intoxicating punch that would sneak up on you after you drank two swigs and before you realized its effects were taking hold, but after you drank half a bottle, which was way too much, it would slowly relieve you of your good judgment and senses.

Soon John's bodily urges began to take control of him like a demon at the steering wheel of a fast sports car; John's body was the vehicle in which this reckless driving demon was veering out of control at a rapid pace while belligerently ignoring the moral road signs about keeping to the righteous. His vehicle bolted sharply left anyway, across the conscious medium of right and wrong way, directly into the oncoming fast lane of sin, with semi loads of sexual desires barreling down upon him as his mind revved up his body with fuel-injected thoughts added by friends to his inner fire of driving fast and hard into these slave women and then crashing there for the night.

Like a progressive driver, he began to join in by just watching the other men up close as they interacted with the slave women at first. That grew into a strange, alluring curiosity that caused him to be aroused with an erection from leering too much.

Next he joined in on what was like frat-house cheering of the other men every time they witnessed a slave girl losing her virginity while they committed these sexual acts.

Soon, unbeknownst to himself as he lurched in closer and closer for a better up-close view of the action, he failed to realize that he was standing in the spot to be next in line, to have intercourse with the girl the sailors held down before him. The other sailor in front had just finished his turn of intercourse with the slave girl and then climbed off while John, still unknowingly, was like a baseball player next at bat—he was up on deck, literally.

There came a tap at his shoulders. It was then that he realized everyone was waiting on him to take the next turn. One sailor playfully shoved him forward, but John modestly resisted, as his vehicle veered back on course across the medium of "keep to the righteous" and "wrong way" for a moment. That's when Bob sneaked up behind him and whipped John's pants down to his ankles, exposing his briefs as all the men laughed and pointed at the sight of John's obvious erection bulging inside them.

"Come on, me bucko, you've got to take care of that woody—you know you want to," a sailor said to John, which embarrassed him, because of his exposed human nature that was revealing what he really had been thinking.

"Oh no! I couldn't," he said, trying to squirm and wiggle his way out of the situation as much as the slave woman pinned to the bunk.

"Sure you can—it's easy. Once you do it the first time, you'll find it easier to do for the rest of the voyage. You've just got to get over the hump of your first time, and hump!" Bob said, smiling. John was trying to apply the brakes to this dilemma, but the pushing from his friends combined with the immoral driving demon spirits from the bottle flooring the gas pedal of his bodily desires kept pushing him toward the fast lane of oncoming calamity.

"That's all there is to it," said the sailor who had just gotten up off the restrained woman and stood beside him naked from the waist down. John looked at the woman, and then they started to chant his name: "John, John, John, John . . ."

"Come on, now, there's nothing like a hot Negro wench to get the blood flowing," the half-naked sailor urged, standing next to him. John stared down longer this time at the young, naked, sweaty, dark-skinned skinny woman, who had breasts the size of firm ripe cantaloupes. She was being held down by four men who restrained each limb of her body across the bed as she tried to struggle free of their grip to get up, but it was no use, for they held fast to her while all eyes were on John as he studied in his mind what to do.

"Go ahead, John," Bob said once more, urging him on in a softer voice like this was his last chance, because others were impatiently waiting in line behind him. "Everyone is waiting." John closed his eye and wiped the sweat from his eyebrows as his mind sped down the conscious medium of good and evil.

"Oh heck!" he said as he pulled down his briefs, and his mind whipped back into the fast lane of sin to join in the merriment of the other sailors, who chanted a different tune.

'Go, John, go. Go, John, go. Go, John, go . . ." and on until his essence came inside the dark-skinned women and the next man took his place. He went from Negro woman to Negro woman the rest of the night while drinking and having fun like the rest of the sailors. John's sinful demon sped him beyond the limits of his body's boozing abilities, causing him to crash for the night. John's vehicle of destruction—his body—was disabled by the unconscious, crashed state of his mind, and no smelling salts could jump-start him as he lay there entangled in the arms of an emotionally wrecked young slave girl, like a victim of a side-impact crash that penetrated deep inside her vehicle's compartment and left many scars to heal. That is where the spirited hit-and-run demon from the bottle abandoned him, like a deserting rat aboard a sinking ship on the high seas.

The ship sailed on through the rest of the night headed for its port destination in Cuba to drop off half its used-up cargo as most of the drunken sailors resembled a pileup of disabled vehicles on Interstate 5, but no authorities would respond to issue citations to the offenders of the violated slave women on board, not even an EMR unit to assist the distraught victims. The women were glad that the sailors' disabled bodies stalled, but their ruined bodies would be repaired in the body shop of soberness, and the same banging, hard, crash-up derby would go on for weeks.

Night after night, nearly the entire thirty-five days of crossing the Atlantic Ocean until they were dropped off at the Charleston, South Carolina, port, this was only one of many voyages to come defiling young Negro women, who would be snatched away from their homeland. It didn't necessarily stop once the women, men, and children got off the boats either. It depended on the type of individual they were sold to, because they became used however the purchaser of them saw fit, just like what happened to the members of the Caucasian race in Egypt at the hands of the Nubian oppressors, who mastered over them.

The boat sailed on into the night while rocking gently on the waves that reflected the light from the full moon in the sky. You could see shadowed images of sea creatures just under the immediate water surface, but soon the night sky steadily clouded up more and more until the moonlight was gone. The waves began to increase as the ship rocked with more swaying from side to side. It was not alarming at first, but became much more noticeable to everyone—even the slaves, who had never ridden on a ship before, as at the break of dawn a storm began to brew. The first mate rang the bell from up on deck to awaken everyone in the wee morning hours to an alert of all hands on deck. The crew now was mostly a bunch of drunken, hung-over, barely conscious sailors drowning in sin through lust, who started to stir out of their beds with every clanging sound of that forsaken alarm bell that seemed like it would never stop ringing to most of them as they struggled to their feet. A few of them crept at a snail's pace to roll out of their bunks that they were sleeping in, while others still shared theirs with the jilted slave women, too afraid to move. Some sailors grabbed their foreheads, bellowing out groans that were equal in every way to the moaning sounds made the night before by the slave girls who lost their virginity while being raped by a dozen men during their first ever sexual experience, which afterward left some of their minds with emotionally scared complexes. The hull of the ship echoed with a "Woe is me" sound as the crew dragged themselves topside.

"John! Get up. We've got to go topside," Bob insisted as he pulled his pants up while trying to keep his balance. Then he walked to the stairs, and a wave of water hit him in the face as he opened the hatch door. The coldness of it shocked him with such surprise that it awoke him instantly—actually sobering him up a little like a cold shower.

"Wow! John, come on, we need you topside now," Bob said, half drenched with water pouring off him, because it was too much to be absorbed by his clothing all at once.

John sat up in a disoriented state. He thought for a second that the room was spinning, but the whole ship was, in fact, because a storm had raged out of nowhere, like the Lord God was angry at what had just taken place. When John finally got himself together, he glanced over to a cowering young girl in the bunk next to him. He noticed that she was very young, maybe nine years old or younger—he really didn't know.

"What! What are you doing here, little girl?" John asked her, but she could not speak his language. "Come on, don't be afraid to speak up." He reached his hand out to calm her obvious nervousness with a comforting touch, but she cowered into a fetal position, which actually almost resembled a small round ball, like an armadillo. Seeing how afraid she was, he withdrew his hand so as not to frighten her anymore.

"I'm not going to hurt you," John said earnestly.

"It be too late for that, mate-tee," a strange, calm voice from above his head said as John looked up, searching to focus his eyes on the being who had bestowed those words upon him. It was the sailor who had been ahead of him last night before he lay with the first slave woman of the night.

"What? What did you say?" John asked, his mind hazy.

"You don't remember—ha, ha, ha. Do you?" the sailor asked John.

"I don't understand . . . Remember what?" John said as he stood to his feet, pulling up his trousers. He sensed something wrong deep inside as he fastened them up.

"Last night, when you were staggering drunk, the men all decided to let you have a virgin . . . for your official ignition on your first slave ship voyage with us, but all the older virgins had been used up . . . so . . ."

"No. I . . . I didn't sleep with that little girl?"

"For sure you did, mate-tee. I saw it with my own eyes, says I." The old codger chuckled to ridicule John's disbelief.

"No! Me?" His eyes widened as he searched through his mind to realize what he had done. He looked over at the little girl still huddled on the bed, but he dared not go near her, for he knew by her previous response that it would only increase her fear and tension, maybe even put her into shock. John slowly started to back out of the sleeping quarters as he looked into the faces of all the women who were in the beds as the crew went topside to prepare the ship against the storm that had crept up on them in the night while they slept. Their faces bore the mark of shame that had been forced upon them, for surely they must have thought that all Caucasian people were evil, because that's what the daughters of Abraham thought about the Nubian people when the dark-skinned man ruled over them in Egypt just a few centuries before.

John felt guilt riddled with remorse. He saw something rolling toward him upon the floor that stopped against his feet. It was the bottle that he had been drinking from last night when all of this got started. He picked the bottle up and stared into it to find that there was only a little left in the corner. Then he slammed the bottle up against the wall out of rage, because he was angry with himself about the little girl he had defiled, which made him realize that he had sinned against God. It scared all the females in the room, for they just figured he was upset with them for not performing without resistance or to his liking. Some of the women had swollen black eyes and huge bloody lips from the drunken sailors who had hit them for resisting.

"That's not going to get rid of that demon inside. You're going to have to sober up really good for a long time or just forget him and go with the flow of things on this ship. The choice is up to you, but for me, I went with the flow . . . It feels a lot better," the sailor said as he pulled his pants up to go topside to help secure the ship against the raging storm. John began to feel that maybe God was going to sink the ship for their acts against these people as his head began to clear like someone collectively pulling himself together after awakening from a traffic accident. It was then that he began to realize the severity of the wreckage that the reckless demon had caused, which he had willing swallowed inside himself from the spirited drink. Instead of being able to laugh and joke like the other men who enjoyed themselves with the slaves, John felt that he had sunk to an all-time low, like the way this ship was being threatened now by this storm. He could hear voices above deck calling out.

"Batten down the hatches! Secure all the riggings, and hoist the main sail! Then get aft and hoist the mizzenmast! Finish up quickly on that foremast!" the alarming voice of the first mate blurted out to the crew. He was a scrawny little guy who got his kicks from being in charge over the other, bigger men and his authority of being second in command as a way of making up in measure for whatever he lacked in his inept size.

John bolted for the short stairwell that led to the hatch opening to get out onto the main deck, where a sprayed mix of rain and ocean water hurled by near gale-force winds hit him directly in the face on the way out. It almost blinded him, because the droplets of water pelting his eyeballs so hard, combined with the saltiness of the ocean water, caused an added lingering effect to the painful stinging sensation that made him stumble-step blindly up the last flight of stairs that led through the opening onto the top deck. He covered his face with one arm, using it alternately to rub his eyes vigorously as a soothing measure while steadying himself with the other arm that clung onto the hand railing. He lurched forward step by step until he got up on deck where he could see what was really going on.

There was enough sunlight peering through the dark clouds to see clearly as the men struggled to hold their footing. The ship was tilted at nearly a forty-five-degree angle at times while they performed the needed tasks to save the sails from being ripped off the mainmast or worst. The sails caught the wind like a parachute, which made it tilt at that awkward angle, but the more they reeled the sails in, the more the ship leveled out, making it easier to walk on. Waves rose high enough at times to cover a good portion of the deck as its water spilled over into the vented openings of the cargo hull, where the slaves were chained on the third deck of the ship. They quickly found themselves knee deep in cool water, and panic arose amongst them from fear that the ship was sinking and ready to take all on board down to the bottom of the sea forever, with them chained to its hull.

John, once he got his footing going, started helping the others secure the vessel as waves continued to knock the men from side to side. They secured all the sails and riggings, which allowed the ship to level out. The waves still tossed large amounts of water up on deck from the starboard side of the vessel that continued to work its way down onto the cargo holds to fill it even more. The adult slaves started wading waist deep in salty seawater while trying to hold the children up above water.

"Man the pumps!" John shouted out an order to the crew. "Or those people will drown down there!" The first mate took an offense to this newly hatched sea guppy bellowing out orders while he was on deck.

"I'll give the orders around here!" he said, bucking up to John, who was at least six inches taller than he was. "I'm the first mate. Now grab some sails and help get us headed into the wind! We're getting too much water over the starboard side. We'll worry about some wet Negros later." He said it like they were nothing more than boxes of dishes, but John manned the pump near the captain's quarters and pumped like crazy in defiance of the first mate's orders. The first mate ran to the captain's quarters, knocking on the door feverishly.

"Captain, Captain!" the first mate shouted as he knocked. John watched him with intent while he pumped the water overboard, more out of curiosity of seeing the captain, who had spent nearly all his time in his quarters since they'd picked up the load of slaves. The door opened slowly and the captain emerged from inside while fastening up his pants. There in his room you could see a young slave girl sitting on his bed crying her heart out.

"What is it?" he bellowed out with aggravation because he had been disturbed, as the first mate peered at the girl on the bed. John took the opportunity to speak up first, in hopes that he might sway the captain to be concerned for the slaves.

"Captain! The third deck is taking on water, and the slaves are nearly under water. I need your permission to move them all up to the mid-deck, sir!"

"That's what you disturbed me for . . . some stinking slaves in water getting a much-needed bath down in that shit hole?" the captain raged.

"But Captain, they'll drown down—"

"Don't 'but Captain' me. I see I need to come out here and run this ship," he said angrily. He grabbed the slave girl, who was naked as a newborn baby, off his bed by her arm and then brought her before the first mate. "Here, maybe you can handle taking care of a whiny slave bitch that's good for nothing after you've busted her virginity, and put her down in the third hold so she can get her bloody ass washed, too." He used the worst, most disgusting phrases he could think of to humiliate this young girl, who could not even understand a word he was saying about her, although she could sense the hatred in his voice toward her.

John watched, appalled, while thinking, *How could he just take the best thing she has to offer a man, then turn around and rape her spirit as well with his words of iniquity?* by damning her this way without a bit of remorse. He squeezed her arm tight as he handed her toward his first mate. She could feel his fingernails gouging her skin, and she turned and bit him on the hand. But the captain only gritted his teeth from the painful bite as he pushed the first mate aside and then pinned her up against the outside of his cabin wall next to a port hole. He pulled out a huge knife holstered in his waist belt and drew back to stab her as John shouted out to stop him.

"No!" But the captain took orders from no one, and he thrust the knife deep into the lower part of her abdomen.

"Ah!!!" she yelled out in pain as she grabbed her stomach

"Bite me, will you, you black wench?" he said with a grunting voice, and then with one quick jerk upward on the knife he slit her abdomen open all the way up to the bottom of her thorax. She wrapped her arms around her stomach in an attempt to hold her intestines in place, as some of them were exposed now and protruding outwardly. John felt a sharp sympathy pain in his stomach; sometimes if you have a good human connection, you can feel pain for others' dilemmas. At this point he knew there was nothing that could be done for this young girl. Tears filled his eyes while he helplessly watched the captain hoist the thin, lightweight girl above his head and cast her overboard into the raging ocean. She still held on tightly to her bleeding abdomen, and with one splash she disappeared—never to be heard from again. One could only imagine the man-eating sharks that followed her down to her watery grave. John curled up into a near-fetal position against a secured lifeboat, like the little girl who had been on his bed when he had awakened that morning to a hideous aftermath of drunken men with defiled women. They included the captain, whom he thought was a madman for sure now.

Rage filled his heart and remorse rekindled his soul as John prayed to God for forgiveness while the two emotions put him in a state of limbo for the rest of the journey.

"All right, now, get everything cleaned up and ready for inspection, and tally the number of dead slaves on board ship and then cast their rotting carcasses overboard," the captain said. "I don't want any of their rotten hides stinking up my ship." Some of the men gave him a double take, but they all went back to work as ordered. Even John, who saw the captain as the enemy of humanity, wanted nothing more than to get off of this ship now as it battered through the rough waves.

By afternoon the hard work of restoring the ship to normal had ended, and the waters were calmer as they headed for the Caribbean. For the rest of the crew it was back to the recreation of hanky-panky as usual with the slave girls, although their only drawback was that they had a third fewer female slaves to use than what they started out with, because of diseases, drowning, and murder. Usually more than half of the black slave women on board slave ships were pregnant by the sailors, after the thirty-five-day voyage that carted them off across the ocean to America. The sailors cared not that it was their own children in the bellies of these slave women being sold off into bondage, for in their own minds they refused to believe that a white man could get a black woman pregnant, like it was a well-known scientific fact that such a thing was an impossibility. But it was all denial, just like some people's frame of mind on God's existence, yet he does exist.

They continued to use the women until they off-loaded them in port to the owners who had paid for their shipping. None of these women were able to communicate what had happened to them on these voyages, but even if they could've spoken the language, no one would have cared much, just as long as they were still strong and healthy enough to perform laboring tasks, and most likely this practice continued after they were sold.

John stayed mostly on deck for the rest of the voyage until it was time to sleep, for he would not join in on the perversity that took place in the crew's sleeping quarters anymore. He found himself continually going to sea after his newfound salvation and rose in the ranks to become an officer, a first mate, and then a captain himself.

The slave trade brought wealth to many men, but John's Christian heart could not endure it any longer as he found himself at odds with the crew, who wanted the benefits of pleasure aboard his ship with the slaves. He began praying more and asking God for forgiveness now; he started humming a tune that he added words to also, which the crew and slaves alike could hear him singing from time to time.

> A—maz—ing grace! How sweet the sound! That saved a wretch like me!
> I once was lost, but now am found; Was blind but now I see.
> 'Twas grace that taught my heart to fear, And grace my fears re-lieved.
> How pre-cious did that grace ap-pear the hour I first be-lieved!

John Newton's mind's eye had finally been opened to the truth as he realized that these people were not different from himself and deserved the same humanitarian rights and dignity that he did, but so many others are self-blinded to the truth of who we are, because the conscious reality of being interracial is too hard for them to accept.

The slaves were continually off-loaded, ship after ship in Charleston, South Carolina, before leering crowds of giddy young boys ages five to fourteen hiding behind crates, whose thoughts were *Let's go get an eyeful of the naked slave girls that just came into port* while the men saw the arrival of slave ships as a free peep show of naked women and men as they marched them from the ship to the auction houses.

John one day decided to get off the ship of burden when it docked, and never looked back. He wrote the words to the song called "Amazing Grace," which is sung in many Christian churches around the world today. It's one of the most famous and well-liked Christian songs in history, but very few know the heart-wrenching events that made this man reach down into his soul to conjure up that song out of his heart to honor the Lord God. Years later John Newton would try to become a fishermen of men by doing the Lord's work to convince the rest of his fellow man in South Carolina and everywhere else that this treatment of the dark-skinned slaves was wrong, but most paid him no attention and kept on doing whatever they felt was right, whereas others became more lenient with their slaves to spread some relief.

# REVERSAL OF IRONY

The number of slaves brought to America and abroad totaled nearly a million, and they were bred for profit so much that one Negro woman was credited with birthing sixty-five children. Their numbers increased rapidly in America, which all but put an end to the slave trade aboard ships. The result was just the opposite of the Caucasian slaves—descendants of Abraham. The more these impregnations of enslaved black women in America by Caucasian man went on, the more the Negro race made the transformation back closer to the 100 percent human white "genetic norm" side. After each generation in America their skin color got lighter, and their hair became longer and straighter as compared with the first Negros who had come to America with short, coarse, black curly hair, and their skin color nearly charcoal black. But soon they had large Afros and their hair color started turning brown, and the skin turned brown as well.

By the next generation more Negro children were born to Caucasian men who for various reasons would not accept them. These often married men hid them from their Caucasian wives, embarrassed to be thought of as, or known to be, sleeping with black women that they considered animals. No one would question making slaves of them; they tried to pass them off as a sub-life form barely above domestic beasts of burden such as horses or mules that no one would consume as livestock.

These kinds of shady dealings went on for a couple of centuries here in America, and some of the Negro women transformed back so close to the white side that some of them were born with blond hair, but through the process known as Kendihuchrodnamixgenesis it turned brunette.

These types of Negro women became more and more appealing to the eyes of Caucasian men as their looks changed to their liking to resemble Cleopatra, queen of the Nile, and so on, with the more white featured traits they possessed through this transformation back to the white side.

Not everyone can be beautiful—or can they? Some Caucasian men were not as handsome as other Caucasian men—let's just say it! Some were just plain ugly, fat, and obese; we have that type of man in every so-called race of people on the earth. These less attractive American Caucasian men, from living off the fatness of life that slavery had to offer, were not able to catch the eye of a desirable, slim, trim, beautiful blond, redhead, brown-haired, or brunette Caucasian female. Some of them would turn to these Negro slave women they owned who had been beautifully transformed closer to the white side and force them to marry them. Some of them were so close in resemblance to Caucasian women by then that if you did not know their mothers were slave women, you would not have been able to distinguish them from other Caucasian women.

Sometimes these men would move to another part of this country to marry these slave women they owned, saying they had met them in another part of the country. Then they would create a false family name and background for them up to their desired social stature with ties to another white family far off enough that no one would bother to check. Then they would settle into their new township to live a somewhat seemingly normal life. To most of these women, it was still bondage with the perks of being considered white—few were ever discovered because of this propaganda.

The Negro race endured many hardships just like the Israelites had in Egypt. They saw their women taken right in front of their faces while they were virtually powerless to do anything about it, just like the Hebrews.

We often don't see the discomforts of others as being dramatic as our own. The dark-skinned man in Egypt did not see the sufferings of the Caucasian man as tragic, nor did the Caucasian man in America see the suffering of the dark-skinned man as tragic. I am telling you all the truth about how these events happened because every time one of you opens your mouth to say, "How terrible it was, the way those people treated our people," your words are nothing more than a testimony against you. You are judging yourself to hell, because you are all interracially made of the same flesh, just with different measures of black and white blood mixed in.

If you curse the name of the white race, you have also cursed yourself, because no matter how black you are, you're still at least 75 percent white. And if you curse the name of a black man, you still have some black in you, no matter how small the amount. Remember, "In the eyes of God a man who robs a candy store is still as guilty as a man who robs a bank," for all have sinned and come short of the glory of God—and isn't that the pot calling the kettle black? You will be judged by your own words on Judgment Day.

Birth for the Caucasian-fathered Negro male child was different, though, because the owner would often have the doctor or midwife delivering the boy untie his umbilical cord and let him bleed to death, just like Pharaoh ordered in Egypt—for you see, what goes around comes around. Thousands of male children were drowned in the Nile, and Caucasian men in America committed the same sin so no one would discover that the dark-skinned male children belonged to them. Since the Israelite children were drowned in the Nile, an equal number of Pharaoh's army men who pursued them into the Red Sea were drowned when it closed up, and the people were still freed.

Since the dark-skinned children were allowed to bleed to death when their umbilical cords were untied or worse in America, the South untied its umbilical cord from the Northern states for not letting the people go. God allowed the South's sons to lie on the battlefield bleeding to death, and the people were still freed.

When the Civil War was just ending, the South went to the bargaining table with the North with one of the first initial requests for surrender: that they be able to keep the slave women and let the men go. This offended many of the Caucasian women in the South, and it was probably explained to them that we just didn't want Southern ladies to wash dishes or clean their own floors. Pharaoh and his advisers, however, presented the same request to Moses when they felt their grip slipping on the Israelite people, and of course the dark-skinned Egyptian women were offended as well, and the same lame excuse was given to them, for when Potiphar's wife came on to Joseph, you can bet that she was lonely and love starved (Genesis 39:6). If Potiphar owned male slaves like Joseph, then he more than likely had female slaves as well who could be forced into doing his bidding.

# TARNISHED ICONS

Let's take a look back into the days of slavery when America was considered young. Indians still lived near some of the colonies that would become states, and future heroes of the Revolutionary War were just young lads under English influence. We'll look in on the actions that caused the quaint little township of Charles Town, West Virginia, to exist, one of the many small towns of then Frederick County, Virginia; it was named after Charles Washington, the brother of our nation's first president, George Washington. We start years back on their father's plantation when he and his brothers were young boys at heart. They were, however, to be raised like polished young gentlemen with stature on the outside, but the inner man is the real tale of one's true autobiography. (University Press of Virginia 1979)

Down the long dirt road to the Strother plantation traveled a two-horse-drawn open carriage with a slave in the driver's seat wearing a uniform, probably one of the obedient servants who had humbly given into the submission of the master's will long ago on how things were run. For his obedience he got things like the cushy coach driver's duties, instead of being a farmhand toiling in the soil under the hot sun while wearing filthy, stinking rags on his body that might get washed if it rained on him long enough.

The carriage was carrying the owner of the house, who was in colonial dress with a white wig on his head under a colonial-style hat. On the back of the carriage were some newly purchased slaves, male and female, along with supplies. It pulled up to the front of a large house as servants hurried to attend the carriage, one placing a stepstool at the side, where the owner was sitting. He was Augustine Washington, the first one to disembark from the carriage, as was standard protocol, and two of his sons came to greet him and inspect the new arrivals.

"Hello, Father," they said.

"George, Samuel, how are my two fine sons doing today?" their father asked of them.

"Well, Father," they both replied as their mother watched from an upstairs bedroom window. She was not as thrilled about coming down to see what her husband had brought home, for she knew, and she despised the thought somewhat.

"What did you bring us this time, Father?" young George, who was eleven, asked with a little excitement in his voice. His father handed down a bag to him that had been sitting on the seat between himself and the coach driver. Then he reached into the bag to pull out two brand new, colonial-style white wigs, one for each of the boys, who placed them upon their heads to cover up their true dark-colored hair. The Viking insults still lingered on to influence fashion trend into this era as well.

"Wow! Thanks, Father," the two of them exclaimed. "Real gentlemen's white wigs."

"Just what young gentlemen like yourselves should be wearing these days," their father said as they headed to the back of the wagon, which is what the two boys were really interested in. The arrival of the new slaves to comfort their lives was sort of an expected thing with them, for their father's financial ambitions and achievements were very impressive; he had amassed a tremendous amount of land and wealth. George and Samuel met up with the overseer of the plantation, who was carrying a musket over his shoulder with a single-shot pistol in his waistband as he approached the wagon. This overseer would soon be left in charge of Strother Plantation after the Washington's moved on to a better plantation.

"One day you boys will be masters of your own plantations, so you help show the slaves to their new quarters to start learning how to master over them yourselves," he said as the new slaves without chains on walked with their heads down to their new dwellings, followed by their future masters.

George's father was one of these men, figuring that a boy was a man at an early age, ready to take care of himself at sixteen or younger, in fact. This was a far cry from Abraham, who kept Isaac under his care for forty years to make sure he was mature minded enough in the ways of our Lord God and not perverted in sexual immorality. They watched their father finish unloading the wagon of a single slave girl he had recently purchased as he eyed her over. She was not led to a shack out back, but into the house, where her duties would be.

George's two eldest half brothers, Lawrence and Austin, from his father's first wife, were home from the prestigious Appleby School in England and already established with plantations of their own—gifts, of course, from their father, who had more than one plantation. George in time would have received his own also, possibly after his father had sent him off to England to be trained in the ways of proper gentry as well, but his father passed away before that opportunity was afforded him as a result of being caught up in a rainstorm, it is said, but the actual occurrence in some parts are pure speculation. Without his father to guide his life or send him off to school to be refined, George at age eleven became the "man of the house" for his mother, who never remarried—women couldn't own property, so she put everything in his name. George assisted Mary Ball Washington for another four years and became a wealthy teenager; in time he inherited Strother Plantation, or shall we say his mother did, and decided to sell it. He sold the property, and with the money he made from the sale, arranged for a home to be completed for his mother, who lived in comfort for the rest of her life.

George began to think about life on the open seas because of the stories he had heard about the partying action that went on below deck every day on return trips aboard slave ships, until they off-loaded their cargo they hauled back to America. That captured his imagination. He began to speak of leaving home and going to sea for his first real job, but what young boy at his age would not have been tempted by the flesh, especially by those in chains who had no right to object?

His mother after hearing of the consideration began to worry and figured it best to seek advice for her young son. At first she appeared to favor his going to sea, but she began to dislike the idea when several friends told her of certain immoral acts with slave women witnessed above and below deck. She offered several trifling objects to her young son of fourteen years, after getting advice . . . "I find that one word against his going has more weight than ten for it" as indicated by a letter from (Robert Jackson to Lawrence Washington, 18 Sept. 1746, NjMoNP: Smith Collection). In December 1746 Mary Ball Washington requested advice from her brother in England, Joseph Ball. His reply on 19 May 1747 lent effective support to his sister's campaign to keep her son at home said:

> I understand that you are advised, and have some thoughts of putting your son George to sea. I think he had better be put apprentice to a Tinker; for a Common Sailor before the Mast, has by no means the Common Liberty of the Subject; for they will press him from Ship where he has 50 shillings a month and make him take Three and twenty; and cut him and staple him and use him like a Negro, or rather, like a dog and as for any Considerable Preferment in the Navy, it is not to be expected, there are always so many Gaping for it here, who have Interest, and he has none. (DLC: Joseph Ball Papers) (In his own words)

Had George taken to the open sea, he very well may have been aboard the same ship as John Newton—perhaps in the bunk next to him—but would a young George Washington have repented to sing alongside John Newton the words *Amazing grace . . . that saved a wretch like me?* Whenever possible GW escaped from the austerity of his mother's home at Ferry Farm to the pleasant plantation of his brother's house.

His half brother Lawrence would take him under his wing, for George's curiosity was growing, so he started making visits to Lawrence's plantation, Mount Vernon. One might think that Lawrence may have cured George's desire for sailing on slave ships like polio in the form of a vaccination, by giving George a little injection of what he craved as a means to build immunity while keeping his antibodies at home in Virginia.

George soon started making friends in his young adult life. Thomas Turner, who would later own Walsingham Plantation, played him at the age of sixteen. GW won 1s shilling. 3d. pennies from Turner by gambling in a game of billiards. The gambling bug had bitten George, who came to love gambling at cards also, and even years later in January 1768, he recorded losing on the 16th 3s. 6d. and on the 18th 11s. 3d. by playing cards all day. (Fithian, 25n)

After staying with at Mount Vernon with Lawrence, who had married into the rich Fairfax family, to whom he introduced his young brother, GW became a frequent visitor at Belvoir, the beautiful estate of William Fairfax some four miles from Mount Vernon. He soon became an intimate of the family and formed a particular friendship with George William Fairfax, Colonel Fairfax's son, hobnobbing with the filthy rich as both became sexually aware at the same time with slave girls at their disposal.

The Fairfaxes were deeply rooted within political empowerment to the crown—especially Lord Thomas Fairfax, sixth baron of Cameron, born at Leeds Castle, County Kent, and educated at Oriel College, Oxford. He received from the king of England a large parcel of territory that spread from Fredericksburg, Virginia, on up into what is Morgan County, West Virginia, today—though no one bothered to forewarn the Native Americans of this arrangement, although they had been here since centuries before. (He was a recluse and misogynist and lived 1693-1781.) He hated women, and had had many young slave boys at his disposal for whatever acts he preferred, which is why he was so reclusive. He hid his true desires in the closet, which left some young Caucasian female alone during this time period. If she had turned to a male slave for satisfaction, she would have been ostracized by most others within her culture's society. One might be inspired to say about Lord Thomas Fairfax that he lived a gay, happy life.

It was natural, therefore when George William was sent as Lord Fairfax's agent on a surveying trip that GW should be asked to accompany him. Part of that surveying meant venturing into the territory of what would soon become Charles Town, West Virginia, with major streets to recognize George Washington and his family's legacy. George was the robust type and thought of himself as a rugged man's man. At the age of sixteen he thought of it more with pride than any surmountable feat at that moment, but he would grow in more ways than one to become a somebody.

His brother Samuel was more on the polished side. One might think *frail* a better word once knowing him, but soon he would take the job appointment of being the Frederick County, Virginia, justice in now Charles Town, West Virginia, where he built his Harewood Plantation, and George would build upon his Bullskin Plantation nearby.

While surveying they came upon another place in particular that was of quite a bit of interest, a warm spring that the Indians had been using for powers to heal rheumatism since long before the settlers came.

Upon finding this warm spring, George noticed that the local European settlers, who had homesteaded there in the area around 1730, seemed a little upset by their arrival. He mentioned that they followed them, and some were indignant toward his survey party to a certain degree. They probably figured that Lord Fairfax had sent them to rid the land of them or charge an excessive amount of rent in order for them to continue living there. GW wrote of the warm springs by mentioning that there are those here today who believe that the spring may have been the "fountain of youth" for which Ponce de Leon and De Soto were searching, but all they needed to do was look between their legs in the most unobvious spot to find it.

After the surveying job had ended, his brother Lawrence had taken ill, so he told him the springs were supposed to have healing powers. Desperate for a cure, he traveled back to the springs, hoping the famed place would heal him. When they went back, they found the treatment was unsuccessful, but now the place had even more occupants, who had all but run the Native Americans out of the valley although they had been using the springs for an untold number of years. (Bath that Seat of Sin, Morgan County Public Library 1993).

The Honorable Lewis Burwell, Esquire, president of the colony (governor) returned from the medical springs, where he had been for some time, saying he had benefited from the waters. This was even more reason for George and his brother to travel, but all they really got was a new change of scenery. David Strother wrote that the whole scene resembled a camp meeting in appearance, but only in appearance. Here, day and night passed in a round of eating, drinking, bathing, fiddling, dancing, and reveling, while gambling was carried on in great excess and horse racing was the daily amusement.

When the Indians realized that they were no longer welcomed to the valley of the healing waters they had once shared with open arms toward the Caucasian people as friends, they came back to them as enemies. The truce since the pilgrimage of Thanksgiving was called off, so they killed and captured some of the people. Among the captured was William Smith Jr., said to be the first white child born on Sleepy Creek, and his two sisters. William was carried west, but a few years later was helped to escape, but his two sisters were taken to Canada and were not returned until 1763 in an exchange of prisoners with the French—their condition was unknown. (MCPL, 1993)

George and his brother left that place and went to Barbados in search of a recommended cure, departing September 28, 1751. The two stayed in the company of a wealthy slave-trading family named the Clarkes, who brought slaves for resale to America, mainly South Carolina. Clarke's sister Deborah was the wife of William Fairfax, who owned Belvoir next to Lawrence's Mount Vernon, where George was accepted as family. Surely if they needed the services of slave men or women during their stay, they were provided or could at least be rented.

They became dependent upon these slave traders during their stay on the island, which was under British control like most of colonies in America. While in Barbados George's brother Lawrence still did not get the healing he was looking for. He told George that it was best that he go back home, but he would stay longer in hopes to get better. He agreed, but before he left Barbados, GW became a witness to the trial of one Benjamin Charnock. According to GW's writings, Charnock was a man of opulent fortune and infamous character. He was indicted for committing a rape on his servant maid and was brought in guiltily and saved by one single piece of evidence (he swore upon 'his reputation as a gentleman before the almighty God' of his innocents) while laying his hand upon the bible. Then he was set free, and no doubt reclaimed as his rightful property the slave girl, who accused him as he left the courtroom.

Probably upon reaching his home he took the girl to his bedroom and beat her nearly to death and then ordered her never to tell anyone of any of his affairs concerning her ever again. But if someone had gone back to the courts saying that they'd just witnessed Benjamin Charnock take the slave girl home and beat her to death in retaliation, the courts merely would have said that he had the right to beat her to death if he chose, although not the right to rape her—so much for justice.

This Benjamin Charnock probably never married, since he left all his slaves with his remaining fortune to a friend named Dowding Thornhill, because he had no heirs when he died in 1783. That meant that some young Caucasian female had to wait longer or was left without a husband—perhaps she gave into promiscuous affairs with someone else's spouse for satisfaction, but this was a common thing with slave owners. An old adage goes, "Why buy the cow that you have to feed and take care of, when you can get all the chocolate milk you want for free?" Where did unmarried respectable gentlemen like Benjamin get their satisfaction if no Caucasian men were to be found guilty of defiling Negro slave women?

GW left his brother on that island and then headed back to Virginia for Mount Vernon. Sometime later Lawrence wrote his family that he was coming home in much poorer health, and shortly after he arrived home, he died as the result of his illness. George ultimately inherited the responsibilities of ownership right away, overseeing the slaves—men, women, and children—as the widow grieved. She probably spent less time at the Mount Vernon plantation, and George loved everything about Mount Vernon—everything!

From 1752 at the age of twenty until 1759 at the age of twenty-seven, George Washington had a virtual harem of slave women at his disposal as he came and went to service for the English Crown army during the French and Indian War. George found himself coming home beaten, tied, and exhausted to a mansion full of slave women, who could not marry unless he authorized it, time and time again.

The ideal notion that he remained a virgin; this sexually aware boy, who wanted to sail aboard slave ships (used like a Negro or dog to serve, but intercourse with these slave women on board as reward seemed to balance things out for serving amongst these considered worst of riffraff.) after the stories that he'd heard often enough from other boys near his age. Being his mother a lady of promise, if she could hear of these atrocities then he certainly a virtual man at the age of fourteen had to hear of them. Which is why she dragged him away kicking and screaming from this seaward notion with her austerity, until he literally ran off to his brother Lawrence's home for satisfaction, which consequentially GW would come to own everything at Mount Vernon. (UPV)

# FILTERED IMAGE

The image of George Washington's past has been filtered and boosted up like the voice of a pop recording artist with acoustic sounds in a recording studio, but the realistic truth is that this puffed-up version could fall hard like a Milli Vanilli image. The worst thing one could do to George Washington is to pump him up to a demigod image next to heaven so that it would fall back to earth like lightning, for others to realize that he was in fact just a man. He remained there unmarried during and after many years of fighting wars—which means he was under constant pressure for a few years, and everyone needs a release from time to time—but content with his bachelor status of drinking free milk, for any thoughts of marriage were not much of a consideration at the time.

After the war he felt discriminated against in pay and other things, compared with what the English officers received, while equally risking his life time after time. At this point he needed money to pay his debts to English credit lenders who were calling in his debts. An opportunity presented itself to him in the form of one Martha Dandridge Custis, a wealthy widow of Daniel Custis, who was twenty years senior to his eighteen-year-old wife when they married. His father, John Custis, the wealthiest man in the colony, had objected to the arrangement, which probably meant that he felt Martha was a gold digger who wanted to upgrade her second-class society status. Then what about his son Daniel? Did he feel that he was a user, who had many slave girls around to do with as he pleased? There was no pressure for him to wait around until age thirty-eight and then marry Martha to use her young body as a baby factory to produce an heir to his plantation throne. Who's to say that he was any more honorable than she was?

Daniel Custis, by passing away, left Martha at age twenty-six with the responsibility of managing a 17,500-acre estate, but women were not allowed to own property so she would have to marry soon or relinquish her rights to ownership. This law was fought by Abigail Adams, who had her husband submit petitions in the 1700s. She later said that if the laws governing the people did not conform to include amenities to favor women, they would revolt. Abigail was inspired by a playwright of that time whom she admired, named Marie-Olympe De Gouges, who was considered very extreme by expressing some Caucasian women's feelings in scenes of her French plays. The scenes showed Caucasian men feverishly desiring the flesh of young Negro slave women while casting aside Caucasian women to be left alone and love starved in their bedrooms. De Gouges, a pioneer of women's rights who demanded fairness, wrote the following?

> Man are you capable of being just?
> It is a woman who asks you this question.
> Who has given you the authority to oppress my sex?

Martha met George Washington while on leave from the French and Indian War; he had some debts with his English creditors at the time, and gold digging might have crossed his mind once or twice. Not to say that any of it was attributed to gambling, but George did like to gamble, even once he was filthy rich, with Daniel Custis's money that was Martha's dower, now under his control by English law. Martha had delivered four children—two survived—but she was possibly still attractive.

The question that remains is, Was GW a virgin until he married Martha Washington? One thing for sure Noah has shown us, if nothing else, is that the longer you stay a virgin, the longer you will live without incident. The journal entries of George Washington in his early drinking years of consuming alcohol from 1754 to 1759 before he married Martha on January 6, 1759, in New Kent, were expunged by the very people who puffed up the image of the first president of the United States for the betterment of the nation's youth to look up to when they published his diaries. Those entries made up a large chapter of that time when he was youthful and sexually aware. Martha was a wealthy widow, but she had one thing that probably attracted George Washington more than anything else: many slave girls and money to buy even more slave girls. Believe it or not this was a major consideration with all of her suitors, knowing the men of the time. They also knew that once if they married Martha, her entire fortune under British rule would revert to her husband's control.

One of the first purchased slaves after GW had Martha's money in his control was a slave named Hannah, whom he bought from William Cloptan for eighty pounds on June 16, 1759. The price for her didn't make any sense, because Martha came with more dower slaves than they actually had room for at the Mount Vernon estate. Also in the will of GW when he released his slaves, Hannah was still at the Dogue Run Farm, which listed her in June 1799 at sixty years of age, as partly an "ideot" (probably meaning nearly mentally retarded) after his death, virtually forty years after he paid that amount for her when she was twenty years of age. (gwpapers.virginia.edu/will/slalis/dogue.html).

Who in their right mind would have paid that much money for a mentally challenged slave that today would have ridden the little short, square school bus to and fro? They were nearly impossible to sell, and most often the slave owners were stuck with retarded slaves or killed them off. Why then, when he needed more carpenters to make room for all the dower slaves Martha brought with her? You can't say GW had a bad business sense, because he was all about profit.

One possible conclusion is that Hannah, although she was lacking the mental faculties of an adult, may have had the body of a teenage beauty queen at age twenty. Maybe GW was renting Hannah's services from Mr. Cloptan, and she became impregnated by someone more intellectually confident than she was who figured she would be too inept or afraid to tell anyone of what had happened to her. A person with that state of mind could be easily willed by most any manipulation, especially that of a master, whom she might fear or feel was superior to her, unlike the slave woman who charged her master in Barbados. Hannah was a good choice if a slave owner wanted someone *submissive to his beckoning whim!*

"Hannah, get on that bed and take your clothes off," is all a master would have to say.

"Ya sir, now what?" she would have replied.

"I'll do the rest from here. You just lie there."

"Okay!" I'm sure this was Hannah's mother's greatest fear, when she saw the young, attractive, naive girl sold away from her. Thus if GW was renting Hannah's services, he would have been responsible for overseeing her care while in his employment. Then perhaps he had to pay the demanded high price to her master for her altered condition by whoever, because it was indicated in his diaries that Hannah was "with child." That was most likely by a white male, because she was not married, which also could have come out an idiot. Some six years later, around 1765, she was married off to Morris, one of Mrs. Washington's dower slaves, and then sent to the Dogue Run Plantation. GW was said to refer to his plantation workers as either *his people* or *his family*, and since it was said that GW never told a lie, it should be taken literally that his only offspring were black.

On New Year's Day 1760, George Washington complained that Mr. French's great love of money was disappointing to him. French had committed to selling some pork to GW for 20/0. Then he raised the price to 22/6, because of a shortage. GW on January 2, fearing disappointment elsewhere in pork, agreed to Mr. French's terms, but soon GW was consumed with a greater love of money himself.

A year later after his marriage to Martha on Saturday, January 12, 1760, GW set out with Mrs. Basset on a journey to Port Royal, but after reaching Occoquan, Virginia, high winds forced them to lodge at Mr. McCraes in Dumfries, Virginia, where he sent the horses to the local tavern. There George Washington was informed that one of the guests at his home—Colonel Cocke—was disgusted while at Mount Vernon and left, because he had seen an old Negro (most likely a teenage boy) there resembling his own image. GW let out a hearty laugh as he chugged down a mug of ale, thinking, *He won't talk publicly of my Negro kids any more.* Cocke and GW feuded over the Negro child issue until each despised the other, and on February 26, Cocke demanded a higher price of GW for cattle than he did of all other bidders.

Obviously these two men were having sexual relations with their slave girls like most of the other colonial gentlemen of the time, including American presidents-to-be. Whether it was rape or not is unknown, for no trials were held in Virginia for this kind of crime against slave women if it was committed by their owners. These slaves had no ears to call upon except God, for this was a closed society in which other's affairs not directly affecting you were looked away from. However, Cocke envied GW's success—and forgot the rule.

There are only two reasonable answers why an old slave resembling Colonel Cocke was now in George's service at Mount Vernon. One is that he was the result of a slave girl offered as part of Southern hospitality to Colonel Cocke for a night's visit a long time ago at Mount Vernon or the Custis plantation by either George, Lawrence, or Daniel Custis. Since Cocke was a colonel in the military, he probably knew the Washingtons a lot better.

The second possibility is that Colonel Cocke owned the slave and his mother and figured to sell him off farther South to hide his embarrassment from his wife and children. If so, he didn't sell him far south enough, because he wound up in George's possession. He probably even initially believed the myth that a Caucasian man could not get a Negro woman pregnant, and that it really wasn't considered sin or sexual relations by religious belief. I'm sure it was the top discussion laughed about while GW held gambling card parties with beer in plentiful stock for a long time to come at the Washingtons' Mount Vernon plantation by saying, "George, did you see the look on Colonel Cocke's face when he walked into your living room and saw his own eyes looking back at him from a slave?"

"Yes, I did, in fact. He was about as flabbergasted as Thomas Jefferson would be if he read a newspaper article about himself and Sally, wouldn't you say? Ha, ha, ha." Oh, how the laughs must have rolled at those drinking and gambling card parties—the boys' nights out that GW hosted, although it was known that he hated to lose at cards. During this same time it was noted in the diaries of GW that Rev. Isaac William Giberne was licensed to preach in 1758 and came to Virginia the next year to find a parish. Men of God are usually suppose to marry only virgin women, but he married a wealthy widow also, which seemed to set a trend here amongst the colony's most elite eligible bachelors. A hard drinker and avid card player—which GW liked—and an active Whig, Giberne was generally considered the most popular preacher in the colony. (Fithian 25n).

A look at GW's diaries from 1760 spanning a little over a weeklong period from January 26 through February 6 show a drastic change in his disposition after he received Martha's money. Dates and events are exact and some language paraphrased.

Saturday, January 26: He wrote that there was very white frost about the ground, and the river was frozen hard. He rode to Williamson's Quarters, now a part of his Mount Vernon plantation, after Benjamin Williamson lost it. Upon arrival GW found that the overseer, Mr. Robert Stephens, and son had not showed up for work that day, maybe because of the severe cold that froze hard the running water of the Potomac River.

Sunday, January 27: GW wrote that high wind from the northwest blew fresh air.

Monday, January 28: "The river ferry was closed again, and the ground was very knobby and hard with the wind south. The air blew fresh and about cleared the river of ice." Then George Washington went to his overseers with harsh words of reprimand on his mind. (One can imaging the conversation went much like this.)

"Now look here, Stephens, I'm not going to let you take advantage of me. I came here on the twenty-sixth, and neither you nor your son were here to watch my slaves or put them to work. I lost profits. Now, if you two don't get your acts together, I will replace you both, and I'm bloody well docking you r pay for this. Not one shilling more than you earn will you get," George said angrily.

"I tried to get my horse to carry me here, but every time I headed him into the cold wind, he ran right back into the barn with me. Look, Mr. Washington, anytime running river water freezes over solid, it's too cold to work here that day. Besides, no barely clothed slave is crazy enough to cross a frozen river. The cold night air would kill him if the freezing water didn't," Stephens enlightened to get some understanding from GW.

"I don't care. I pay you and your son to do a certain job, and I won't be robbed."

"I was thinking of what was best for your slaves."

"I'll do all the thinking for my slaves—got that?"

"Yes, Mr. Washington. Then you need to start by deciding what to do with Cupid in there, because he's not doing well at all."

"What?" George said as they went to look in on Cupid. They opened the door to find him balled up with one thin blanket on the floor, incapacitated and chilled to the bone.

"Come on, Cupid, get up. Let's have a look at you," George ordered, but Cupid did not stir. "Cupid, did you hear me? I said get up. That's an order—right now!" He said it like he was ordering his troops, but all Cupid did was moan out a word and then continue to shiver. George came over and rocked him back and forth by his shoulder. "Cupid?" When he didn't respond, George realized that he was seriously ill. "What's wrong with him?" he asked abruptly.

"I know I'm not supposed to think for your slaves, but I fear that he has a death of a cold, which might kill him if he doesn't get rest and warmth. Nearly all here are ill with colds; it been unseasonably cold this year. It's not weather fit for man or beast to work in, and I would suggest much warmer clothing for them, Mr. Washington, and resting them as long as the river remains frozen."

"Do you know how much extra clothes for slaves costs? They don't need a break—they're tougher than they look." George shook his head in disgust and then looked at Cupid.

"It was just a suggestion. They're your slaves to do with as you wish."

"Bloody rotten luck! I've already lost four slaves this winter. All right, load him onto my wagon . . . That's all I need—to lose some more profits." Cupid was loaded onto the rear of the wagon and taken back to Mount Vernon, where Morris was still getting over a cold illness that had kept him bedridden from the third of the month.

Tuesday, January 29: "White frost on ground and wind at south, but not very cold," GW wrote. He also noted that Darcus—daughter of Phillis—had died, which made four Negros lost this winter. Three of them were dower Negros, so GW tallied their loss as if they were livestock. GW appraisal records lack amounts for all entries.

Beck—appraised at fifty pounds—

Doll's child born since—

Darcus appraised at.

"Belinda, a wench of mine in Frederick," he wrote at perhaps Bullskin Plantation.

Belinda was most likely a bed wench used for home-away-from-home pleasure when George traveled for business to Frederick. Her main task was probably just to wait there for his visits, until he called upon her services. He probably replaced her as soon as he found someone else young and appealing enough to his desire. The question still remains that if male slaves appraised higher, why would he pay eighty pounds for Hannah, who was considered a nearly useless worker? When Beck was appraised at only fifty pounds—perhaps Mr. French offered GW some

Southern hospitality and he didn't want the embarrassment Colonel Cocke had suffered, so he purchased Hannah at the high price to cover his tracks.

Wednesday, January 30: "Very cloudy. Wind at south till 9:00 at night, when it instantaneously shifted to the northwest and blew a mere hurricane. Cupid was extremely ill all this day and at night. When I went to bed I thought him within a few hours of breathing his last," George wrote. Yet George still worked his other thinly clothed slaves in this extremely cold and torrential weather.

Thursday, January 31: "Cupid was somewhat better; the wind continued to the northwest all day—it was very cold and clear."

Friday, February 1: "Wind, and snow till 9:00, then cleared and became tolerably warm. Visited my plantations. Found Foster had been absent from his charge since the 28th. Left orders for him to come immediately to me upon his return and reprehended him severely."

George Washington laid into Foster severely, the same as he had done to the Stephenses, which he had written about. He ran his plantation 365 days a year like it was an army boot camp, which usually lasts only twelve weeks today—his word was law. Foster, even though on another plantation, had the same concerns that it was just "too cold" to come to work or for the slaves to run away with the minimum amount of clothing they were afforded, because they would've frozen to death in the ice water of the Potomac. Besides he warned GW that the slaves were coming down with pneumonia conditions daily, but George pushed on, insisting that he was wrong. No matter how much these overseers tried to explain to George about the severity of the elements, he refused to listen, and saw only dollars, cents, and profits.

Saturday, February 2: George rode out to his plantations again that he was building with Martha's dower money, where he saw his carpenters, and Robert Stephens working hard with an ax—*very extraordinary!* George thought, but Stephens and his son were beside themselves after the scolding tongue lashing GW had given them. They probably despised the sight of GW right now by the way he talked down to them like dogs or worse yet, slaves.

GW then desired to ask Stephens for a favor. He asked him if he would go see after William Nations's rent, for he had died just the other day. GW wanted to collect his rent first, before the other creditors came calling for their debts to be paid, leaving nothing for him. Stephens must have been knocked for a loop, thinking, *Here you are insulting me one day for not driving your Negros to their graves for money, and now you have the nerve to ask me to go knock on some grieving family's door to ask for your rent money, because you don't have the guts to do it yourself, and the man hasn't even been respectfully laid to rest yet.* At that very moment Stephens must have thought George Washington was one of the lowest forms of life on the planet. Hence George became absolutely corrupted by greed, money, and power. But his closed mind's eye could not see it.

Sunday, February 3: "Very white frost again—and wind shifting from south to east. Now Breechy was laid up with pains in his chest and head with fever."

Monday, February 4: "White frost and southern winds, sent Foster to Occoquan for barrel of corn.

Tuesday, February 5: Breechy's pains increased and he appeared extremely ill all the day. In suspense on weather to send for Dr. Laurie or not"—money was probably the main consideration. GW visited his plantations again and found two more Negros, Greg and Lucy, sick at. GW also found that the Stephens were at work this day as ordered. GW decided to call for Dr. Laurie after calculating a higher loss of profit if the slave died. GW visited his plantation again to find Stephens at work constantly, and Greg and Lucy no better. George noted when passing by his carpenters who were sawing wood in the freezing weather that they had milled only 120 feet total since the previous, when the ground was covered with white frost. George sat in his carriage before them to observe, because he felt that his slaves weren't producing enough.

Then George stared them down like any penny-pinching boss on a job site. They made an effort to work faster and harder with his eyes upon them until he left, but GW calculated how many board feet they produced in that hour and sent word that he expected at least that many board feet all the time now for every working hour of the day; he wanted nothing less from them ever again—no matter what the weather. He only measured from sunup to sundown in an hourly production rate, not taking into consideration that the reason they did not produce as much as before was that their hands were freezing in this weather, as the overseers had informed Mr. Washington before. The days went on the same, and GW became even more of a penny-pinching Scrooge. At least Ebenezer let Bob Cratchit off for Christmas.

Saturday, February 9: The ground crusted with a "remarkable white frost," Washington noted as he left early in the morning to visit his plantation. He also wrote that he "forbid that Stephens was keeping any horses upon my expense." George, who complained that Mr. French's great love of money was disappointing, had gone over the deep end with greed himself.

Stephens had to ride his hungry horse to work, and if it nibbled at one flake of hay that belonged to George Washington, the chips were going to fly—Stephens felt like Bob Cratchit adding a single chunk of coal to the heating stove and then being disciplined for it.

Soon Robert Stephens and his son became fed up with George Washington's greed and belittlement and parted company with him. GW hired Turner Crump to oversee his carpenter slaves. GW offered Turner one-sixth of what the slaves earned, to ensure Turner's greed would be the driving principle behind making the slaves work harder like beasts of burden, and one-seventh more the next year if all went well. GW failed to see that he went beyond Mr. French's greed of cash for pork bellies fourfold by putting money before people's health!

Even Roman Catholic churches here (not clarified in GW writings whether church or priest owned them) were noted to have slaves, mostly for farming, although some had slave women under their control as well, like Father George Hunter. This was a bad combination when the clergy were allowed to gamble and drink to their hearts' content, because few have proven able to handle it.

# MISSING LEGACY

GW was usually specific about what he wrote and the time spent at the tasks, but quite often when he rode out to visit these plantations, which could have been considered love nests away from home, he wrote only "Rid," like some August 1771 diary entries. Perhaps it was because one of his slaves ran away during that month. He recovered him and felt his presence was needed to keep the others in check, for George ran his plantations like he did his military troops: he expected perfection and loyalty, and deserters and runaways were punished.

GW had a few slaves run away for reasons one can only speculate about. Perhaps he was a harsh taskmaster and expected his orders to be followed without rebuke from male or female slaves. It was noted by his military commanders that at age twenty-two, GW, though lacking experience, learned quickly to meet problems of desertions with brashness and native ability that earned the respect of his superiors, which probably meant he had you whipped like a slave for running away.

At age twenty-three, he was promoted to colonel and appointed commander in chief of the Virginia militia. In 1758 he took an active part in General John Forbes's successful campaign against Fort Duquesne. From his letters during these years, Washington can be seen evolving from a brash, vain, and opinionated young officer, impatient with restraints and given to writing admonitory letters to his superiors. How much more was he that way with his common servants and bonded slaves? Robert Stephens certainly enlightened a few people's minds. The eight volume set of GW diaries Pg 26 indicate missing pages without explanation, after his Barbados trip with his brother Lawrence. Nothing indicated 'GW took a break from writing' during these periods when most young men are sexual active. Much time after that is filled in with public accounts.

George showed signs of becoming consumed by money, wealth, and power. There didn't seem to be enough to satisfy him. He probably even envisioned himself possessing more land than Lord Fairfax from time to time. He became a moneylender like Ebenezer Scrooge, counting and recording every shilling of the dower that Martha's first husband, Daniel Custis, left her. In January 1768, while doing some foxhunting with friends, GW noted that Captain Posey joined them. Posey was being destroyed by enormous debts that he had acquired over several years. GW was a primary creditor, holding mortgages on his land and slaves for a total of 820 pounds in Virginia currency with an annual interest rate of 41 pounds. But Captain Posey was strongly opposed to selling his property to clear his books. He *begged* GW several times to lend him more money to avoid the end, but GW refused to advance Posey any more, although he agreed to act as a security for a 200 pound sterling loan from George Mason for him.

During the next few years George built upon not only Mount Vernon, but five other plantations at the same time, each with beautiful living quarters to accommodate his tastes. At the same time he was building up the United States government, which has transformed into the great nation it is today. GW endured many conflicts of war, as he heroically led men into battles against impossible odds. No man can doubt the great contributions that he made to this nation. All Americans owe him and many other men a great deal of thanks because of their work for the freedom and continued establishment of this country of ours, "one nation under God," and the freedoms we all enjoy.

But to deny the possibility that he had feelings for his slave women, which he would have had to hide for obvious reasons, like so many of the other continental leaders of the United States, is to deny acceptance of them entirely, because of their human nature. Saying we will love them only if they were morally superior enough to never touch a Negro female—if this is the appreciation that Caucasians, who are an interracial mixture of black and white blood, would have for GW—means we don't love or appreciate the sacrifices he made for us all.

None should look down on him for the follies of his ways, for not all slave women in America were the victims of rape—some relationships were consensual—for there is only one judge eternal. This is why so many of these political leaders hid their affections, from Thomas Jefferson on down to some recently discovered twentieth—century political leaders who slept with Afro-American women while strongly opposing the civil rights struggle of equality, to appease their people as they ran for president of the United States to lead this country with fairness.

In the beginning it was not as much so with slave women, but the lighter the skin, and the longer the hair—genetic traits of the next generation of slave women conceived from raping by sailors on these ships and men like the slave owner accused of raping his female slave in Barbados—the more of a common occurrence it became. Slaves wanted to shelter the mind's eye of their children from these things. But at the age of five, slave girls had to be informed with sexual knowledge as a fortification to prep their minds against what could happen to them at any instance in their life. There was no other way. They had to be exposed to this knowledge, to help with possible traumas that might confront them if it happened to them at an early age. Things were getting so bad for the dark-skinned race that in a few short decades, finding a slave girl who was a virgin over ten years of age on some plantations was a rare event in itself unless she was really ugly, and let's be fair—there is ugliness in all so-called races.

This was the beginning of why Caucasian women in America would march in 1875 for women's right to choose. They often felt trapped in their own home like slaves, as Martha Dandridge Custis Washington wrote. "I think I am more like a 'state prisoner' than anything else, there are certain bounds set for me which, I must not depart from." In one of her surviving letters, Martha Washington confided to a niece that she did not entirely enjoy her role as the first First Lady. It seemed wherever Negro slave women were present in the Caucasian world, the Caucasian women lived in misery, which they expressed in writing. They saw their men being more sexually interested in affairs with these captive Negro slave women.

In Europe, women had like struggles. Marie De Gouges published pamphlets to spread her ideas about equality. Sure, there were certain social boundaries to which most women of Martha's stature were accustomed, though she actually meant life in general with George Washington, who set very controlling boundaries and demands for her like he did his overseers, the Stephens, his slaves or troops. She kept herself looking as elegant for GW as she possibly could to keep the interest of lovemaking alive.

She had married him upon his outward reputation within the community as a gentleman and a scholar with some wealth—surely he failed to mention the creditors breathing down his neck for past due payment of his bills and gambling debts. No doubt a lot of these upper-class gentlemanly character traits attracted her to him in the beginning, but now they had the opposite effect on her, for they were the public masquerade that allowed him to obtain his desires without being suspect, which cut her like a knife the most. Now Martha took less satisfaction in "formal compliments and empty ceremonies" and declared, "I'm fond of what comes from the heart." Abigail Adams, who sat at her right during parties and receptions, listened to her every woe—to praise her as "One of those unassuming characters, which create love and Esteem." Even though George was outwardly good to Martha, a marriage takes a lot of work inwardly, and outside interference is usually the cause of most couple's dissatisfactions. (www.whitehouse.gov/history/firstladies/mwl.html—Biography of Martha Washington Pg 1,2)

She wrote to a friend, Mercy Otis Warren, "I can not blame him for acting to his ideas of duty in obeying the voice of his country." As for herself, "I am still determined to be cheerful and happy, in whatever situation I may be; for I have also learned from experience that the greater part of our happiness or misery depends upon our dispositions, and not upon our circumstances." Perhaps she may have meant, "even if your husband prefers to sleep with slave girls more often than you!"

It was well put what she wrote—perhaps these words should have been relayed to a certain Princess of Wales to strengthen her character. In effect many Caucasian women thought of themselves as slaves of sorts, for the man ran the home without question. The bedroom could be a woman's holding cell, where she was trapped like a queen bee in a hive or an ant inside an anthill. Despite how lavish the golden bars of Martha's surroundings were, which GW saw fit to purchase with *her* dower, they only served as a reminder of her state-prisoner-like confinement and the master's control, when a man disciplined like this lorded over the home.

Martha's situation with GW seemed moderate compared with a few others, who felt used as heir-producing trophy wives to wealthy slave owners. Martha had been used by Daniel Custis while propped upon the lower plantation's throne and was virtually love starved. These women knew that if they were ever found adulterous with another man, their husbands could beat them into submission like any other slave and then divorce them—leaving them penniless, even if their dowry was as large as Martha's. In Tennessee it was legal to beat your wife as long as the disciplinary rod used was within certain measurements, though most Caucasian men used this policy only if they caught their wives cheating. Nevertheless these Caucasian women comprehended the fact that they were prisoners (semilegally slaves) under lock and key within their own homes.

Publicly, Caucasian men sleeping with their slave girls was for the most part a well-kept secret between American slave owners. A reinforced unwritten policy between male American slave owners said, "If you don't tell on me, I won't tell on you" to keep the Caucasian women from being upset by this becoming general public knowledge. It lasted for a long time until an Irish foreigner who edited a newspaper ratted out Thomas Jefferson for his exploits of Sally Hemmings, to expose a scandal that awakened many American Caucasian women to the truth that some of their men preferred darker-skinned slave women over them.

Then mysteriously the Irish editor who wrote this breaking story was found drowned in a river, supposedly while taking a bath. One might think that the paradox to this was Thomas Jefferson saying to the Washingtons and other high-profile colonial revolutionary figures at the time, "If he's telling on me, gentlemen, then he's telling on you as well." One might think that Thomas Jefferson was a conspirator to murder, but how could this be? We don't place statues on Capitol Hill to honor murderers and rapists of the past, no matter what great stature they may have achieved in life. Surely our government would not look the other way on such crimes, so therefore, Thomas Jefferson is innocent! Right—along with all the others, just like the man in Barbados, upon sworn testimony of a *gentleman's* character.

It came to a point where slaves would try to mate or marry their children off young, so that they could be pure for one another their first time, which strengthens and holds marriages together. But some plantations slave owner, especially farther south, responded viciously out of spite by castrating the slave men, and maybe leaving the biggest Negro males off-site from their women for breeding more slaves. That is, after the master got through pleasuring them first, because this would ensure that the slave women had to come to them first when they were maturely ready to desire sex. Another unwritten policy; which most Caucasian men knew of from would be Maine to Florida, but shielded from most Caucasian women.

George's family soon started occupying the areas in the western portion of Virginia, which would soon become Charles Town, Jefferson County, Berkley County, and Morgan County, West Virginia, where George Washington obtained a 453-acre parcel of land. The parcel became Bullskin Run Plantation, on the outskirts of Charles Town in Summit Point. He used one slave, Mulatto Jack, a dower Negro from the Custis estate, as a courier to the Bullskin Plantation, which he soon expanded to two thousand acres from the time he had purchased it at age eighteen. In no time he had a lot of slaves, men and women. In the 1798 house tax report for Berkeley County, General George Washington was listed with the following:

1. house valued at $315.00, occupied by James Riley;
2. house valued at $420.00, occupied by John Dimmett;
3. house valued at $315.00, occupied by Thomas Griggs;
4. house valued at $262.50, occupied by Hollis Bun;
5. house valued at $131.25, occupied by John Bryan;
6. house valued at $157.50, occupied by J. Boley;
7. house valued at $1,890.00, occupied by George Washington;
8. house valued at $157.00, occupied by H. Craghill;
9. house valued at $131.00, occupied by George Boston;
10. house valued at $133.00, occupied by Edward Violet;
11. house valued at $1,500.00, occupied by John Avis.

Lawrence Washington had a house valued at $157.00 and one at $262.50 occupied by John Lock. Samuel Washington's house was valued at $1,260.00 and had another valued at 210.00, and Corbin Washington had a house valued at $262.50. In 1797 the Washington family paid taxes on the following: Samuel Washington on 700 acres; Thornton Washington, executor, on 333 acres; Lawrence Washington on 1,468 acres; and George Washington on 1,528 acres. They were the largest land and slave owners the Charles Town area had ever known. Most people remember only Mount Vernon, where a much older and wiser George lived after he had possibly sown many wild oats that would have resulted in severe punishment or death for slaves who would dare open their mouths like the newspaper editor did about Thomas Jefferson back then. The Washingtons controlled what was legally and morally right in the Charles Town area.

In 1771, George Washington's brother Samuel was appointed justice for Frederick County, Virginia, and vestryman (church warden) of the Norborne Church. Then in 1776 he became sheriff, which meant one of two things: by wearing both hats as county judge and church warden in this area, he could have administered great justice to all or could have blocked every avenue of hope for all, especially slaves seeking justice from cruel punishment—possibly like GW's slave Harry, who ran away. GW paid to get him back on August 2, 1771, after writing letters all day. Samuel was married five times and widowed five times with seven children. All his wives' deaths were deemed natural, by whom else—Samuel. No one could accuse him of foul play, because Samuel did the investigations and the closure. His wives were Jane Champe; Mildred Thornton, who had the same name as his brother's wife; Lucy Chapman; Anne Allerton; and Susanna Perrin.

The Washington's believed in the encirclement of power, because it could keep all secrets hidden and your sparkling, flawless reputation intact from all looking in on you. If one of George's slaves ran to the church for help, his brother Samuel was the one to decide their fate. If they ran to the steps of the courthouse pleading for mercy, his brother Samuel would decide that, too. None of the Washington's needed to fear being dragged into court for an embarrassing trial like Benjamin Charnock had been in Barbados. Samuel got this position by political appointment like most others who agreed to go along with the immoral practices of slavery influenced by the Church of England, which was run by wealthy families. The church had split, probably because other ministers of faith disagreed about the moral aspects of slavery and the goings-on at the city of Bath in warm springs VA (now called Berkley Springs WV) southwest corner of Fairfax and Mercer streets, which became known as the "Seat of Sin" it was the mirror image of Bath, England, which was noted by John Wesley as Satan's Headquarters.

The established church in Maryland and Virginia was the Anglican Church of England, where priest or ministers were assigned to their duties by the mother church under the control of the Crown of England. Appointments were dealt out on the basis of political consideration more than on spiritual leadership. Many of the ministers appointed were alcoholics, gamblers, and immoral, such as General Alex Stevens's brother Adam Stevens, founder of Martinsburg, Virginia. The general's life was one of promise in politics, business, and the military, but his achievements in each were overshadowed by his personal life of drinking, reveling, and promiscuous living that went on at the Warm Springs he visited, where he hobnobbed with the "best families of Virginia." George Washington made note in 1769 that he attended church service there, believed to be held by Parson Allen. They had tea and dined with the likes of Lord Fairfax, and he stayed for over a month.

By the close of the 1775 season the patrons of Warm Springs had increased to about four hundred, and the facilities for lodging and bathing had been somewhat improved. A visitor of that year was Rev. Philip Vickers Fithian, a Presbyterian minister from New Jersey. He made notes on the ministers of the established Anglican church, particularly Parson Allen, of All Saints Parish, in Fredrick, Maryland, and Parson Wilmore of Virginia. He said of Parson Allen, "It is said that he was mobbed by the ladies," and Parson Wilmore, he said, bore the reputation of being the "varriest buck in town." It was said that a Methodist preacher was heard over some distance haranguing the people. The Anglican ministers looked upon the Methodist exhorter of that day as "sour grapes," because they could not get a license to preach as required by law from the Church of England, of course.

It was said that Parson Allen got his appointment as reward from Lord Baltimore, a powerful friend of the English Crown, for perjured testimony against some nobleman in a lawsuit against him. He plunged into politics and found himself at odds with Walter Dulaney and Samuel Chew, two of the most prominent members of the Maryland parish. He challenged Chew to a duel, but fail to show up. He complained to the governor that the income from the Annapolis parish was not enough to keep him in liquor. Under pressure Governor Sharpe moved him to the Fredericks All Saints Parish, where he read prayers and the twenty-nine articles of induction to a congregation of two. One was a tippling barrister that made him eligible to collect the tithes amounting to 1,000 pounds ($5,000) annually. After being barred from the parish, he spent the summers at Warm Springs gambling and drinking in the company of such as the Washingtons.

Like most of the ministers of the Anglican church, he was a Tory. He returned to England after the Declaration of Independence, where he continued his fight with the powerful Dulaney family and then challenged the elder Dulaney to a duel and killed him. The case of Parson Bennitt Allen was not unusual, and conditions in the Anglican church in Virginia, where the Washingtons and Fairfaxes received guidance, were worse than in Maryland. However, it is not fair to say that all the priests were immoral. Some were devout men who had left, but the church affiliation where the Washingtons and Fairfaxs and other rich Virginia families with rapport to the Crown received their moral instruction was Virginia. It is said that sheep are led by example, and as long as you were on good terms with these families, then Samuel Washington, church vestryman, sheriff, and justice, usually had no reason to come knocking on your door.

# PLEA FOR COMPASSION

Francis Asbury and Apostle of John Wesley both compared the city of Bath in England to Bath in Virginia, which they openly protested against. Needless to say they were not invited in on the red carpet of Satan's Headquarters, as they called it. The people at each Bath were generally members of the Church of England, and they were taught the rituals of the church and received its sacraments as a matter of outward form and appearance. If you bathed regularly, dressed well, and conducted yourself properly in public, then you were righteous and blameless in all matters in the sight of their society, which gave you the "word of a gentlemen" like Mr. Benjamin Charnock in Barbados. Sin, immorality, and intemperance were practiced without remonstrance from the priest. In fact, the priests in many cases were the worst offenders, like Parson Allen and Parson Wilmore, from whom the Washingtons, Fairfaxes, and nearly every rich slave-owning family in that area received similar religious beliefs, so it is not presumptuous to assume that in their minds, they didn't think it was wrong to be promiscuous with women if done with gentlemanly finesse, especially if they were slaves, considered to have no rights except what you allowed them to have as their lord and master. Parson Allen may have been the one who held the service for Colonel George Washington and Lord Fairfax in 1769 at Bath.

Less than six weeks after Francis Asbury turned his back on Warm Springs ("The best and worst place I've ever been in—good for health, but most injurious for religion") the Virginia Assembly chartered the Town of Bath. Several things were unusual and wrong in the chartering of the town. First, the fourteen trustees were all nonresidents of the

"Little Bush Village." The trustees—Bryan Fairfax, Thomas Bryan Martin, Warner Washington, the Reverend Charles Mynn Thurston, Robert Rutherford, Thomas Rutherford, Alexander White, Philip Pendleton, Samuel Washington, William Ellzy, Van Swearington, Thomas Hite, James Edminston, and James Mourse—were all among the first purchasers, as was General Washington and many other prominent colonists. Nearly all were wealthy slave owners mostly associated with the Church of England, but the Indians who first used these waters and openheartedly shared it with the white settlers were excluded. These once pleasant Native American places for healing were now just an exclusive resort for bathing, prostitution, drinking, and gambling, and catered exclusively to the "colonial elite."

GW also had an entourage in 1777 with the likes of Thomas Jefferson and the signers of the Declaration of Independence and Constitution, two Revolutionary War generals, and half a dozen members of the Continental Congress, who came to visit at Harpers Ferry and Warm Springs. The county and high school would be named after Thomas Jefferson, who no doubt toted Sally Hemmings along with him, and they all had a favorite spot at Warm Springs, which was their private party hangout for the colonial elite, B.Y.O.S.G. (bring your own slave girl). If you didn't have one, one could probably be provided for a fee, but Thomas Jefferson was way ahead of everyone. Freeborn Garretson, one of the most effective exhorters of the Methodist Doctrine, came to town that same year, in 1777, but because of their conflicting past association with the English church, Methodist preachers were frequently beaten, ridiculed, and jailed by the revolutionaries (posse to Sheriff Samuel Washington) in the presence of their wives. Mrs. Charles Carroll of Maryland, wife of a signer, Mrs. George Washington, Mrs. Fielding Lewis, and others were present during that time period as well, but they kept on preaching anyway.

Samuel loved his brother George, who quite often kept him out of debt acquired most likely from his personal life of reveling, promiscuous living, drinking, and gambling losses in between wives. George wrote in 1781, "In God's name how did my brother Samuel get himself so enormously in debt?" George continually bailed Samuel out of financial pit falls, perhaps for the special favors as sheriff to settle disputes, like when George was accused of land grabbing during his surveys by his neighbor.

Colonel George Lewis purchased two lots, number 58 and 59, for George Washington that overlooked the warm springs on the southwest corner of Fairfax and Mercer streets at the original auction of the new town of Bath in 1777, with money to spare. George Washington expressed his appreciation to his brother Samuel by writing "it was always my intention to be a proprietor at the Warm Springs." This was the place that Francis Asbury called the Seat of Sin, and GW loved it.

The combined powers of the Washington brothers—George, Lawrence, Samuel, Austin, and Charles—whom the town is named after now in this family's era was astounding as it rivals that of kings of foreign nations, and the surviving family members conquered victoriously a year earlier in the Revolutionary War against the thousands of Englishmen who came after them. Then the mere slave in chains stood not a chance in hell against them. They were politically empowered like the Kennedys, but the Washingtons had slaves, and the Charles Town area was their Hyannisport where they established their family domain and which they totally dominated, and Bath was their Palm Beach resort. The Washingtons' sexual exploits or family embarrassments could be totally hidden away or, if need be, sold farther south. They say every family has a black sheep in it. Possibly these Washington colonial giants with the power to completely miss abuse had theirs as well. It was around this time that John Newton wrote the words to "Amazing Grace" after his experience upon ocean-faring vessels, which GW's mother steered him away from.

GW noted in his journal May 26, 1785, that he rode to Muddy Hole and Neck plantations (no explanations given). Immediately upon his return he found Mr. Magowan, Dr. Coke, and Mr. Asbury that GW wrote he had expected them yesterday, who were sent to America by John Wesley as missionaries to superintend the Methodist movement in this country. They were at Mount Vernon to ask GW to sign an antislavery petition, which was to be presented to the Virginia legislature. Coke later wrote that GW informed them "he was of our sentiments, and had signified with them,"

Still, when Philip Dalby came to enlist GW's support in recovering a slave who was lured away to freedom by a group of Quakers while he was visiting in Philadelphia, GW was more than happy to oblige. Dalby inserted a long notice warning slave owners about the "insidious practice of the Quakers" in the *Virginia Journal* of Alexandria on March

30, 1786. George without thought or hesitation wrote to Robert Morris: "If the practice of this Society of which Mr. Dalby speaks, is not discountenanced, none of those whose *misfortune* it is to have slaves as attendants, will visit the city if they can possibly avoid it" (April 12, 1786, DLC: GW) Eight vol. collection. He added that although he deplored the institution of slavery, its abolishment must come through legislative authority. He had refused to use one very small drop of ink to sign a petition for Francis Asbury and Thomas Coke on May 26, 1785, just eleven months earlier, for the freedom of slaves, but with enthusiasm he willing used a quail pen full of ink to bring a freed slave back into the bonds of servitude.

The Washington brothers would entertain important foreign guests after they took America from the hands of the king of England. At his brother Samuel's plantation—Harewood—they entertained such visitors as General Comte de Lafayette, who gave Washington a set of dueling pistols, and Frederick the Great, who presented him with a sword. The French make no qualms about it—they love their wine, women, and song, so while visiting the Washingtons they did not go without the true southern hospitality whether the wine or slave women were properly aged, willing or not, without fear of the press like Thomas Jefferson. These gifts were no doubt the way to express their gratitude for all the comforts they received during their stay. The State of New York Library in Albany now owns these artifacts. During this time Martha and Abigail felt sympathy for Marie De Gouges, who after writing the Declaration of the Rights of Woman and the Female Citizen in 1791 was arrested, found guilty of treason, sent to the guillotine, and beheaded. It was said that she inspired many women in other countries.

George's brother Charles, who owned and operated a bar—Rising Sun Tavern—was somewhat of a drinker who surrounded himself with friends, some of whom were drinkers without restraint. All were naive about the effects of alcohol back then, which quite often made for hostile tempers and bad moral decisions in their own lives while exercising direct control over others' lives. This was often a very frightening thing for slaves, especially small children, and particularly the young girls.

Every major road connecting the main street in Charles Town, West Virginia, is a constant reminder of the control the Washingtons had in the area—good or bad. This does not necessarily depend upon the side of the street you were born on, because when some slave owners with conscious minds conceived slave children who were Caucasian looking at birth, they sometimes brought them over to their side of the community without much fuss, unless the children got too dark in the summertime and started prompting questions. Some descendants of Charles Town's Caucasian community are the direct result of very light-skinned slave women being tied to all four bedposts and forced to conceive. These children were then raised in the shadows, told that the slave women attending them were not their real mothers, but just their nannies. Surely this thought would have been a lot harder for some of them to conceive than a woman who had had a hysterectomy.

George Washington later led a life full of adventure that most men would consider a marvel of achievement. He has been touted as sinless and never telling a lie, which puts him up there in demigod stature with God and Jesus. It slightly rings a tone parallel to descendants of Egyptian Pharaohs, who proclaimed their leaders as gods—the morning and the evening stars. Ludicrous! Which proves the power to rule over slaves can be more intoxicating than vintage wine, which few can handle.

GW's life neared old age, and on December 6, 1797, Mount Vernon endured a steady stream of visitors, which put quite a strain on Mrs. Washington. What made it worse their steward, housekeeper, and cook Hercules had run away sometime in the early fall. This had all the signs of something wrong in the departed of greedy obsession and power hungriness. George and Martha had between them 276 slaves total at the time of George's death as indicated in his will, 146 of whom were servants of adult working age, not counting the ones rented from Mr. French.

They could have easily pulled servants from the other five plantations they owned. Often you see some elderly person who needs some pampering and attention so they call on the local police force to rescue a cat from a tree branch six feet off the ground. All indications of this confirmed that when Hercules ran—he'd best keep going until he passed out. GW wrote several friends asking them to help him find either a housekeeper or a steward, and a cook, either slave or for hire, but Mr. Washington's infamous Scrooge ways and high-pampered expectation were well known throughout the colony. Virtually no Caucasian wanted to work for them, but the slaves had no choice unless they fled successfully. He also inserted an advertisement in the newspaper for a house "keeper" competent to all the duties of a large family—for such he would pay $150 per annum, but many white servants were not interested for twice that much, especially Robert Stephens's family.

Life being as true as it is calls us all sinners. No less was done in Egypt, I say to you all. The real heroic thing that George Washington did was not being a Revolutionary War hero or becoming the first president of the United States, but in fact was something he did for many other people who thought that they did not matter in his life. While he lay on his bed near death, he was probably being nursed by a woman named Sally (Sall for short). Perhaps some of her children belonged to GW. She came to him one evening with a single request. To be more exact, it was a plea.

She looked at him as he lay there with his eyes closed, resting, trying to reserve what little strength he had left in his body, which in his youthful state he had considered somehow invincible. George Washington in his later years wrote in his journals of visiting "ye fam'd warm springs," that "seat of sin," nearly a dozen times, hoping that the spring would cure his ills. Perhaps this included impotency also; with hundreds of young slave girls and a wife around, he also may have dreamed that it was the famed "fountain of youth" for which so many explorers had searched the world, but he soon came to the realization that it was not, and he was in fact dying as he lay there on his bed. She had come into the room nearly a dozen times before, clinging to her hopes when they were alone. Each time she tried to gather up the nerve to make her plea, while coerced by the prudent urging of the others lurking in the hidden background of the kitchen and slave quarters. They knew that because she was his favorite, Sall could sway him, even after all these years with younger slave girls in his presence. *Okay*, she thought finally; she would do it by summing up her nerve. She breathed in deeply.

"Master Washington?" she said softly. Almost instantly she wanted to take back her initial words, because of her nervousness. He lay there motionless, not moving a muscle. Figuring that he was asleep, she started to get up and walk away from his bedside, and would probably never have gathered the courage to ask her question again.

"Yes, what is that you want, Sall?" George asked her as he slowly opened his eyes. He was awake when she turned around to see his weakened eyes looking back at her, not strong and bold like the first time when he took her into his heart at the sight of her blossoming into a woman, but with humbled eyes of a man bedridden by the approaching rider of death, while trying to fight back the eternal sleep that was slowly covenanting his body day by day, like the great floodwaters trying to cover the last of the highest mountain peaks of the great alps when God sent forty days of constant rain on the earth. She knew this was her last chance to ask him, because highly distinguished visitors came over more and more every day to wish him well. He was rarely ever alone anymore in the last days he was awake. She had to do it now, while Martha was not in the room, because others would undoubtedly interfere and mess it up for her. "Go ahead, speak up," he said. Then she began speaking softly.

"Master Washington, I have a great burden weighing on my heart, about which I need to ask you a favor."

"I'm listening. Go on," he said.

"I and some of the others have been in service to you for a great many years, some of us nearly all of our lives. We have been wondering about our futures, if that matters at all to anyone. I've heard you say to others that you think the Lord is about to call you home," she said soulfully.

"Death is a humbling thing . . . isn't it? You don't want to die, and we don't want to stay in these tired old, sore, aching bodies anymore either, but what is it that you want? Please be brief, for I am growing more tired by the minute," he said in his raspy voice.

"Master Washington, we want to be free. Once you pass, we will be sold or given to others, who will use us to no ends." He made a *tsk* sound with his lips, almost sounding like he didn't want to hear it.

"Please, just listen to me . . . just this once," she pleaded with him. He let out a deep sigh of relief and then settled halfway back to listen as he had with Mr. Asbury, Mr. Magowan, and Dr. Coke on May 26, 1785, after he had returned from Muddy Hole and Neck plantations.

"From that very first day that you took me, I had a deep, burning feeling against all slave owners, but my heart has changed over the years, and I have realized why. I figured all people could change if the right words of wisdom were spoken to them. An old slave woman told me not to hate, because we are all brothers and sisters. No matter what one brother or sister does to another, you must pay them back with goodness anyway before you leave this world and let God be the judge of what was right and wrong, so all these years I've given you dedicated service to pay you back for what you did to me." (Pg 215 referred to his people or his family, DLC GW)

George looked at her oddly, for she had his full attention now. "In my position, I'm last, at the very bottom of meaningless people's. It was a hundred times harder for me to forgive, but I did it. If I could change, I realized surely someone on the top all the time could change also, and that is why I have served you as faithfully as I have, George. I've done it without complaint in hopes of winning you over, not because I fear you, because I don't fear even death anymore—looking at it from many of our positions, it would be a welcome sight, and not even you, who conquered a kingdom, can conquer death, George. I've learned to love everyone . . . yes, even you, George. What did you gain when you conquered that kingdom, George? A piece of dirt that you got to name America with many mansions, or what?"

You could see him pondering it in his mind. Then she spoke again. "You gained your freedom! And all that king did was ask you people for *some* of your money, George. I would have given him every penny of money in my position to live in a hollowed-out tree for a roof over my head for the rest of my life—happily. I see the only way for me to be free is to give up my last remaining possession, my body—like you are about to give up yours, and then perhaps I will be free at last, free at last, George, but think. Will you be free, or are the wages of sin waiting, crouched at your door to demand some payment once you try to pass through it after death? And if you can't pay . . . then what? They say hell enslaves forever, and it's a lot harder to conquer than any king of England," she said mournfully in an attempt to reach him. "All King George asked you all for was your *money*, George, and you called him a tyrant! But George Washington asks us for *all* of our body and soul. Then how do you see yourself? You fought that king with words and then said, 'How terrible it is that he doesn't listen or understand.' I heard these words right out of your own mouth, as you live and breathe; now for once in my life I find myself here using my words to quarrel with you, George. How terrible it is that you don't listen or understand that your demands of payment from us are even higher than that king asked from you."

George closed his eyes as his own words started to convict his soul. She had only a little time to convince him before someone might come walking right through that door to mess up her only chance. She looked around to make sure no one was coming.

"Just think of what will happen to us once you are gone. We have children by you, George—the only children you have in this world are slaves, some of whom are your daughters. Is the only bloodline left to represent the great George Washington to be consumed by greedy slave owners? We've kept this to ourselves all these years. Please, George! Let our children be free—your children, George!" she said as her voice started to break up a little while trying to hold back her cry. "God be my witness, I forgive you from this day of everything you've ever done to me. It's paid in full. All I'm pleading is for you to let us go, George. Please let us go so we're not scattered to the wind amongst the wolves. Don't let what happened to me happen to our children, for they might not have the strength to forgive, and be devoured by sin crouching at their door in death."

George just lay there staring up at the ceiling now without saying a word as she soulfully cried on before him. George had a little bit of black blood in him, even though he never realized it or cared to know about it, just like everyone else in the world like him. Even if it had been mentioned to him at that time in life, he would have denied it.

Minutes later Sall came out of his bedroom still crying, but silently as all the Caucasian people in the house looked at her with strange eyes.

"Look at her! She really loved her 'master' . . . That's just like George. He's done nothing but good to everyone all of his life," one man said. They thought that she was grieved to see him going away, because beloved George was a good master of the house who never told a lie.

She made her way back into the kitchen, where the other servants had gathered to await her return. She walked up to the doorway with her face full of tears, and that's when all of their hearts sank to an all-time low. Everyone just looked at her as she leaned back against the wall to prop herself up while looking upward. She wiped away the tears that were streaming down her face as though she were calling on the Lord's name for help.

"Oh, Jesus!" she mumbled while crying a little more. Then one of her daughters, who was as Caucasian featured as one could be, yet was still considered black enough to be a slave, with the Washington family nose, asked her mother in a downhearted voice, "What did he say, Mother?"

With everyone looking on disappointedly as she struggled to get herself together enough to formulate the words," Sall then uttered, "He said he's going to set us all free."

One of the other servant girls instantly screamed out with a shriek of joy, "Oh my God!" The sound could be heard throughout most of the house, grabbing every visitor's attention and causing one man to come and investigate. All the slaves standing nearby covered her mouth as she began to compulsively do a jig, bouncing up and down in one spot while shaking her hands loosely as though someone issuing discipline had smacked them a good whack with a ruler. They could hardly contain her, like the Holy Spirit had just hit her in a church service. Tears started to flow from most everyone's eyes presently, because the energy floating in that room could have lit it up from pure joy. Suddenly one of the visitors popped his head into the kitchen area.

"What's going on in here?" he asked abruptly.

"Nothing, sir. The girl thought by the look on my face that Master Washington had passed," Sall said.

"Well, keep it down in here. He's a sick man, you know," he reprimanded callously.

"Ya sir," said the elderly servant man standing there with them.

"Dumb jackass Negros," he uttered while exiting the kitchen, but his insults could not get them down at this point.

"All of us, Mother?" her other daughter asked her.

"Yes, baby, all of us that he owns." They all quietly cheered her for convincing him and bringing back such great news. They kissed, hugged, and prayed, and then they hugged and prayed some more that day, because their worst fears of being split up amongst his family members, who were circling like vultures in the living room, awaiting death to dine on the wealthy material body George had built up over the years, had ended.

Back in his bedroom many days later, George Washington prepared a new will, this time alone, without, as he attested, any "professional character being consulted or having any Agency the draught." George's mind's eye was truly open for the first time in his life, as if he had been visited by three spirits like Ebenezer Scrooge to look upon the GW of the past. He did not like what he truly saw, and then he sought to do the right thing, so he did it in secret, because he knew his greedy beneficiaries would try to count him mentally ill and incompetent. Though

George was a very smart, tactical general—for he knew the enemy and opposition in all campaigns that he waged, which is what made him the most successful military leader in our country's history—he knew his family would prevent him from doing the last good deed he could do for his lower-class countrymen, and after finishing, he called Martha to his side.

"Beloved Martha, you are a great blessing to me, and I can't see how I deserved such a gift."

"Oh, George, you are sweet, kind, and very much deserving of greater," she said.

"If only that were true." He sighed, for something had changed his heart—it was liberation like he had not even felt on Independence Day, July 4, 1776, after the signing.

"What did you want, dear?"

"Call the executor of my estate. I want to present my will." He dated the will as the work of many "leisure hours," the ninth day of July in 1799, probably the date that he finished making the final copy, and put his name at the bottom of all but one of its twenty-nine pages. It was like signing the Declaration of Independence in July again for the lower-class citizens.

"George, are you feeling well, dear? You already have a will prepared. What do you want him for again?" she asked.

"I want to set something right. Something that I should have done a long time ago," he said. So she called for the executor to hear her husband's demand, but when others in his family learned what he was proposing to do, they tried to talk him out of it. His slaves became worried that they would get him to change his mind. They even tried to sway the executor when he came that perhaps he was not of sound mind in his last days.

"George, I must ask. Are you sure you want to release these slaves?"

"Yes," he said.

"What is your name?" the executor asked him.

"George Washington."

"What are the names of three of your brothers?"

"Samuel, Lawrence, and Charles."

"And you are of sound mind and body while you make this decision, George?"

"Yes, I am," he acknowledged, and then George ordered, "Martha, destroy the first will in the fire so that I may see it burn." She did as he asked, and he watched the flames consume the papers like it was a signed agreement between him and the devil that freed him as much as it did the slaves from the potential heirs of his family, who wanted to get their hands on as many of the slaves as they could once he passed, especially the men, whose eyes consumed the now even lighter, practically Caucasian-looking slave women created by George, his family, and other Caucasian males. But George held fast in his decision to release them.

The slaves were still filled with joy that he gave them through their freedom; they never forgot what he did for them, so they kept hidden within the walls of the small Negro family community the secrets that have virtually faded out of existence. Some might think that they kept these things to themselves because they did not want other people to know the shameful things that happened to them in bondage, but the real reason is that George Washington never did a more valiant deed in his life than he did on this day. He led armies against impossible odds to conquer a kingdom, and helped to form a nation, but none of those can compare with the fight he fought on his back to set people in bondage free. That made him a real hero, like Moses following God.

George did not sign an antislavery petition in 1785 for Bishop Asbury to present to the Virginia legislature. What George Washington did do was to present an antislavery bill to the Virginia legislature in the form of a living will, which was the most powerful and influential document in Virginia's history. It makes George Washington not only the father of our country, but a true hero of American legacy for all. After GW's death, his estate was not settled until June 21, 1847. When were these salves actually freed? Who knows? Some may have still died as slaves some twenty years later.

# FREEDOM FIGHTER

Thomas Jefferson proclaimed himself the greatest freedom fighter of all time in America, though when a timid slave woman named Sally came forth to ask him for the freedom of their children he had forced her to create, he showed his true side.

"You know, Sally, we have tried to talk to that king of England, but he is a stubborn old goat. He actually considers us lesser subjects, like peasants or slaves, that he has papers on to own us, plus he demands the money we work for. Well, I tell you, he has another thing coming if he thinks we'll let him get away with this, because people are created equal and need to be free." He thought of words to write into the declaration he was drawing up. "Hey, I could use that phrase in this Declaration of Independence I'm writing. 'All men are created equal.'" Then he started drafting it, and hearing this gave Sally hope that she might gain freedom, so she gained courage to ask him later.

"Thomas," she said, but he wouldn't let her call him by his first name in public or amongst other Caucasian people—only in private.

"Sweet Sally, you must remember not to use my first name in public—it's *'Master,'* because you almost slipped up yesterday in front of some very sharp-witted ladies, whose loose lips sink ships. I'd hate to be written up in an embarrassing newspaper article. Now, what can I do for you?" Thomas answered calmly, for he genuinely loved her, but he didn't truly love her.

"Yes, Thom—I mean, Master. Well, do you remember when you were talking about the king of England and how wrong his rule over you was while saying that everyone was created equal in that Dec-lar-rasin thing and should be free?

"Declaration, yes, we won our freedom from the ruthless tyrant ruling over us. Thank God Almighty, we are free at last. Why do you ask anyway?" he asked mystified.

"Well, I was hoping that you would let me and our children be free, Thomas, for all our years of service to you.

"No!" he said. "I can't do that, Sally. Besides I treat you good enough here. Believe me, you wouldn't want to be free anyway, because you're like a child. You need me to make good decisions for you, Sally. Oh, you may not know it, but there are some men out there who would take complete advantage of you," he said.

"You mean like making a bed wench out of me all of my life while making me have their children, but not marrying me, and then using me up completely like that nonunderstanding king of England?"

"Yes! Exactly," he said, and then he thought about it as he looked into her eyes: that's exactly what he had done to her. "No, I mean, not like me, of course you know that everything I've done was to protect you out of love, right?" She was slow to answer him at first, but then she spoke.

"Right, Thomas," she said sarcastically in a mildly downhearted voice.

"See, there's the difference," he said to her."

"Then at least do this for me, Thomas, I beg of you. Since you say you are the greatest freedom fighter in America, let our children go, and I will be your devoted slave for the rest of your life, and also to whomever you will me to hereafter—please do that!"

"I'm sorry, Sally, I can't do that for your own good. The answer is no." She put her head down, sighing with a heavy heart. "Life with me will be better for all of you, you'll see. Don't be so downhearted," he said as he reached over with his two pointer fingers to lift the frowning corners of her mouth up to place a man-made smile on her face. "Now, that's the smile I like to see on my Sally gal." But as soon as he let the corners of her mouth go, they fell toward earth again like a meteorite. He paused as he tried to figure out what was wrong with her. "Hey! I know what's wrong. You want something from me, I know just what will make you feel better. Now get over on the bed and take your clothes off. I'm in the mood to pleasure you. That'll put a smile on your face." He said it like he had come up with a brilliant brainstorm of an idea in the subconscious of his mind.

He really believed that all slave women's sole desire was for a Caucasian slave owner to have intercourse with them. No matter what problems they were dealing with in life, this was the cure-all. This egotistical stigmatism was burned into the minds of young white males at an early age in those days, just like the one saying that Negro girls were ready for intercourse at a younger age than Caucasian girls. This was only a crutch to nullify the guilt of being a pedophile in their minds, for defiling very young slave girls like Sally years ago. Now much more mature, she looked at him as if to say, "I can't believe your nerve." It was almost enough to cause her to revolt for once in her timid little life, but she quickly realized her no-choice bondage position as his little joy toy.

Even though he never put shackles on her, it didn't mean she could refuse his advances of intercourse like a Caucasian woman at the dislike of his choice of words selected by ignorance. Remembering this, she knew that nothing would help; he could have her killed if he wanted, and the only penalties he might have received would have been stares of *How could you?* from his peers. The regrettable thoughts of how he had used her over the past years started tormenting her mind, but she submitted humbly to his request.

"Okay, Thomas," she said with her dimly lit eyes looking tranquil, like she was feeling the early effects of overdosing on a bottle of sleeping pills. She did as he instructed by disrobing like she was a nearly lifeless zombie. Then she climbed into the bed with as much enthusiasm as one getting into a casket to await death, for her desires in life were over. It was like she handed Thomas the remote controls to her flesh and said, "Do with this walking corpse as you like, until the rotting flesh falls off this carcass, if you please. I'll just lie in wait for my Lord God to take my soul out of it when you're done defiling it as usual."

She lay in one spot upon the bed like nothing mattered anymore. Moments later when he climbed upon her, she turned her head to the side. She became as motionless as a dead codfish, and it seemed to her that he went to the bathroom inside her. She realized now more than ever that he had been just using her as a waste pot to discharge himself into for a longest time. She became like a veteran plumber, who was not fazed even slightly by the most horrific bathroom toilet plumbing mess ever encountered in the profession, as she would lie down like a lady of the profession, numbed by the disgust of her johns treating her like manure for the rest of her days.

"Come on, Sally! I'm not feeling you here," he said as he continued to hump on top of her, and never would he ever feel her again.

George Washington soon passed in 1799, and his slaves were freed to move out of the state of Virginia, because one year later they could have been legally made slaves once again by the family members who desired to have them back. The Caucasian members of that community thought that they held George Washington's name in high honor, but the dark-skinned slaved community that served him from what is now Charles Town, West Virginia, to Mount Vernon, Virginia, held him in much higher regard for not giving up his greatest fight for them. When he was down on his back, he was their hero in a lot of ways by fighting the most treacherous battle of foes ever, who tried to proclaim him unsound and unfit to make good judgments while bedridden near death.

In the back of their minds at that very moment it was not the tune of "Hail to the Chief" that they were playing, but rather way down south in "Dixie, George, You Abolitionist." But the ex-slaves, who mourned him as the "first black president of the United States by Virginia's 1662 'one drop rule' law" kept his secrets until they faded from everyone's mind, and now in this day when it is proclaimed that all of mankind are an interracial mixture of black and white blood, no one can look down on General George Washington any more than they can themselves.

He created a cascading effect on others, like Martha's grandson George Washington Parke Custis of Arlington, Virginia, who freed every remaining slave on the three plantations he inherited from Martha. George Washington had the right to free only the slaves he owned, which he willed free after his death. There was also the legal process known as the Manumission Act, which should ring as a loud and clear testimonial that all Caucasian men are not devils as some have suggested, just like in Egypt—we're all the same. George did divide up and give his family the remainder of his monetary possessions; his great-nephew Colonel Lewis William Washington got some of the gifts that were awarded to George Washington by foreign guests and alike with distinguished reputations—on the outside, anyway.

# FREEDOM AT ANY COST

Years later John Brown, who led the famous raids on Harpers Ferry with some followers, seized Colonel Lewis William Washington, grandson of Samuel Washington, near Flowing Springs Run, and then held him hostage until Brown's capture at Harpers Ferry. Once inside the house John Brown and his followers must have read the captions for the weapons that thanked George Washington for the "warm" hospitality.

"What are you doing with those? They were gifts given to my great-uncle George Washington, the first president of the United States, by Comte de Lafayette and Frederick the Great. Now they're mine. Put those back!" Colonel Lewis Washington demanded. With the wave of a hand from John Brown, two of the men just thrust him down into a chair, forcing him to sit.

"Shut up!" they insisted with a gun pointed to his head as they responded to one another with cheap shots at this branch of the Washington family with frightened females around.

"I wonder what services a slave had to perform for the master of the house to earn these gifts for him," one said.

"She probably had to lay on her back, Southern-hospitality-style, for these," said the Negro man with John Brown. "I wonder how many slaves in this house have to do the same thing."

"They're well crafted . . . I think I'll keep them," John Brown's son said while sticking them in his waist belt, and another man took the sword. They figured to keep the items as mementos for their cause. John Brown's raid on the Harpers Ferry gun factory, if successful, would put guns in the hands of Negro slaves, to free themselves from the dominating oppressors like the current Washington family member they held hostage. John Brown could have been triumphant, but he "did not want to murder" the unarmed Conductor A.J. Phelps riding on the caboose of the train, who had recognized him. At the next stop he reported seeing John Brown the abolitionist with his men at the Harpers Ferry train station, thus foiling their plans to rob the gun factory to arm slaves in the South so that they could walk off the plantations there with drawn weapons. This plan would never have worked just for the very fact that it would have taken the men two weeks to train escaped slave men how to shoot the guns with any type of accuracy each time they freed one, but American slaves were working with desperation like the Hebrews who tried increase their numbers to gain freedom. Individual plights grew worse every day as revolting slaves took on more violent solutions to gain freedom, even if it meant risking their lives.

Nat Turner's story was one of the worst revolts recorded in the area at the time. He led a rampage that killed sixty-five Caucasian people. Nothing like that had ever happened in America before, but what was it that he endured that would drive him to do such a rash thing? It had to be more than just being forced to work six or seven days a week in the master's fields. Even dogs—man's best friend—usually have to be provoked into doing some of the rash things that they have been accused of by humans. Did Nat see the master of the house take his wife right before his eyes and dare him to even say a word about it? Did he see his brother being beat nearly to death while being told to stand idly by and not interfere? Did they try to take his sister, as the dark-skinned Egyptians took the sister of the redheaded young man who tried to protect her when Pharaoh ordered that she be brought to his bedroom?

Whatever the case, Nat Turner took it upon himself to kill. Perhaps sixty innocent Caucasian people lost their lives that day because of five stupid Caucasian men whose daily thrills came from abject humiliation of the dark-skinned race. They not only raped the women, but raped the men of their pride and dignity in any way they could, just like in Egypt. Nat Turner went around getting satisfaction by sticking guns in the faces of innocent Caucasian people as well as the ignorant ones, demanding that they all call him master or he would shoot them in the head. The fatalities would have been higher, but most of the Caucasian people swallowed their pride and called him master for a day. Sixty-five stubborn ones did not, and they never spoke again. It was a sad day for all mankind, because of the failure to communicate with each other's hearts.

Nat Turner along with his friends knew that their chances of escaping were futile. Revolt was their real intent, though they had hoped that it would lead to the light of freedom at the far end of the tunnel. Their attitudes, and the courage to rebel, were just the type of slave mentality that John Brown had hoped to find once he got the guns away from the arsenal in Harpers Ferry, a site selected by George Washington while he was president. Nat, like John Brown, figured that many slaves had the same type of attitudes to join their cause.

Would John Brown's plan have worked if he had gotten the guns? Probably not, because although the death rate might have been 650 a day, both black and white in the beginning, later on this avenue of freedom would have resulted in more Negro lives lost than would have been freed. Once the slave owners in the Deep South realized any chance of their slaves being freed by the ever increasing army of freed slaves joining in with their people—like the Israelites had hoped to do—it would have caused them to pull all their remaining male slaves out while chained together and shoot them all dead to keep them from joining this onward marching army of slaves. John Brown's failed attempt created a better chance for the Negros to be freed through sympathy. It made the nation take a good look into the South's cruelty, which gave the Union Army the legitimate excuse it needed to take up the battle of defeating the arrogant ego of the South that resulted in fewer Negro lives lost than Southern Caucasian men. Human lives lost of any type is a *complete tragedy*, but word is coming that will bring healing to all by letting them see that God is real to unify man.

John Brown was captured, and tried at the Old Court House in Charles Town. Many people from all around the country came to see the famous court battle—really just his hanging; they knew the outcome of the trial before it ever started.

The confiscated items from the house along with Colonel Lewis William Washington, who had been held hostage by John Brown and his associates at the time of the Harpers Ferry raid, were all returned. The artifacts taken were the pair of commemorative dueling pistols presented by Comte de Lafayette and a sword presented by Frederick the Great, which are the same artifacts now owned by the State of New York Library in Albany.

The type of life that the Negro was living was one of complete hell in most situations, but not all. This was the reason that John Brown along with his associates would risk losing thousands of them to free the rest of them.

# ONLY ONE QUEEN BEE
# PER HIVE

The Caucasian men in the Southern Confederacy of America lost everything, including the respect of most of their women, who wanted to be in control of their own lives after the Civil War. As quiet as it has been kept, Caucasian women were infuriated as they witnessed the seemingly infinite number of dark-skinned slave women carrying lighter-complexioned babies fathered by their Caucasian men over the centuries.

They started bringing other women to their side with stories like the one at Belle Grove plantation, near Middletown, Virginia, built in 1794, which was later purchased by a bachelor named Benjamin Cooley in 1860—just eight years before slavery ended. He moved in with a few slaves, including Harriett Robinson—spelled Harriette then—who was given run of the house and ordered the other slaves as though she were Cooley's wife. She was probably his mistress for many years—no less than a decade—and the mother of his children after he had most likely taken her virginity. With the authority he bestowed upon her around the home, she took it upon herself to assume the position of a common-law wife—outside the public eye, of course.

Well, it was not long before Cooley, who was getting up there in age—perhaps forties or early fifties—decided that he wanted an heir to his meager fortune. He most likely skipped the formality of informing Harriette of this change from his bachelor swinging days with her to the new husband-hood lifestyle with someone else, which was commonplace back in those days.

A short time later there appeared a new resident on the scene in the mansion: Benjamin's new bride, Hetty. This incited insurgence in Harriette, which she displayed toward Hetty in every way. She felt as though she stood on common ground with her before Benjamin, because of the lover's favoritism that she had amassed over the years, which seemed to be true.

Before long, Harriette and Hetty were having some knock-down, drag-out fights, which Benjamin would have to referee. It was like Abraham, Sarah, and Hagar, when Sarah asked her husband, Abraham, to cast the Egyptian slave and her son out of their home, for the sake of their son Isaac's life—and perhaps hers, too. Abraham found it difficult to decide between them on most matters, but God instructed him on what to do, so Abraham gave freedom to the servant woman and her child and then sent them away. It's certainly well known that Hetty often confronted Benjamin with pleas to get rid of the slave woman.

"Benjamin, I am your wife and this slave woman fights with me, when I only ask her to do things without ordering or making demands. Please get rid of her!" He refused to intervene, but merely scolded both women while ordering them to stop fighting like two children, because he had affection for both of them.

One day Mrs. Cooley came up missing. She was found alive but beaten and burned in the smokehouse, and surely as she lay there smoldering like a nearly used-up ember of charcoal, she came to realize that she had stumbled into the love nest of a queen bumblebee, and the male bees make them fight it out to the death. Hetty died soon after without being able to tell what had happened to her, but a trial was held and circumstantial evidence convicted Harriette, who died in prison.

Hearing similar stories of how some Negro women were given higher privileges in the home made Caucasian women look to make their own choices in life now. It led to a boiling point that resulted in a rebellion by the Caucasian women (as Abigail Adams foretold it would) for their freedom from the dominating ways of the males within their own so-called race and society. Slavery was abolished, and with no slaves left to command, Southern Caucasian males, who were used to dominating everything, found it hard to just pick up their homes and be on equal terms with their women to raise their children together. Southern males' minds had been trained to control for so long that subconsciously they turned toward their women and children, because they were the only ones left for them to reign over, and they would need rehabilitation to learn how to walk down the aisle of matrimony once again.

However, there came a wrench in the works of this rehabilitation process, because many of the Caucasian women and Negro males started to unite with each other once again in marriage and relationships, like when Noah's ark came to rest and during the establishment of the one world government. The years of being on top were just too hard to shed overnight for the Caucasian male—just as it was in Egypt for the dark-skinned male trying to reunite love with their dark-skinned women after the Israelites left. Joseph and Potiphar's wife weren't the only Caucasian male and dark-skinned female to have encounters, and some of them went all the way—willingly, too.

It brought insurrection with it for the Caucasian women, who looked to make their own choices in life now concerning everything they wanted to do, even in deciding to marry Negro males and raise families with them if they pleased. This highly upset most—if not all—of the Southern Dixieland Caucasian males, which caused them to voice their disapproval, and when voicing their disapproval didn't work, they set state laws into motion against these marriages, and when the law didn't work, they formed the Ku Klux Klan, who made havoc to sever these so-called mixed marriages.

# WHO'S WHO

The war ended and slavery was finally abolished as the nation for the most part seemed to be off to a fresh start, but only the people who truly lived these lives, rather than the descendants who passed it all on, really know the detailed truths of what happened back then. Giving honor to any man needs to be taken with a grain of salt.

Now the scene back then was one of despair for people on both sides of the war, but there was one group that felt happy—the freed slaves, for they were used to having nothing, whereas being free meant everything—owning yourself! Then you could see young, recently freed slaves running to pace alongside the Negro Union soldiers on horseback, who were like heroes to them, because they looked like powerful men by wearing guns at their sides to some of the former slaves, especially children.

"Hey, mister, is that a real gun you got?"

"Yes, son, and don't you touch it or you might get hurt."

"Wow!" they exclaimed. It was not John Brown who put the guns in their hands illegally, but the Union Army legally—though John caused it to happen. This sight of seeing Negros with guns positively confirmed in their minds that they were free, because they learned from Nat Turner that slave owners feared this more than them reading books so they made it a crime punishable by death for any slave to touch a gun for any reason.

They had the same significance as a police officer who walked down the street with his gun unconcealed, because it was the instrument used to hold Negros in bondage, not the lack of knowledge in the capacity of their minds as initially claimed by the churches run in England so they could be deemed on the level of beasts of burden to be worked like horse or oxen—certainly not to have sexual intercourse with. Even some Caucasian women viewed them with a new form of powerful respectful, yet they were humbled without arrogance by the mortification of slavery, which caused an attraction between them as the dark-skinned man began to find pride in himself like he had never known in America before.

Over at a burned-out plantation in Georgia sometime just after the Civil War, an uncovered wagon was being loaded up by a Negro Union soldier of a light brown complexion with four other shades of Negro soldiers like a band of angels standing by with their Caucasian captain looking on. A young, slender blond-haired Caucasian female sat in the front passenger seat. She was looking at the Negro soldier as he loaded on the last of her things.

"Well, it's all loaded," he said. "Are you sure you want to do this?" he asked her shyly in front of the other men.

"Yes, I'm sure," she said softly, a Southern belle in every aspect of the word: intelligent, beautiful, of respectable stature, pure and innocent in every way—the whole works.

Then a woman came hurrying toward the wagon. It was her mother, followed by two of her other daughters as she called out, "Ashley Spriggs, you get down off that wagon right now, and that's an order." Her mother sighed deeply as if to say, "Not again. I thought this was settled."

"Mother, we have been through this before, and I have made my decision. Now let it go." Ashley placed her hands to her forehead like this conversation was giving her a headache.

"I won't let it go . . . You're my daughter, and I won't see you running off with some dirty, stinking Yankee Negro," her mother said, because the stereotyped word *nigger* did not yet have the stigma that it acquired later when referring to the so-called Negro race. All the soldiers looked on drenched with reverence, though trained not to do anything to a woman even if she was insulting.

"Ashley, please come to your senses and come down from there." Her two sisters pleaded with her, but Ashley would not even respond to their attempts to persuade her. Then the father with her two brothers came toward the wagon. One of the boys had a shotgun in his hand as he approached.

"Gun, Captain!" the soldiers on horses shouted while drawing their weapons.

"Ma'am, tell your son to drop his weapon. We don't want to see you burying anyone out here today," the captain said.

"Clay, put the gun down," the two sisters along with their mother yelled. One sister went as far as to confront him by placing herself between him and the soldiers, who had their guns drawn now.

"Hold it, Clay," his father said in a rush, as he limped with the support of a cane. "I've already lost two sons to this damn war, and I don't plan to lose another." He was older looking than his wife by quite a few years. Perhaps she may have been a second wife.

"Spread out!" the captain ordered so that if he shot, he would get only one of them, maybe, before they got him.

"Please don't shoot him!" Ashley asked the soldiers. "Clay, put the gun down, please!"

"Don't raise that rifle or they'll have to shoot," the captain commanded as he stood high in the saddle, taking aim at the foolish lad of about twenty.

"She's our sister and she is not going to run off to marry some ex-slave from our plantation," Clay shouted.

"I'm wise enough to make my own choices now," Ashley insisted to her family as all kept their eyes on the boy with the gun.

"That's a matter of opinion," her mother said.

"Yours, Mother?" she sputtered back to her disrespectfully.

"Don't you sass me back, gal. I'm your mother."

"Then act like it and be happy for me," she pleaded with her mother, who put her hand to her face in frustration, because she was tired of trying to sway her daughter's mind.

"I forbid you to do this, Ashley," her father said angrily. Ashley had decided to get married to the ex-slave with whom she had secretly fallen in love over the years as a girl on the plantation. Once her parents found out, they had sold him far away north to another plantation two years earlier, figuring that that would put an end to the relationship. Her last sight of him was when he was carted away wearing torn, filthy rags for clothing, but he had joined the Union Army a year earlier, after being freed by a raid on one of the northernmost plantations within the Confederacy. He had never forgotten Ashley, and when his unit marched through town freeing the slaves on her father's plantation, she saw him face to face, dressed in a clean uniform while toting sidearms, and it was like they had never been separated.

"And Clay, you put that gun down right this instant!" Their father saw that his son was debating in his mind whether or not to challenge all these fighting soldiers, for he was not used to Negros looking him in the eye and not backing down—it was a new concept that he found harsh for his mind to deal with, as did so many of the other Southern-prided rebel men. Odds are he would have lost, too, and left his family with just more added grief to deal with, because coming down the road was a garrison of Union army troops escorting a disarmed group of captured Confederate soldiers—many with injuries that caused them to limp and some with life-threatening wounds on stretchers being hauled by horses to an army prison in the town. The other brother took the shotgun from his hands to keep him from doing something they would all regret.

"There are more Union soldiers coming, you fool," Andrew said. The number of them was about twenty.

"Ashley! Don't you ever come home if you marry him, because I will disown any of my family members who have half-breed Negro children," said her mother, about to cry.

"Well, mother, you've just disowned Father, Clay, and Andrew, because between the three of them, you already have about sixty half-breed grandchildren and stepchildren, with about twenty more on the way. I would think with a few more that you probably wouldn't be able to notice the difference," Ashley said. Her mother's eyes welled up as she began to cry softly, because the truthfulness of the words from her own daughter Ashley cut her deep like a butcher's knife.

"She doesn't have any half-breed grandchildren or stepchildren," Clay blurted out in a fury. "Because we don't claim 'em. Right, Pa?" His mother just bent down to her knees, accepting the truth, and started crying uncontrollably as her husband looked at his son, who had just made that absentminded remark without thinking clearly.

"Ashley!" her sister Caroline said. "What's wrong with you? The Edwards boy is tall and handsome and wanted to marry you, but you refused, whereas most white women can hardly wait for a white man to come calling these days—better yet for a good-looking guy like Johnny!"

"And do you know why most white women in the South have to wait so long, Caroline?" Ashley asked her with attitude.

"Why, Ashley?" Caroline debated back with her.

"Because just like Clay and Andrew, you'll have to wait until they have finished sowing their wild oats, until they're nearly forty years or more on every black bed wench they can get their hands on. Then when they decide that they need to produce an heir to their huge plantation thrones, they come seeking you out like a prizewinning filly for breeding at an auction, to be their wife. Just like the forty-year-old Edwards 'boy' to be the baby-making factory in his life, and once you're pregnant, most of them will even continue on in practicing their old ways—right, Mother? Like the many nights you lay in bed crying alone, but the men don't know any lonely nights—do they, Father?" Her mother just kept on crying as Ashley spoke out like Abigail Adams with her threat of revolt. "I feel sorry for the two women that will marry Clay and Andrew unless they have a miraculous change of heart. Well, at least with slave women being released they might have a chance for a happy marriage, and I realize all of our Southern men aren't like that, but what's left that's decent for me to choose from—a twelve-year-old boy I'll have to wait for to grow up to become an unsoiled man, now that the Negro women are free. Odds are he'll probably get shot while guarding our Dixie front to help keep the black women in the beds of our fat-eating, high-on-the-hog plantation owners."

The horse-mounted Union army battalion came by at that instant with their prisoners held at gunpoint as the leading commander of the troops stopped to salute the captain before he passed by.

"Any problems, Sergeant?" the captain asked of him as he glanced at the family of people on the ground and said.

"A pitiful day, captain it is," the sergeant said.

"What happened?" the captain asked.

"This group we captured is nothing more than a bunch of kids in uniform with a few nonfighting men meant to spoof us." The sergeant's eyes dimmed as he paused to talk. "We shot at some before they gave up . . . I shot and killed a boy, twelve years old! For what reason would they risk the lives of young children?" The sergeant questioned the captain, who knew, as Ashley had just explained it seconds ago to all of them. She was wise for her years, because her mind's eye was open to the truth—not closed in racial self-pride. "Now I'm going to have to live with this for the rest of my life!"

"Carry on then, Sergeant," the captain said while keeping his eye on Clay.

"Will do, sir." The sight of the Confederate soldiers who came by was a miserable sight for anyone to behold; the look of defeat was on them all, especially the wounded ones.

"Mother, I'm not doing this to hurt you, but to try to find true love, and whether you understand it or not—I love him. You always told me to be a virgin and find a virgin man when I got married. Well most of the slave men and Southern belles are virgins—why is that, Mother? And look at what you're telling us women of the South to choose from," she said while pointing to one of the Confederate prisoners being hauled on a horse-drawn stretcher with a bandage over his one bloody eye socket and both legs missing. "They're not fighting for us; we're not in chains. They're fighting for the black slave women . . . to keep her in chains, for 'their way of life.' Because I can do my own dishes and clean house, thank you, but their mind's eye can't see that." The wounded soldier cried out in agony.

"My eye is gone!" he said as he clutched the bloody rag with one hand while feeling for his legs with the other hand. "Uh. I can't feel my legs! Where are my legs?" He gasped for air, as if he were being dragged along.

"Shut up! You're just making it worse by complaining. Now suck it up like a real Confederate soldier," said his companion, who hopped alongside with the aid of another fellow soldier under one shoulder and a cane under the other. He had lost one leg, also from the knee down, and knew great suffering.

"He will never even be able to work a plow or gather supplies ever again," Ashley said. "What can we do with him but nurse him for the rest of his life? If he were fighting foreign invaders to save us from being raped, then I'd gladly take him, but then with a slap in the face, for the first terms of surrender they asked to keep the 'black women' and let the men go. Why didn't they ask to keep the men around us and then let the women and children go? Surely the men can do more work in the fields and the house, to put food on the table for us, or was the most important work caring for the bedrooms? I may not be a formally educated woman, but I'm smart enough to see through what's going on here. I feel for him—I truly do. I pray God wakes up everyone's mind to the truth here, so that we can become a nation of peace. I'm not the only young Southern woman who feels like this, either, but if I were, then everyone could say that I'm all screwed up in the head and go on about your happy little lives. I might only be one out of every three who feels this way here, but that is still a lot when you consider every house of the South," she said with one hand pointing to herself and the other pointing to her two sisters, who had long faces now while understanding her pains. "Maybe no one will ever repeat my words, but they are long overdue, since this country got started, and for once they will be heard—I'm just the unfortunate one who had to say it exactly how a lot of us Southern belles feel. Because our men don't seem to take hints very well from us about having to play second fiddle to any woman, better yet a slave woman." She paused for a breath. "Like Abigail Adams, I see the day coming when to keep Southern women in these homes you will have to make it a law to do so." Everyone stood silent. Not one person said a word as the last of the prisoners escorted by the Union army went by. Ashley sat down again in the passenger seat, looking forward. "I think I've said enough. Now, goodbye." The feelings were the same in Egypt when Pharaoh lost his slaves in almost a single day by returning without most of his army that had been swallowed up by the Red Sea; a lot of Egyptian women then felt like Potiphor's wife had toward Joseph, being second fiddle, while their husbands looked toward their Caucasian Israelite slave women. Whether we want to admit it or not, man has taken advantage of women's positions for a long time.

"Its time to head out." the captain ordered to his Negro troops, feeling there was nothing more that needed to be said.

"And what kind of a white man are you, helping young white women run off with Negros?" Ashley's father said harshly. The captain sneered at the remark with his eyes, and then gathered himself to speak.

"It's not my place to judge, sir. My orders are to inform everyone, on every plantation, that they are free, and to assist anyone wanting to leave from said plantation."

"But she is white!" her brothers said.

"Again, sir, I say I cannot be the judge of that. Just yesterday on the Edward plantation a few miles up the road, where I was ordered to free the slaves, a very light-skinned slave woman, if I may say so, came to me saying that the master of the house was trying to hide her daughter from us and had her chained in the uppermost room of the mansion. When I went into the room to make sure everyone was released, I found a nervous-looking young woman with long, blondish hair who looked like she was hiding something under the bed from me. I thought perhaps she was hiding the slave child, so with my gun drawn, I ordered her to stand and let me see what she was hiding under the bed. When she lifted her hands, it was a heavy pair of shackles. I asked her who was chained to the other end. Nervously she said, 'No one, sir.' I didn't trust her so I looked for myself. The other end of the chain was bolted to the bed, and the other end was shackled to her wrist. Then the very pale slave woman came running in, saying, 'See? That's my daughter; she is chained to the bed.' The chain was so heavy that she could barely lift it, so she rested it on the floor near the bed. She wasn't trying to hide a slave from me; she was the slave woman's daughter. After I freed her, she told me the master of the house had hidden her away and ordered her not to speak, because he was not intending to let her go with the others. Then this *almost* Caucasian slave woman thanked me for freeing her daughter as we all left that place together. So again I say that it is not for me to judge who is a slave and who is not a slave, because it's too hard to tell down here in the South who belongs on what side of the tracks, and the young lady here has given me a good explanation of why that is so. I'm ordered to release whoever asks to be released from any home." He turned his horse around and gave orders to the men. "Move out," he said, clucking to his horse twice as they all rode off with their guns still drawn. But after a few yards, they all holstered their weapons one by one as the Negro soldier looked at his Caucasian wife-to-be, who nodded her head yes, and the wagon took off and she left with them.

"Bye, Mother. I still love you all, whether you love me or not." Those were her last words to her mother and family as she drove off out of sight.

"You're just letting her go with her Negro lover, Pa. That's all you're going to do!" Clay said angrily. He could not stand to see a dark-skinned man with a Caucasian woman, especially his sister—no matter how many slave children he had already fathered. He was raised with the understanding that he and others like him had all the advantages. All the women in America belonged to them, so to see this before his face was a cut against the grain of his thinking that he'd had been brought up with as well as a serious blow to his falsely inflated alter ego.

"Shut up, Clay!" his mother responded angrily. "She has just spoken the minds of what a lot of Southern women have been feeling for a long time now—too long, as a matter of fact. I always knew she was a Joan of

Arc. I just pray that she's not right about us having to make laws to try to keep our daughters home because of some Southern men's greedy ways."

"Joan of who?" Clay asked. It was obvious that he had not read many books in his lifetime even though there was no law forbidding him, for most of his time was spent defiling Negro slave women and disciplining slave men's backs with his whips, which he figured was his rightful duty and would last forever, but that well had just run dry.

"Shut up, Clay!" his two sisters exclaimed as Ashley rode out of sight with the armed escort while they began to feel her pain that they had overlooked concerning their male counterparts in their society although they knew some of the painful resentments that ones like Ashley were feeling. They were not affected by it as much as Ashley, because they'd learned to accept things the way they were and felt it better for themselves to be with their own kind. Maybe it was because Ashley experienced more of her mother's pains late at night than the other two, or perhaps Ashley had just found her soul mate in this man of darker color, no matter what caused her to be forthright enough to speak her mind while standing by her final decision. She did it just as openly as the men in her family had flaunted their time of dominance over the Negro slave women.

"I just pray she's not right about the laws, because that will mean that this a widespread plague on our society," her mother said once again as she sobbed a little while clutching her breast in her own arms, but her hopes were wrong; they did make laws against Negros and Caucasians marrying shortly after the war had come to an end, because more and more former slave men started marrying these Southern belles—if they weren't castrated. The Negro male for the most part was healthy and strong, whereas a lot of the desirable, good-looking Caucasian Southern males had been killed, shot up, or blown up in the war. The Negro males had a few scars on their backs from the many whips that often visited there, but most of them could work a plow, harvest a field, and work the farm. Some even had good money saved up from their Union army pay to buy land and proposition the willing, beautiful Caucasian women of the cathouses, like Rhett Butler in *Gone with the Wind*, to keep warm at night, whereas most Southern males saw themselves tossing Confederate dollar bills into a fire to keep warm, which burned to the core of their emotions. The Negro men were looking at a choice of either marrying these Caucasian women, who were mostly virgins like themselves for obvious reasons, or a slave woman who had already been forced to have up to five, six, or more babies by their Caucasian masters who ruled over them. The South was in a shambles now, and it needed to rebuild in the worst way—morally.

# Jim Crow Surfaces

The first laws against interracial marriage to be enforced came out after droves of Caucasian women and Negro men started to wed in holy matrimony. It was enacted like the drunk driving law. After seeing so many incidents happen, the law was set into motion by hypocrite ex-slave owners, who were used to having intercourse with their Negro slave women just a short time before. Now seeing beautiful Caucasian women in the arms of ex-slaves, they proclaimed that Negros and Caucasian people could not marry or interact sexually in the Southern states or you had to move out or go to jail, even though many transformed, almost Caucasian slave women were allowed to marry Caucasian men and the society of Caucasian men looked the other way during slavery.

Another key reason that prompted the law was like in the case of Martha Washington. Everything reverted over to her husband's control anyway, and the enactors of this new marriage law certainly did not want to see Negro ex-slave men inheriting plantations, money, and power from beautiful, young Caucasian Southern belles. Thus these Caucasian women were forced to give up any rights they had to any land or anything of value that was a part of that state. These laws were set into motion by the very men who were guilty of starting interracial mixing during slavery in America in the first place.

It was plain to see the obvious jealous motives that inspired these un-American Southern state laws into action. The Negro male and Caucasian female could see right through it, and that these laws were intended to prevent their interaction only. Some Caucasian women were happy about the law, but most others were enraged by it, even if they didn't intend on marrying a Negro male—the restraint-controlling factor was the issue with them. Surprisingly enough, though, they still continued to get married and move out of the state, for most Negro males owned nothing in the state anyway, and nearly every Caucasian woman was disinherited anyhow by her family, who now owned worthless Confederate dollars. Not much was lost for them either by leaving nearly worthless plantations that had been burned to the ground by the Union forces.

Realizing that this method did not work to their satisfaction, they tried another ploy—gang retaliation, which in a few years after slavery ended would transform into the Ku Klux Klan. Its sole purpose was to drive a wedge between the Negro male and the Caucasian woman by scaring Negros, who still had lingering fearful effects from slavery's physiological domination over them, like the Israelite people just after being freed from the Egyptians, who pursued them with the advantage of weapons to the Red Sea—literally scared out of their wits. Few were brave enough to take a stance against any enemies at first like Caleb or Nat Turner. When Moses said the Lord told us to take this land for ourselves, they fearfully refused, so he made them wander in the desert.

The Klan first started their malicious tirades by stampeding into shantytowns during the middle of the night, like ghostly riders on horseback firing shots into the air from their Confederate-issued firearms to frighten the superstitious, fainthearted freed Negro inhabitants, who came to the towns daily to work cheaply for the local merchants. Most of them were trained to be scared of their own shadows from birth during slavery, but it was mostly the firing of the guns that gripped these unarmed, financially strapped Negro people with fear. The only way for them to get guns was to join the Union army, who really didn't need them anymore since the war was over.

These Klansmen came in small family groups at first, some not even wearing masks, like raiders in the night hollering threats from the bushes, but when scaring the Negros away did not work anymore, they started to become more violent, at first beating the men who had been seen courting beautiful young Caucasian women into unconsciousness, hoping that they would wake up remembering the terrible thrashing so to never again want to even glance upon another female. But with some Negro men who were bold to walk publicly with Caucasian southern bells, the Klansmen had to take more persuasive measures.

Their renegade rebellion against this form of love resulted in the first murder of a Negro male since slavery had ended. True, an investigation was launched; unfortunately it did not divulge the devious murdering perpetrators who committed these hideous crimes of sin. They were never given up to the authorities by their heinous cohorts in crime, but the conclusion of this murder investigation by the Union forces only led to one thing: disguises!

At first just like train robbers they used handkerchiefs to cover most of their faces with hats to hide their hair. Then finally they used the dreaded hooded white robes symbolizing their unity like an illegally established private army, and they became a secrete hate society of organized crime funded by the more wealthy Southern Caucasian merchants. The merchants realized the Klan's potential as a group of mercenaries for hire, which would ensure that their Caucasian daughters were restricted from the limbs of dark-skinned males embracing the soft, pale skin of their Southern belle daughters.

Once under a tree sat a young lad of about sixteen or seventeen years of age. He didn't know his real birth date or even who his parents were, but judging by his a medium to dark brown complexion, they were both probably Negro slaves, who maybe watched him being sold away from them when he was about three or four years of age with very little memory of them. He did not hate because of his situation, for he was a humble boy by nature as well as by the iron rule of slavery that had once dictated his life.

It was this type of individual mentality that some Caucasian females of the South found as appealing as their physical traits during this time period. They felt very unappreciated, but this quality is very rarely seen in today's Afro-American males, compared with the newly freed slaves who were used to having nothing. They were very appreciative of having their own women back that the slave masters had discarded as worthless, tarnished pennies after using up their virginities. They valued the love of a beautiful virgin woman (ex-slave or Caucasian) as an uncovered rare treasure chest of their very own to cherish, and didn't have to watch the slave owner cart off to his bedroom to count it for them. The next morning, the owner would tell them of the beautiful jewels he'd touched inside and how much he had enjoyed himself as he spent the night in it frolicking through the precious pirate booty. Then he would bring back the little trinkets that didn't interest him at the time, although if he saw you taking notice in it, he might even desire it back again.

The lad was happy just having his freedom, and food to eat from a nearby river teeming with fish that he mostly got by means of a single fishing line and two hooks he cherished like fine gold and kept in the pocket of his tattered clothing. I'm sure he never thought by being a former slave from a nearby plantation, now living in a shantytown filled with other former slaves, that he'd have anything good in life when it came to possessions, and he still didn't desire them.

She was the daughter of a local food store merchant whose business was still able to thrive by accepting only Union money now, but he worried not of his daughter's afternoon stroll-about. She was a sweet, charming young girl, who because of the war did not get to complete her days of finishing school, but she was so naturally sweet that she must have taught the educators of etiquette a thing or two. She was the proverbial Alice in Wonderland; she spoke with proper pronunciation and syllabication, trailed by a silky sweet Southern accent.

They first met on the side of the very stream where he got most of his daily food source while he was trying to catch his dinner. He saw the fishing line that he had tied to a huge log about twenty feet away along the riverbank's edge go taut as if a fish were nibbling at the bait. He got up from his favorite shady spot to attend the line and squatted patiently for three or four minutes with the fixation of a cat focusing its attention on a possible catch. She spotted him there as she appeared in the clearing but really didn't pay him much attention, and sat down under the shady tree in the same spot he'd just left so she could quietly read a book, with her house—one of the few still standing unscathed by the war and visible by the rooftop—just a good holler away or roughly two hundred yards through the trees, which she felt was well within safety from the spot where she sat to read.

He never saw her walk up because he was concentrating on his fishing; he looked up moments later to see her sitting in his favorite spot under the big shady tree that he was previously occupying. Normally he would just go join the person to sit a spell, for there was enough space under there for four people, really, but she was a white girl, he thought, and even though it felt silly after being freed, it was hard to break free of the mind-set rules of slavery ingrained in him like the scar tissue embedded into the skin on his back from whips. Sitting next to a Caucasian woman was punishable with twenty lashes or more from a bullwhip, even if she came and sat next to you. Her face was buried in the pages of the book she was reading, which she seemed to enjoy somewhat.

He figured it was all right, though, and he'd stay there until she was gone. *How long would it take someone to read a book anyway?* he pondered in his mind. He couldn't read, so he had no idea what it entailed, but he remembered the preacher opening the Good Book for about half an hour each Sunday at the plantation he had been freed from, because the preacher begged the owner of that plantation to let him give the Word of God to the slaves. He finally agreed after the reverend's persistent vigil of asking. The book she had was much smaller than the Bible, so he figure that she would be finished in no time at all. Then he would be out of the hot sun enjoying the shade once again next to his favorite lucky fishing hole on this side of the river.

Half an hour passed and she was still there reading, flipping page after page at a good pace, but she was still only near the middle of the book, and he was getting hot. *She must be ready to leave,* he thought in the agonizing hot rays of the Alabama sun; by tomorrow his skin surely would be two shades darker on the exposed areas of his arms and legs as he patiently waited for a fish. He noticed that she peered up at him once or twice not saying a word; he wondered if, she was like the prejudiced multitude, who didn't like seeing the Negro freed. She also noticed him looking at her a few times and tried to figure if he was one of the multitudes who resented all white people for what had happened to them during slavery, because in the short time they had been freed, her people realized that the slaves had been biting their tongues for years. He broke the ice first by saying, "It sure is hot out here today, ain't it?" He spoke shyly, with a southern accent. She just looked at him for the most part without saying a word back for a moment as he thought, *She's not going to speak back. Why did I even waste my time?*

"It sure is hot," she said softly, which surprised him tremendously.

"Is dat tha Good Book you is read-in?" He asked her. She understood him quite well for someone who spoke with such poor pronunciation. She paused to correct him of his ill performance of speech even though she really knew what he meant.

"Do you mean to say, 'Is that a Bible that you're reading?'"

"Yeah, dat's it!" he exclaimed.

"No, as a matter of fact, I am reading from some literature called *The Count of Monte Cristo,* if you must know." She was trifling with his intellect, but the goodness of his candid nature was so fortified against insults that they just bounced off him like bullets off the man of steel, almost as though he didn't even realize that the insulting potshots were being taken at his intelligence. At least she initially thought that he was too illiterate realize it, but it was not the case. His pride had been pierced so many times in his life that it was numb. He would not let self-pride inflate within him ever again just so someone could take potshots to burst it like she had just tried to do. He didn't care that the clothing on his back was tattered, or that his hair was not combed nice and neat or that he lacked the etiquette qualities of a gentleman. But he was tops at giving everyone due respect as a human being, and he did wash his body when possible to keep his odor at a minimum.

"I's really don't knows much about read'n or stuff, but I's can catch some fish now. I knows dat, and I knows that peoples don't thinks much about me because'n I don't has too much but a fishing strang and knife, wit two hooks. I's happy about dat, though," he said humbly. She felt a little remorseful after he said that, because even with the South in its downtrodden condition, her family still owned a general store; all people still needed food and supplies. They weren't poor, but they weren't rich, either, she had thought until she met this boy; then she realized her position in life was pretty damn good. She selected some kinder words for him to hear from her mouth this time that naturally flowed out. She hadn't realized until now that she had been trained to reserve those for others who weren't slave people at finishing school.

"Well, have you had any luck today?" she asked him nicely with a little more enthused interest in what he was doing.

"They is bite'n, but I hasn't caught one just yet." He sounded hopeful, though, and suddenly there was a bite at his line that quickly drew the line straight and tight like the string of a high-press compound bow of a marksman.

"Look! Your string—I think you've hooked something," she exclaimed as he whirled back around to see the line pulled tight. Then he latched onto it excitedly and started to pull the tight, heavy line in.

"Ah! Fool's gold," he said in a disappointed voice.

"What's wrong?" she asked while looking on from the shady tree with real interest. She put her book down on the grass to stand to her feet for a better look and walked closer.

"Da line is too heavy. It must be hooked on a drifting log or something," he said as he continued to pull on the string steadily. "Dang it! I's only got two hooks." He gasped as she came near to him.

"Can I help?" she asked.

"I's don't know."

"Maybe I can hold the string and you wade out into the river some to see if you can snag it free," she suggested to him. He was kind of leery for two reasons: first, snapping turtles, and second, which he feared the most, was that she was standing so close; he had never been this close to a Caucasian woman before without having been reprimanded.

"I's guess," he said softly. At six foot two inches tall, he seemed a boy in a man's body even at sixteen. Hard work as a slave had made his body lean and muscular, which she noticed through the holes in his clothing. She was near his age—maybe a few months older or younger—and up to his eyes in height, probably five ten or so, tall for a girl anyway, with a small waistline and hips that curved like a woman's. Her sweet ways made her seem like a girl in a woman's body, and together they possessed a lot of innocence. She took hold of the line as he started to follow it out into the water.

"Just keeps a tight tug, don't pulls, okay?" he said.

"All right." As soon as he got knee deep in the water, the line began to move frantically back and forth across the mild flowing water, tugging her near to the edge.

"Hey! Something is on here; it's moving the line. You must have scared it!" she said in an excited voice.

"Don't let go!" he said anxiously, imagining that it was a big fish. How big, he didn't know, but all his thoughts were on pulling it ashore quickly. He wasn't even consciously aware he was standing side by side with her now, each putting their hand in front of the other to pull in the string, like that traditional bat toss where you catch it and each player places his hand above the other to reach the top of the bat to choose sides first.

"Oh my gosh!" she said. "It's pulling hard." After a minute or so they got it to the riverbank's edge. It was huge.

"Wow!" she said. "That's an enormous fish."

"No, it's not an enormous—it's just a catfish!" He sought to correct her with his minimal vocabulary as she did a double take at him with a perplexed expression, but just shook her head to indicate *Never mind*. It was the biggest catfish either of them had ever seen, and he did a lot of fishing. He reached down to pin its head against the muddy bank while slipping his finger inside its gills to secure a hold on it. Then he flung it upon the grassy bank so that it had no chance of getting back into the water. She held the string tautly as he went to pull the hook out of its mouth.

"That thing could be a record; you should show it to somebody."

"I's is going to show it the way to my belly, and if I's is lucky, I might get some corn bread to goes along wit it," he said, winding up the string hurriedly while she still held the other end of it in her hand; he unconsciously wound up his hands with hers in the string for a second while monitoring the fish, but once he realized that his hand was touching hers, a rushed feeling came over him and he began to be overly apologetic.

"I's is sorry," he said quickly, trying to untangle their hands from the string but making them more tangled by jerking nervously; it began to hurt her arm as he tried to get free.

"Stop!" she exclaimed to settle him down, as he was all wide-eyed and nervous.

"I's never touched a white woman before," he said to her nervously. "You's got to believe me—it was an accident!"

"I know, silly—just be still and let me get it loosened for us," she said to calm him down; with a few tugs on the string, she freed their hands. "There. That's much better."

"Thanks you, ma'am," he said, breathing a little easier now.

"Oh no, don't call me ma'am. I'm not that old yet," she said. "You can call me Teresa." She put her hand out for him to shake. "What's your name?" He just kept rubbing his hands together, like he was trying to avoid her offer to shake hands. Then he rubbed them on the side of his leg to wipe them dry. He acted like Forrest Gump at the sight of seeing his first naked girl.

"My name is Chris," he said.

"It's all right—you can shake my hand," she said, but he looked around in all directions first to make sure that no one was around. After feeling that the coast was clear, he shook her hand quickly.

"That was a start, I guess," she said with the catfish still flopping in the grass. Chris settled down some by placing a wooden stick in the fish's mouth to stake it to the ground.

"Where do you live?" she asked him.

"I's lives over in da woods yonder about half a mile wit some other folks that got freed. I's has to gets my own food, because'n I's don't has no mammy or pappy."

"What happened to them?" she asked. He just hunched his shoulders to say that he didn't know.

"Do you know where they are?" she asked.

"No, ma'am—I means, Miss Teresa," he said. "I's was a young'n when I's was sold. All I's remember was my mammy crying when's dey put me on dat wagon. I's cried too for a spell, but I's remember it was a long wagon ride to dat first place I's was sold. It took maybe three or four days to get there. My bottom was hurting by da time I's got off of dat wagon, and I's remember the first thing that man wit da gun says when we's got off that wagon. I's was only five or six years old but tall for my's age. 'Don't looks at any white woman's, and don't touch any black gals unlessen da master say so, because'n dey belongs to the ma'sa, and never looks a white mans in da eyes.' And I's looked up to say yes'sa. Dat's when he punched me in the stomach and said, 'I's told you to never look a white mans in the eyes.' It took me a few minutes to catch my breath after dat, but I's spent a lot more time looking at my's feet after dat, I know's dat," Chris said, looking down at his feet as he talked to her out of habit.

"Well, you are free now, so those rules don't count anymore," she said naively, because she really didn't understand the way the world truly worked. Chris just hooked more bait onto the hook and then cast it out into the river once more. "You don't want to seek recognition for having the prize fish, do you?"

"It don't much matter to me. I's is happy I can eat and be free like da birds. A man don't needs much more, I says." Then he whistled a short happy tune.

"You are truly a man of simple means," she said with a good feeling.

"Does you's mean that I's is simple like I's is stupid?" he asked. "Because'n I don't care if ya does."

"Oh no, I meant it in a nice way. Like you don't desire owning possessions like a frog or something."

"Nope, I's don't want to own anything living. It would be like owning a slave, and if you have been a slave, you know dat everything belongs free, not in a box or chains—just free."

"Yes, exactly, that is what I mean," she said, happy that he understood, because he wasn't retarded—he'd just never been taught. They paused for a moment with each trying to think of something to say. "It sure is hot over here—how can you stand it?" she asked.

"Maybe we's worked da hot fields so long we's can take it," he answered.

"Well, would you like to come over here in the shade while I read? Maybe I can teach you some words, and then you can read for yourself someday?" she offered, but inside he was inclined to say no. "It'll be fine socializing with me now that you're free," she urged. "I promise you won't get hurt."

"Okay, if you says so." They both went to sit under the shady weeping willow tree along the bank. Soon they were talking about all sorts of things that she hadn't even realized had happened to slaves, like when she asked him why he had certain scars or a brand like cattle on his arm. With his broken grammar he spoke quite candidly about the details, once even causing her eyes to well up with tears as he explained that he was hung upside down naked and then beaten severely because one of his close friends ran away from the plantation. They had never found him, but Chris took enough lashings for the two of them as they questioned him. Even though he truly had no idea where his friend was, the overseers thought he was just holding out, and they figured by beating him long enough they could force the information out. But it was like trying to get blood from a turnip, because he didn't know, and his midthorax was left badly scarred for life.

She learned a lot more through him about the real world of slavery, from which her eyes had been shielded at finishing school, and he plainly spoke of it to her with innocence, candidly describing disciplining events relating to the scars that she would ask about. He was like a five-year-old at a mixed social gathering, naively reiterating a racially biased comment that the child's parents didn't want repeated outside the home in front of others.

She now realized that her eyes had been hidden from the truth, like most proper young ladies of the South. She wondered at how she could have lived so close to such events in body, yet with her mind so far away from the truth. It was like she had had an out-of-body experience and was now back with her eyes open to the truth, and they were both learning a few things from each other.

They would meet fairly often after that day as he came back to his lucky fishing hole time and time again, and she came to the same shady oak tree to read many books. Once her father threw away a shirt that had a huge grease stain on it that would not wash out, so she retrieved it from the trash and brought it to the river, washed it as best she could and offered it to Chris, to see if he would like to have it. His present clothing was in terrible condition, with one sleeve longer than the other and holes throughout. He was ecstatic to receive it; you would have thought that he was trying on a brand new suit from a Brooks Brothers store. "You would be easy to buy for at Christmastime; you even appreciate used clothing." She smiled as he expressed the very appreciative attitude instinctively that a lot of women looked for, and gave her a hug. They did not kiss or show any feeling like that; the thought didn't occur to either of them, but the feelings of real friendship did blossom between them.

Little did they know that they were being watched until Chris looked up to see a strange Caucasian man behind her looking at them. He quickly released his hold of Teresa, causing her to look around to see what was the matter. She recognized the man as an ex-Confederate soldier and now a drifter in town who just hung out with some of the local rowdy sore losers from the war at the town pub. She wasn't familiar with his name, though she knew his face well. He didn't say a word, and then he continued to casually walk on by as they looked at him, wondering about *his* intentions.

*We weren't doing anything really wrong,* Teresa thought to herself as the man walked out of the clearing where they both stood, through some dense brush toward the town and the pub. It left an eerie feeling with Chris, but she figured it was nothing to worry about.

They spent the rest of the afternoon together as she read to him for an hour or so in the beautiful weather. Then their feelings settled back to normal. Too many more days like this and these two might fall for each other, one would think. She had brought a small bag containing a handful of salt that had spilled onto a table, which she cleaned up for him to season his fish with for once.

They parted with a handshake as usual, to say their goodbyes. Teresa spent the night thinking somewhat about Chris; she loved the humble nature that he displayed consistently, like Old Faithful. *He wouldn't hurt a fly,* she thought, *unless he needed it for bait to catch a fish.* Then she chuckled to herself silently while lying in her bed. She thought he might be an interesting subject to write a book about. Yes, the thought of him would inspire her to write books, this innocent, responsible kid in a man-size body. He was giving her a sense of purpose that he didn't even know about. She evaluated to herself about teaching him, whether it was a good thing or not. She knew some of the things she was teaching would change him, so she made herself a promise to teach him only good things, to try to preserve his childlike innocence and behavior or he wouldn't be Chris.

Around noon the next day she came to see Chris at his favorite fishing spot, where she would start a book about his simple character and life, but he wasn't there. *Odd,* she thought, for he was as dependable as a Swiss timepiece to be at this spot, even on days when she didn't come to visit. She had the feeling that something was not right when she glanced over to the riverbank and saw the precious string that he cherished like finely woven gold drawn tight, jerking back and forth like a fish was hooked to it, but for how long, she couldn't tell.

A frightful thought popped into her naive mind. What if Chris had somehow fallen in and then gotten tangled up in the line? She dashed to the river's edge and pulled on the string, but when she reeled it in, she found his favorite catch; a catfish. It was not a record like the one they had enjoyed eating before, but it was a keeper all the same. She looked around puzzled, thinking, *Chris would never leave his line unattended.* Then her mind raced. *Did he fall in the river and drown and float away?*

She then remembered that Chris said he stayed in a small village of shanty like structures just down the river about a half mile, so she started making the trek in that direction while scanning the river for Chris's body as she went along. She had not been this far from her house on foot before, but she found the place, which was almost the exact distant that he had described. It was easy to find from the smoking campfires and children's voices far in the background. When she appeared in the clearing, she found a gathering of newly freed slaves huddled together, encircled around something near the ground just about fifty yards or more outside their camp. She approached slowly while announcing herself, so that she would not startle anyone.

"Hello," she said, just loud enough for the group to hear her. They all had their attention focused forward but turned around almost simultaneously to see her standing there. It surprised them all to actually see her there, although none of them even knew her. Someone said quietly, "Is it her? What's she here for?" They knew it immediately without her even introducing herself, and she heard the comment and actually wondered if they meant her.

"Excuse me, but I was looking for Chris. Do any of you know him? I went to his favorite fishing spot, but he wasn't there, so I thought he might be in trouble." She paused. "He said that he stayed near here somewhere. I just wanted to let him know that he hooked a fish back at his favorite fishing spot, plus make sure that he's all right, is all." Then she looked to see his head just above the other people, who turned to look at her; she could see part of the side and back of his head through the crowd. He looked as though he were sadly peering down at the ground while surrounded by the others; she just figured that he was embarrassed or shy about a Caucasian girl coming around to see him at the camp of his people.

"Oh, there you are," she said as she continued to move toward his direction while nodding respectfully to the people around as she passed. "Hello, and pardon me, please," she said. They parted as she walked closer to him, exposing his limp, dead body, hanging from a low branch. His toes hovered just barely two inches above the ground. She never noticed the rope hanging down as she approached the encirclement around him, because it made him look as though he were standing amongst the group until they parted to fully reveal him. She gasped for breath as tears filled her eyes. His face was badly beaten, both eyes swollen, and a sign was pinned to his pants. His newly received shirt that she had given him with the large grease stain on it was missing, and an old man pulled the note off of him.

"Can you's tell us what dis says, so we's can knows if'n he was stealing or sump'in like dat? We's all can't read no good," the man said, slack-jawed while scratching the side of his face, but now after seeing her, they all had an idea why. She was trembling at the horrible sight of Chris's badly beaten body that had been shot, dragged, and hung, but all who stood around her did not shed a tear, as though they were hardened or immune to seeing such atrocities in their lives. She choked up as she read the letter.

"'All you niggers'—I guess that means Negros—'better stay away from our white women.' Signed, the Ku Klux Klan."

"Da Ku Klux Klan? Who is dey, misses?"

"I've never heard of them," she said tearfully as she tossed the letter upon the ground. Then she turned and ran while crying like the world had come to an end. She ran through the thickets past the fishing spot, where she had first met Chris. She ran farther, until she reached the small town where she lived. She passed by the local pub, where the alleged perpetrators were hanging out in their regular clothes. She paused as she ran past them. There before her was the man who had spotted her and Chris together that day. He was wearing the shirt with the oil stain on it, which fit him loosely, because it wasn't his size. Some of them put smirks on their faces and continued to laugh while boozing it up. They thought to themselves, *She will keep her sweetness at home for now on,* but what they didn't realize was that the very sweetness that made her the object of desire to all men was yanked out of her with the very same rope that snatched apart the vertebral column in the neck of the humble young man whom she loved innocently. These hateful men were the same descendants of the Caucasian European people who told the pure white Vikings that it was wrong for them to put Caucasian people to death because of their darker traits. Even with a person experiencing writer's block, the word *hypocrite* could easily come to mind.

Many women who left their homes to marry Negro men against their family's will, discovered added external inhibiting opposition from others to their relationship along the way while still enduring all the normal challenges a marriage has to offer. For an interracial marriage to survive during this time period meant that their love was truly strong, which validated their marital commitment of oneness. To ones like this the efforts to keep them apart seemed futile. However, some did not survive the test of extra outside interference and fell by the wayside. Soon after the Civil War ended in 1865, these Caucasian women began to protest against their men trying to keep them in their homes through these newly established laws concerning marriage, which were enforced through the unwritten policies of the Klan.

Ten years later the Caucasian females mustered up enough courage and support of many other like-minded women to say enough was enough. In 1875 a rally for women's rights took place in New York to proclaim that they were able to make decisions for themselves concerning all choices in their lives. There had been many female pioneer advocates to speak out against the ways their lives were being dictated like Abigail Adams, but a small group put these words into action and later became known as the Suffragettes. Some of these women from the South had been kicked out for marrying outside their so-called race, but they had made only small amounts of progress before 1875 during the first three or four years, heard only by small audiences in parks or town halls at first. Some were even jailed, beaten, and buried with very little of their stories ever heard, because some of them were considered troublemakers trying to get other white women to join their cause. They felt as though the Negro race had been freed and they in turn were enslaved in their places, but Martha Washington exposed the truth long before when said she felt as though she were a "state prisoner" being kept home by laws created to soothe the egos of their male counterparts, by limiting their choices.

Even the menacing ways of the Klan were directed toward these women who were considered rabble-rousers, but not many people know of their fights and run-ins with the Klan, who beat, raped, and murdered them with no justice to vindicate them. Yes, even the female Caucasian suffered at the hands of the Klan, and their stories should be hanging in the so-called black museums about atrocities toward blacks, because even though they were Caucasian, they were still part black also.

# PLESSY V. FERGUSON

The black and white issue boiled over in the South during the Reconstruction Era. People were literally awed by who was who, but that didn't keep some from trying to draw a defining line between the races. The original black bloodline was so diluted that it looked like a weird Picasso painting dabbled in *colored* to shades of black. Out of the ashes of the burned-down South emerged the hidden proof of the Caucasian slave owners' sexual tirades in the form of thousands of transformed white freed slaves. It was direct proof of how DNA worked, but no one even knew what DNA was in that era. They had previously been hidden on the plantations of the richest slave owners and usually hidden from their wives. Some slave owners like George Washington had many plantations, and even Martha didn't even get to see all the virtually white slave children produced. Now Caucasian women viewed the mass numbers of virtually white slaves who had been hidden from their eyes to deceive them. Now their eyes gazed upon what had gone on behind their backs as these white-looking slaves were freed, and they knew that many Southern gentlemen had hidden them for the most part. In some ways they felt scorned and betrayed by each and every light-skinned and white-looking child in the arms of these freed slave women. *Who's your baby's daddy?* they most likely wondered. *Could it be my spouse?* In the Reconstruction period they tried to separate whites and blacks, but this proved impossible, for most of the freed white-looking slaves sided with the freed black slaves. This caused problems with the newly emerging Jim Crow laws, even though the law still existed that black men and white women could not marry. It presented a problem when black men went to marry white-looking freed slave women, because it looked the same as if they were marrying white women who were never slaves. Often these couples would be stopped by mobs and police to be arrested because it was thought that they had defied the two-faced marriage law that had soothed their pride for so many years as slave owners. The thinking had been, *We can sleep with your women, but you can't sleep with ours.* It presented another problem as well. The upset white women who weren't slaves saw it as an interracial marriage also, and would question "Why is that white women married to that black man?" "Oh honey, she was a slave. She is not white!" 'She's as white as I am or ducks don't quack! Well, I guess I see how our Southern men spent a large part of their time in the slaves' quarters when our backs were turned." These ex-slave-owning men now experienced two losses. Their wives were now mad at them because they realized the truth of how these women were changed to white. And the ex-slave women were resentful toward them for having been forced in to sexual acts with them as property. Worst of all, young white women seeing this became rebellious—"If she can do it, so can I. She's just as white as I am." It was the very reason Reconstruction failed. Virtually for the most part the only ones who wanted everyone to stay with their own kind was the white Southern male. Black men felt okay if one of them wanted to marry a white woman; it seemed more like retribution in their eyes. Everyone basically forgot what had happened in Egypt for nearly 400 years when the black men took white women, raped them and turned them from Caucasians into Jews, like the Caucasian men in America for more than 250 years had turned black people into colored people or near white. Eye for an eye, tooth for a tooth. Man's inhumanity to man is usually only remembered by the ones abused, and it seemed that God had created the perfect situation from these enslavements to judge all men who open their mouths to cry foul.

Turmoil ensued in the South, and the Jim Crow laws started to rear their ugly head in 1890. Segregation was the only option Caucasian men would settle for from this situation that they had created here, especially in the South. And the freed black people from the state of Louisiana set to challenge it, as now came forward one Homer Plessy, born three months after the Emancipation Proclamation in New Orleans in 1862 to a family of mixed racial heritage. Homer's great-grandmother was of African origin, but they considered him seven-eighths white and one-eighth black, a civil activist who became vice president of the Justice, Protective, Educational, and Social Club. These Jim Crow laws included the Separate Car law for black and Caucasian passengers traveling on trains in and out of Louisiana. The group hired a white New York lawyer named Albion Tourgee and challenged the law. The plan was to get a Homer on the whites-only train. One look at Homer and he was the obvious choice. He was more than white enough to pass for white on the train and then get himself arrested. Homer Plessy was selected and the plan was set.

Homer walked up to the ticket booth where a Caucasian looked upon him kindly. "I'd like one ticket for passage on the train, please." The man issuing the ticket took one look at Homer and gave him a ticket for the whites-only without hesitation or question. Homer didn't even have to ask for the whites' car passage. The ticket agent automatically assumed Homer belonged in the whites-only car. Homer boarded the train and none was the wiser. Everyone greeted him with pleasant salutations—not one person was offended as children pleasantly smiled back at him. Now all Homer had to do was wait for the train conductor to come and ask him to get off the train. But something was wrong: no one came, and the train was ready to leave any minute now. All of Homer's black friends outside realized this, too. *We have to do something,* they thought. The plan was not going as planned. "Go tell the conductor there's a black man in the whites-only car." They hurried to save their plan, and one of them raced to the conductor. "Mr. Conductor! Mr. Conductor. There's a black man sitting in the whites-only car."

"What? A black man!"

"Yes, sir." The conductor reacted with all speed to get him off that car as quickly as possible. Upon reaching the car, he climbed aboard to rid the invader. The conductor's eyes rapidly scanned the entire car of passengers, but he paused with a bewildered look on his face. Then anger started to build inside him.

"All right! Who's the practical joker that thinks it's funny to waste my time with this joke?" He turned to look at the black guy who told him there was a black man in the whites-only car. "Boy, is you trying to make fun of me?"

"No, sir! He's sitting in the third seat on the right with a dark suit on." The conductor reentered the car and scanned the passengers one more time. This time he spotted Homer with the dark suit on. But he wasn't sure. What if he approached Homer and accused him of being black and he lashed back at the conductor and belittled him in front of the whole passenger car? The conductor approached with caution.

"Excuse me, sir, could you please state your race?" the conductor said in a mild respectful voice.

Homer answered, "I bought a first-class ticket for passage on this train." Now the conductor felt the right of empowerment and became vociferous with authority.

"Sir! I said state your race, please," the conductor said, amplifying his voice enough to grab everyone's attention on the train as all on board looked onward to see what was happening. Homer merely repeated himself. "I bought a first-class ticket for passage on this train."

"Boy! You need to get off of this car right now and ride in the Negro car." But Homer refused to answer his request. Now the sheriff was called to the scene and told that a black man was refusing to get off the whites-only car. He entered the car as all of Homer's friends watched from outside.

"Where is he?" the sheriff demanded in a stern voice. The conductor pointed in the direction of Homer. The sheriff looked at Homer and then scanned past him for a person with darker traits and then back to Homer again. The sheriff didn't believe his eyes, so he looked back and asked the conductor, who made a slight hand gesture toward Homer to indicate yes, he's the one. The sheriff studied him over to be sure. "Boy! State your race."

Homer again said, "I bought a first-class ticket for passage on this train."

"I'm giving you one more chance to leave this car, and get back there in the Negro car." But Homer didn't respond to the request. "That's it! You're coming with me, boy." The sheriff grabbed Homer and placed him under arrest as Homer and his friends planned, but because Homer possessed such white traits, the plan was almost ruined. Homer didn't resist and was taken without incident.

Now he appeared before Judge Ferguson, and just like all the others before him, he viewed at Homer with disbelief and the applied charge, because homer looked white.

"Mr. Plessy, you have been charged with occupying a passenger car restricted to whites only by the state of Louisiana. Do you understand the charges against you?"

"Yes. But the law is wrong and violates the thirteenth and fourteenth amendments.

"Well, I'm sorry you feel that way, but the state's laws will be enforced."

"Mr. Plessy, even though you look white and are seven-eighths white, you are required to ride in the black car of the train, and I am fining you the maximum amount for violating this ordinance". If Homer even now had said he was white, the charges would have been dropped. They gave Homer the chance to say that he was white, even up to the court proceedings, but Homer stood his ground and claimed his black heritage. Now the trial was in the hands of the Supreme Court. Judge Harlan dissented, based on the "one drop rule" and the "any variation from white adopted by various states. It was used to keep black people as slave no matter how white appearing they became was used as determining factors in the case. Justice John Marshall Harlan, a former Kentucky slave owner, was the only judge in favor of Plessy. He wrote that segregation was a "badge of servitude" and that "the Constitution is color-blind." He warned the Caucasian people who wanted to keep the blacks from riding in the same cars as them that as long as a white man could be distinguished from a black man, they were all safe to have this segregation, but by their using the "any variation" and "one-drop rule," they could be including themselves if it was ever proving to include them. Besides, this would include them and their grandchildren to come. "Are you sure you want me to do this?" Harlan asked. "Yes," they replied. That day in 1896 when Justice Henry Brown slammed that gavel, he made everyone in America black, including himself. Homer and his friends walked out of that courtroom thinking they had lost. But they had actually won, for they had succeeded in changing everyone in America to black. No one should have been allowed to ride in the whites-only car, for whites were all extinct! When the gavel was pounded that day, George Washington officially became the first black president of these United States, because of the 1662 one-drop rule. At times it's the small, unseen victories that you don't see that have the biggest effect. After the Supreme Court decision, Homer and his wife, Louise, had children while continuing in religion and social activities around the community. Homer also sold insurance while working for People's Life Insurance Company. In 1925, at the age of sixty-one, Homer Plessy died and was placed in an aboveground tomb in New Orleans, Louisiana. He was placed in the Debergue-Blanco family tomb in St. Louis Cemetery 1. Today a park is dedicated to honoring him. This was not first case of this kind in the American political arena, for you see, in the 1850s Senator Charles Sumner had advocated abolitionist to free slaves by proving that there were white slaves purchased Mary Botts from her slave owner. Judge Neal from Alexandria, Virginia, for about eight hundred dollars and taken to New York to be paraded around to all the political figures and their communities. She was likened to the mythical Ida May character in a book, who was actually Caucasian of European descent living up North. When she went on a trip to the Deep South, she was taken and enslaved by a slave owner, who accused her of being the little runaway slave girl for whom he had been searching for the longest time. Mary was dubbed the real Ida May, so white looking that you could not tell her apart from any American president's daughter and taken to town meeting after meeting from Boston to New York. Sumner used this to his advantage by striking fear in the Northern states' parents, saying, "What if you're taking a trip down South and your little girl is snatched up by some drunken crazed slave owner. No telling what awful things they may have done to her by the time you find her—pray not the awful things they did to change these black people into colored or, as you see before you, white people." Sumner kept his vigilance up and finally caught the attention of many Southern slave owners, who were very displeased that their wives and women now heard from Northern women, "It appears your men like slave women better than you," as Sumner pushed the issue ever harder on the Senate floor of the U.S. Congress. Then while in the middle of a session on the Senate floor, while Sumner was writing at his desk with nothing more than a pen in his hand, Preston Brooks sneaked up on him and beat Sumner savagely with a cane to shut him up good, like Irish editor James Calendar for telling on Thomas Jefferson. They didn't appreciate Sumner stirring up so much commotion with white women in the South and damaging the reputation of Southern gentlemen, who claimed they never touched black slave woman. But Mary Botts, Homer Plessy, and thousands of others like them begged to differ, and even after the Civil War they were paraded around New York like a spectacle to be seen. On January 30, 1864, *Harper's Weekly* published an article "As White As Their Masters" Visualizing the Color Line. (Source: mirrorofrace.org) Enslaved by the one-drop rule established by Virginia law in 1662, the law of *partus sequitur ventrem* to keep these beautiful, virtually white slave women, or new people, the result of miscegenation and mulattos in the United States as slaves that slave owners didn't want to let go to fill their sexual desires. Three virtually white children were used to make their case. Substantiating the existence of "white slaves" in the South, the *Harper's* engraving unveiled what the accompanying editorial referred to as one of the most loathsome secrets of the slave system—the "seduction" of "the most friendless and defenseless of women" by Southern "gentlemen." These "white slaves" were the incarnation of the racial transgression in the South, extant proof of the sexual exploitation of black slave women by their white masters. *Harper's* was bent on exposing the depravity of the slave system, affording its subscribers "a terrible illustration of this truth of the outrage of natural human affections" in the form of the engraving. Finally these virtually white-looking slave women who had not been completely absorbed into the Caucasian race and allowed freedom in that way were free of being forced to sleep with any Caucasian man who owned them. But the separating of who's who and what was accepted as white or black proved to be a bigger challenge than anyone had expected.

# UNITED TOGETHER

The Niagara Movement soon developed, and in August 1906, an early civil rights organization met on the campus of Storer College in Harpers Ferry, West Virginia. This meeting was symbolic, because it was the first meeting on American soil. The Freewill Baptist ministry opened Storer as a mission school for educating former slaves, opening in 1867. Storer was the only school in West Virginia that offered African Americans an education beyond the primary level. The first objective of the collective Negro males was to seek education for their people while also seeking their rightful place as equals in American society. Sources: (Jefferson County Black History Preservation Society, American Public University System, www.studyatapu. com. www.nps.gov/hafe/Niagara, West Virginia Humanities Council).

It became known as the Niagara Movement, because Dr. W.E.B. Du Bois organized the first meeting held at Niagara Falls in July 1905, at the Erie Beach Hotel in Fort Erie, Ontario, Canada. Where they found sympathy for their struggle. Racial prejudice forced Du Bois to move the meeting to the Canadian side of Niagara Falls when accommodations were refused the group in Buffalo, New York, the very same state in which the women's rights movement started in 1875. Each drew national attention to the biased governing ways of American law.

Harpers Ferry had been carefully selected as the location for the second meeting because of its connection to John Brown and his 1859 raid to free the more than 4 million slaves held in bondage in this country. To look at John Brown closely you could see he was one of the converted white slaves given freedom. Like Moses he wanted to free his people. In fact the meeting was promoted as "the 100th anniversary of John Brown's birthday, the fiftieth jubilee of the battle of Osawatomie." (Brown was actually born in 1800, making this the 106th anniversary of his birth.) The connection to the martyred Brown was powerful indeed; they met there with the National League of Colored Women (NLCW), which was a separate group then, but supporting the same fight for all equality.

Convening on August 15, these men undoubtedly carried strong hopes that their voices would be heard and action would result. Their demands only aggravated the local enforcers of segregation. Many of the Niagarites, as they were called, were drawn to this organization by common goals and desires. They had tired of the Booker T. Washington's theory of "accommodation" and sought to actively seek equality for their race, because all accommodation did was allow leverages to be set in the lawmakers' favor—of biased Caucasian males, who also enforced them to their advantage.

Mary White Ovington wrote of the participants, "Their power and intellectual ability is manifested on hearing or talking with them." In 1909 Ms. Ovington became the cofounder of the (NAACP) National Association for the Advancement of Colored People.

A professional agenda of accounts were kept. Speeches, meetings, and special addresses filled the week at Storer; a highlight for the participants, men, and women was John Brown's Day, August 17—a day devoted to honoring the memory of John Brown. A light rain fell as Owen Waller, a physician from Brooklyn, New York, led a silent pilgrimage to the Murphy farm, site of Brown's fort. The Niagarites, numbering one hundred strong, removed their shoes and socks before treading this hallowed ground. Richard T. Greener, former dean of the Howard University Law School, offered a prayer and stirring remarks. Then in single file the assemblage marched around the fort singing "The Battle Hymn of the Republic" and "John Brown's Body." Many others offered stirring sentiments with words of encouragement as well. Henrietta Leary Evens, whose brother and nephew fought alongside Brown at Harpers Ferry; Lewis Douglass, son of Frederick Douglass; W.E.B. Du Bois; and Reverdy C. Ransom, pastor of the Charles Street African Methodist Episcopal Church in Boston. Ransom's address was described by many as a masterpiece and according to Benjamin Quarles in "Allies for Freedom" was the most stirring single episode in the shortlived life of the Niagara Movement."

Dr. Du Bois commented, "[W]e talked some of the plainest English that had been given voice to by black men in America."

The second annual conference of the Niagara Moment held in Harpers Ferry concluded with an "Address to the Country." Penned by Du Bois, this document was a five-point resolution demanding the following:

1. [W]e want full manhood suffrage, and we want it now, henceforth and forever!
2. [W]e want discrimination in public accommodation to cease. Separation . . . is un-American, undemocratic, and silly.
3. We claim the right of freemen to walk, talk and be with them who wish to be with us.
4. We want the laws to be enforced . . . against white as well as black.
5. We want our children educated . . . Either the United States will destroy ignorance or ignorance will destroy the United States.

The third demand was directed toward all the Caucasian women in America and shockingly came as a bold public invitation to unite with particularly the Suffragette women. It meant that if they or their daughters wish to protest united or be with a colored man in a relationship, or vice versa, then it is all right by us, because the colored women, like members of the NLCW, were already there walking and talking with the colored men without any noticeable outside interference, unlike during the time of slavery, when the Caucasian men coveted both kinds of women in a shroud of secrecy—like in Egypt.

The Suffragettes, however, were still gathering in number to march in protest with force whenever possible for complete freedom within their communities as well. Later it was rumored that the suggestion of affiliating the Niagara Movement with the Suffragettes or Caucasian female members, to increase in number and strength, even though the timing was right to unify, may have caused a cracking in the infrastructure of the Niagara Movement, with some members feeling it might cause undue resentment among the colored female members of the NLCW, who weren't even directly affiliated with their group yet, though they were directing their concerns at the same opposition. This mistake would cause the Negro people another fifty-seven years of unnecessary hardships, and afterward colored and Caucasian youth of both genders united openly in relationships anyway.

The address also said, "We will not be satisfied to take one jot or title less than our full manhood rights! We claim for ourselves every single right that belongs to a freeborn America, political, civil, and social; and until we get these rights we will never cease to protest and assail the ears of America! The battle we wage is not for ourselves alone, but for all true Americans." That itself questions why the merger never happened with the Suffragettes. Sounds of thunderous applause could be heard as the Harpers Ferry conference drew to a close. Recalling this conference years later, Du Bois referred to it as "one of the greatest meetings that American Negroes ever held."

The Niagara Movement continued until 1911, at which time various factors contributed to its demise. In 1911 Du Bois wrote to his colleagues advising them to join the new National Association for the Advancement of Colored People. Niagara, as an organization, ceased to exist. Du Bois must have figured that it was better for people to belong to some kind of an organized group that pursued the rights denied people than none, but its principles and the ideals that evolved continued to gain momentum into the twenty-first century. Perhaps it would have benefited the nation better if they had called the NAACP the National Association for the Advancement of Christian People to include the Suffragettes and even Christian-minded Caucasian males who believed in the equal rights agenda, which may have yielded better results in less time.

Pictures of the colored groups meeting in Harpers Ferry at the time showed how some members of these organizations bore a striking resemblance to the Caucasian race anyway. They obviously had been fathered by their mothers' slave owners and were still maturing inside their pregnant mother's womb when their mother was freed. Then they were born as free children, narrowly escaping the threat of having their umbilical cords untied to hide the embarrassment of the Caucasian slave-owning fathers for coming out too light in complexion or worse, as George Washington laughed about in a bar, resembling their father, as happened to Colonel Cocke. These types of reminders made the leaders of the Suffragettes often realize what they were fighting for after many years later.

These Suffragette leaders became smarter, realizing that other women wanted their own choices as well, but not for the same principal reasons that they had started up the Suffragette organization for originally. To lure them, they changed their tactical ploy to women's rights in general, addressing such issues as the right to choose motherhood; the right to birth only as many babies as they agreed to, not just how many their husbands desired; the right to vote on issues directly concerning them in general and not letting their male counterparts decide what was best for them; and so on. The tactic worked, and more and more women joined their cause to choose the freedom to govern their own lives. It was the first time in history that women elected to be set apart from the men of their own kind, as if threatening to live an Amazon life existence by choice or at least with other men. Everyone voiced a gripe against the Caucasian man at this point in time. American society seemed to ask, "Why can't you see yourself in the mirror?"

During their struggle for an amendment to the U.S. Constitution to give women the right to vote, Suffragettes held parades, rallies, and petition signings across the country.

In 1917 police began to arrest Suffragettes who were picketing in front of the White House like Alice Paul, the president of the National Women's Party. Miss Paul was placed in solitary confinement in the District of Columbia prison and fed only bread and water, causing her health to decline.

The warden transferred Alice to the prison hospital, where she went on a hunger strike. Prison doctors placed Miss Paul in the psychiatric ward and force-fed her three times a day for three weeks.

Guards at the Occoquan Work House in Virginia beat up thirty-three jailed Suffragists, and after five weeks in prison, Miss Paul was released.

News about the force-feedings and beatings of the Suffragettes angered the people and won support for the voting rights of Caucasian women.

Public outcry forced President Woodrow Wilson to make an announcement on January 9, 1918. For the first time Caucasian women all over the United States were stirred up to the point of revolting against their own men. Never in the history of the world had such a thing ever happened. It all started with a marriage law made policy right after the Civil War with the Jim Crow laws, which was drafted by the very violators of interracial mixing during slavery, who incorporated its principals into the Klan's criminal acts. Finally President Wilson made the announcement. "I support an amendment to the constitution giving women the right to vote." This was exactly what Abigail Adams and others spoke out for more than a hundred years earlier, and their daughters benefited from their initial uprising.

# DIVIDE AND CONQUER

Though the Caucasian race still needed to heal from past infidelity, their women slowly learned to forgive and forget, which is a good and natural thing to do. However, the constant reminders of the past were still ever present as some Caucasian women still sought relationships with some Negro men, feeling empowered to do so with the right to vote and choose. The Klan was up against the wall with this issue still, because if they still went out hanging Negro men for being in relationships with Caucasian women, it was sending a clear message of limited choice.

They soon realized that this was the same as saying, "We gave you women the right to vote, but you still have to do what we say concerning your choice of men," essentially saying, "We're still in charge and your vote is powerless and doesn't count." They knew it would trigger another rally or riot from amongst their women, this time maybe even fatal to the now delicate strands holding their relationship together. How to get around this perplexing problem? The solution came in the form of allegations.

Ruthless Klansmen found that the use of forked tongues became beneficial to their cause. By accusing Negro men of raping Caucasian women, they found that the mood shifted from them looking like they were overly jealous of some Negro men in interracial relationships or utterly denying Caucasian women their rights to choose, to becoming their saviors of the day, heroes merely protecting their women's sovereign rights from being violated by ravenous, snarling, white-female-flesh-hungry Negro males. According to the Klan, those males sought nothing more than to sexually exploit and defile white women of their pureness, so then it became stereotyped that all black men wanted to rape white women. Naturally, any race of men with common sense would say, "We don't want blacks in our communities to be near our women or in our schools near our daughters," which was the principal reason behind segregation, to keep the Afro-American male and Caucasian females separated. This gave them time to straighten out the mess started by their forefathers, who founded America, from sailors to slave owners and on through political figures as high as the president, because the Caucasian women's diligence after the Civil War for women's rights with marches, and the triumphant Suffragettes' protests during voting struggles, had widened the gap between Caucasian men and women even further.

These false accusations did, however, work on Caucasian women who were sightless to the fact of nearly fifty years earlier, besides it made most of them feel desired above all other women whether they were beautiful or not. Feeling desired, not raped, is what all women want, especially those women love starved during slavery like Potiphar's wife in Egypt or Martha Washington in America—whether by choice or not, slave women were spending more time in their husbands' beds than they were. They realized that some black men considered them beautiful and would give them this attention even if it meant risking death, which was sometimes the result. This made the basic truth understood—now *yours* desire *us*—like a tit-for-tat childhood spat.

Klansmen soon realized that publicized accusations against Negro males raping Caucasian women yielded results for repairing the gap between the Caucasian relationship. The relationship was like a painting of a Confederate soldier standing alongside his beautiful Southern belle wife that was torn right down the middle by the insults to these women's faces of Negro women carrying light-skinned children conceived by Caucasian males during slavery. Each time a Negro male was hanged for the accusation of raping a Caucasian woman, the rope around his neck became just like a symbolic piece of thread with which to stitch the torn Confederate relationship canvas back together. The more publicized and hideous the accusation was, the more thread it yielded, like the Rosewood, Florida, and Greenwood, Oklahoma, incidents, which manufactured spools of symbolic thread for repairing the torn Southern relationship canvas.

It also made some Caucasian women feel longed for by all colored men, whom they felt had to have them more than a man needs air, food, or water to live on. They were made to feel that they needed protection like priceless fine jewels by the white knights eager to kill, so that only they could have their flesh. That in turn made them feel even more like damsels in distress, but all good, decent women sparkle like fine jewelry; thus the more attention they received, the more rescuing some needed. In this way the lesser gifted Caucasian women who were not as beautiful or attractive as some of the more physically blessed Caucasian women felt this attention and pampering was directed toward them also, *and all women love attention and pampering. It's in their nature, so for some, the more they got, the more they wanted.* And this unfortunately was the only way for some of them to get it.

In this modern-day century of 2000 if the police announced that a serial rapist was on the loose, having victimized five Caucasian women, five Afro-American women, five Latin women, and five Asian women, all in their late teens to early twenties from the same college campus neighborhood, even some women up to ninety-eight years old who lived in the vicinity would feel in jeopardy and threatened with lustful desire. They would feel like they needed rescuing by a constant vigil from neighborhood watches by local bravehearted men like knights or law enforcement men to escort them to and fro, double and triple locking the entrances to their homes, even though there would be nothing to suggest that ninety-eight-year-old women were at risk. Men will dedicate their time just for the opportunity to be seen with favor in the eyes of certain beautiful women. Point-blank this is how it was back then. Someone had to pay the piper.

Back then most of the Caucasian women who were still dating these Negro men, mostly undercover—like heavyweight champ Jack Johnson—did not know if the charges against the Negro men they dated were true or not. If they bothered to ask questions of the police, the fire department, or the physicians, judges, and jailers that the court systems relied on for testimonial response, they were often found to be members of the Klan. Negro men were already lynched most often, and it's pretty hard for a dead man to testify to his own innocence, so they would have to rely on the word of the men and women of their own race, who had accused them of the crime in the first place, to make sense out of what had happened.

These biased men started out usually by paying women from the local tavern or cathouses to accuse them. These women were also needing to repair their not-so-good ladylike name and reputation within the town while receiving blood money in the beginning to make the allegations, and as an added bonus they received the attention and sympathy of others after the ordeal, to totally restore their ladylike status in the community, because if all the men who paid her said, "Your status is good again," then it was, for it is men who most often give women bad names anyway, like the woman who loved Jack Johnson suffered. Then these cathouse women were considered desirable once again—just don't hang around bars anymore!

While the Caucasian women, who were still virgins or not and were escorted around by Negro men, were labeled as prostitutes who had lured these ravenous Negro men into the community to rape decent Caucasian women, which caused nearly the whole township to practically alienate themselves from them, even if they were pure virgins, they were stigmatized as worthless white trash, traitors to the *white race* that really doesn't even exist anymore.

The accused Negro men's lynching crimes reciprocated such good response from the less desired Caucasian women and gave justified confirmation for segregation to keep other Caucasian women and colored men apart as the minds of prejudiced men wanted, so it became like the Salem witch hunts. More and more accusers came forth giving the evildoers just what they desired to achieve their goals of ending what they considered race mixing by legal separation—segregation. The Negro male and Caucasian woman realized that their wanting to be together was causing more hardship on other people within their communities. So-called mixed relationships developed less and less because of the ruthless tactics Klansmen criminals exploited by hanging and driving the segregation wedge between the Negro and Caucasian races, which encountered significantly less opposition by federal and local authorities of law enforcement as time went on like the Suffragettes, who were jailed and beaten by the same authorities who controlled the trials of the aforementioned.

It also benefited another cause or angle they wanted: the youthful Caucasian women who were virgins coming of age would not dare date these Negro men, even though they didn't know much about what had happened in the past during slavery, because it was being shielded from them now. They knew that they didn't want to be labeled and looked down upon as prostitutes of the community who brought these ravenous

Negro men into their sect. They were now stereotyped with only foretold desires of raping decent, innocent, sweet Caucasian women within these redneck communities. Such young women as this would have been regarded as dense, knuckleheaded fools, equal to someone bringing home a pit viper as a pet and turning it loose in the living room of their community like it was a newly weaned puppy dog.

Why, hanging out at the local brothels, taverns, or cathouses and labeled as a cheap floozy by the people of well-regarded social stature within the community would have brought them a better reputation than being seen in the company of even a well-known and respected Negro minister. Damned if you do, and damned if you don't, they say.

Lynching is defined as the extra-legal killing by three or more people of an individual "accused" of a crime or of violating a social code—such as in, Don't mess with our Caucasian women, whether they want to or not. The U.S. House of Representatives failed in 1900 to make lynching a federal offense, because Southern lawmakers used filibusters.

Scholars estimate that 4,743 Americans—3,446 of them black—were lynched from 1882 after Caucasian women marched in New York to have the right to choose whatever they wanted in or for their lives through 1968, when civil rights were won for all. Lynching occurred in all but four states, predominantly in the South, according to an article published Wednesday, May 15, 2002, in *USA Today*. The Klan used every incident, no matter how minuscule an infraction it was, to do their evil deeds.

# SCARED STRAIGHT

On May 31, 1921, in Oklahoma, the deadly Tulsa race riots were such a reflection. They were incited in the community of Greenwood, and a definitive study on the riots is being prepared by a state commission, to be presented to government officials, according to a report in the *Washington Post* on Thursday, March 1, 2001.

The Greenwood State Commission study completed in Oklahoma study say thirty-nine blacks were killed, while the blacks attests nearly three hundred died.

The riots were triggered by an encounter between Dick Rowland, a Negro youth, who worked as a shoeshine boy, and Sarah Page, a Caucasian teenager, who operated a downtown elevator. It is now believed that Rowland, who rode the elevator May 30, may have accidentally tripped or bumped into Page, causing her to scream.

The probable scenario went like this. By 1921 the Caucasian race was using mythical superstitions to keep the youthful members of their race from becoming interested in the youthful members of the Negro communities that sometimes thrived around them; one such myth was that if a black person touched you, you would in fact nigrify, 100 percent without a doubt. How could that be? The 100 percent black race was also extinct now. This mythical exaggeration at the time ranked even higher upon the scale of terror amongst Caucasian children, than say, the "boogeyman," who was thought to be the undisputed *numero-uno* scary person with all the children around the world.

Young Sarah Page, who normally greeted riders with a pleasant personality as though trained by Macy's Department store personnel in New York City, operated the downtown Drexel building elevator in Oklahoma as a shining example of the community's youth as well as a poster child for women doing jobs outside the home. This usually pleasant candor had become a trademark that she had displayed proudly quite often before. But it would soon be discovered that her usual congenial candor was reserved for the likes of her "own kind," as one would have put it back then.

Entering onto the scene now came one eager, youthful, mild-mannered, respectful entrepreneur named Dick Rowland who worked for a shoeshine company. He was hustling to make an earnest wage by shining a pair of shoes for one of his regular Caucasian customers downtown who was a good tipper and perhaps was running a little behind schedule to get to his office or use the restroom.

Sarah spotted Rowland—a young Negro male probably in his midteens—approaching the elevator, which at this time was probably not yet segregated or indicated by any such public signs or notices. Her usual pleasantries and smile of generosity were now withdrawn, closed up tighter than Fort Knox the very instant she realized that he was going to board *her* elevator. His negritude triggered her attitude.

Rowland inaudibly entered the elevator and took a position in the center of it closest to the door and adjacent to Sarah, who was poised at the helm of the controls that drove the elevator. Both youths like so many others well understood the unwritten policy of that era, which overemphasized the rule that blacks and whites don't mix, like oil and water. It was recited to them more than enough times by now that each instinctively knew what the other one was subliminally thinking. Also, what reconnaissance measures should they take in almost any given situation?

Rowland, thinking of an intuitive safeguard, placed his heavy wooden shoeshine box, which probably carted all the tools of his trade, his heavy lunch, and snacks fit for a growing boy so that he would not have to run all the way home across town with it at lunchtime, as a segregating barrier between himself and Sarah. She, also as a safety measure, put a look of disgust on her face to assure all onlookers who might peer at them that they were not an item. In essence they personified the image of a couple not speaking to each other after accusing the other of cheating—seemingly millions of miles apart on the plain of understanding. Both of these youths probably intuitively felt their safeguards were a smart thing do, like actors putting one foot on the floor during the bedroom-filming scene.

Sarah waited longer than usual to see if anyone else was going to get onto the elevator with them; that way she would not feel like she was serving an inferior person, who in the back of her mind was taught not to see them on an equal plain. No one outside the elevator appeared to be showing any signs of concern or discussing the fact that the two were alone occupying the six-by-six-foot room. The doors would soon be closing, giving them as much privacy as any two people in a motel room.

This did not seem odd to anyone at the front desk or loitering in the lobby area who obviously saw the two about to embark on the elevator ride together. The reasoning was that there was nothing wrong—they were two innocent-looking kids with semi-innocent thoughts as well! The only thing wrong with these two children were the dangerous segregated thoughts that had been placed in their minds, which through sound reasoning, caused Roland to err by placing the heavy shoeshine box between himself and Sarah as a physical barrier of segregation while standing straight legged as though in a military lineup like the straight-faced guards at the entrance to Buckingham Palace, to pivoted his balance.

There now came casual, careless glances from people outside the elevator in the lobby area, because the elevator sat so long in one spot as Sarah's hopes of another Caucasian rider boarding dwindled. The ever beaconing lights and indicators on the operator's panel continued to flash and buzz for pickup service on the upper floors, calling her to duty.

Sarah, feeling annoyed but unthreatened, began to close the electro-mechanical doors with a painful expression of obvious disgust still upon her face to instinctively show anyone who cared to notice that she was brought up right and offended by the presence of a Negro male standing next to her. That would have gotten her a great public review of approval from the few biased individuals present who agreed on keeping separatism alive amongst the so-called races. That way they'd have a fighting chance to forgive and forget to patch things up within her so-called race, which was torn by heart-wrenching events during slavery while they casually occupied the lobby. The doors began to close off all view of the lobby as they both peered straight ahead while standing directly parallel to each other. Sarah's tenacious mood made her want to get this ride over much quicker than any other ride before.

That's when in her hastiness she erred by bolting against her training, causing the biggest, most fatal riot misunderstanding every triggered in the history of all Oklahoma or the United States in a single day. Neither of these two could interpret the laws of physics as she, out of defying abstinence, jerked up on the elevator controls. Her action drove the huge electric motor, which did not have modern solid-state "soft start" electronics incorporated into its circuitry, to thrust the six-by-six compartment up toward the sky by snatching it up a few inches—more than enough to cast Dick Rowland directly broadside onto Sarah Page, briefly pinning her against the wall until they fell to the floor together within the bouncing elevator.

Sarah instantly went into a state of panic, for the eeriest ghoul ever mentioned in her childhood nightmares was now literally upon her—a Negro male! The boogeyman was mere child's play in comparison with this ghastly creature that sent sheer, stark raving terror shooting through Sarah's warm blood. The heavy weight of the shoeshine box combined with the weight of his lunch was too much of a downward thrust upon his straight-legged stance, amalgamated with the upward fractional g-force thrust of the elevator on his body's inertia, toppling the equilibrium of young Dick Rowland, who clung tightly onto the shoeshine box to prevent its cargo from spilling. That proved that his initial decision of switching the box to his other hand to guard as a physical segregation barrier between himself and Sarah was wrong, because it would have cast him away from her originally. Instead it brought them together with a hard impact when she jerked the control lever in such haste to get the thirty-second ride over within ten seconds if she could. Page was now screaming at the top of her lungs, because Dick Rowland had made skin-to-skin contact with her, which strongly magnified her so often reinforced belief in her mind that she was now experiencing nigrification. It increased her adrenaline flow as she swatted while screaming in fury at Rowland's hands, as though they were agitated, highly aggressive, swarming African killer bees that were trapped inside the elevator with her and solely hell-bent on trying to sting her with metamorphosing Nigrosine.

She was completely oblivious to the fact that her frantic striking out only thwarted every attempt Roland made to place his hands on the elevator's sidewall next to her, so he could merely brace himself to stand, because in her present state of mind, she was now gripped with the fearful thought of nigrescence. She had a paranoid phobia that had been induced in her mind via collegiate dictionaries, racial prejudice, and communications with members in her own society since she could remember, so her mind rationalized that each skin-to-skin contact with Roland bitterly carried a worsening altering effect on her genetic form that would ultimately result in a fate worse than death for her—she'd become black! Then she would be ridiculed and scorned as a third-class citizen by her family, friends, and other children of her society, as she had often witnessed happening to the Negro members around her community—she didn't want that to happen to her.

Dick Rowland with each incidental touch of her realized more and more that he needed to get to his feet, like, yesterday. He too now frantically struggled to get up, so as to soothe her deafening hysterical screams, which pierced his ears as she continually hindered each and every attempt he made to get to his feet with defying kicks and rebellious slaps to his hands and arms. In his mind, he could not get up or out fast enough.

Her panicky screams sent chills up and down the spines of everyone in the lobby, as the first thoughts conceived in their minds were that this had all the classic, telltale signs of some screaming for help while trapped in a burning elevator car, and simultaneously getting electrocuted to death. The volume of her screams indicated that she was expending great amounts of energy from this adrenaline rush.

The elevator had virtually never even left the first floor that it was on. Good police work could have deduced some sound reasoning out of what happened. But here was a Caucasian female in distress, which needed a knightly rescue, and there could be no justifiable reason at all for this girl shrieking out a horrifying scream of that magnitude, except wrongdoing.

Finally young Dick Rowland made it to his feet with welts on his hands from her slapping and frogs on his arm from her kicking. He backed away from her as far as he could in the back corner of the elevator as the panic-stricken Sarah Page stood to her feet to operate the controls to open the door while gathering her breath. She was nearly depleted of strength, like she had just sprinted the entire length of a heated one-mile race during the panicky, uncontrolled flaying of her limbs. She had scratched the skin on her on arm, and probably even flicked a button off the front of her dress.

She finally scampered through the partially opened elevator doors like a frail rabbit leaping through the narrow opening in a thicket to avoid a starving predator. Some men were on the outside of the elevator trying to get in to assist the panicky teen, whose screaming had subsided into a faint whimper. Once outside the elevator doors, she ran right past the men into the middle of the lobby, where she collapsed upon the floor. A few women who worked there came to embrace her with comfort to calm her down.

"What happened?" one of the ladies who worked in the lobby area with her asked.

"He touched me!" she said. "I want my mother!" she uttered before breaking down into uncontrollable, nonresponsive crying. Everyone standing near heard clearly what she'd said before she went into this despondent emotional meltdown, but after that they weren't able to get anything else out of her, eye-witnessed the desk clerk aiding her.

"Honey, what do you mean, he touched you?" one woman asked, but Sarah in her transfixed sobbing state was not able to tell them anything more. She became like a blob of gelatin as they attempted to lift her dangling, limp body off the floor, She was still trying to deal with the horrifying fact in her mind that she was going to turn black at any given moment.

All eyes were now focused upon young Dick Rowland to make quick common sense of her delirium as he stood in the elevator, still looking mystified with humility, bewildered with shame, and totally embarrassed for reasons he could not elaborate upon. Some say he ran and others he stayed. Sarah Page's state inside the elevator was just as mystifying to him then as it was to them now outside it, but the reasoning behind this scenario would soon be deciphered for him as some men encircled about him on all sides as they prepared to question him. He knew by all the signs of this situation that things just didn't look right, and he had heard numerous stories about Caucasian men accusing colored men of attacking Caucasian women, but he had never figured in his wildest dreams that this would be happening to him. They began speaking to him in abrupt tones.

"Boy! What happened in here?" the first man demanded to know.

"Nothing. I's was standing there—"

"Don't tell me nothing, boy! Something did happen in there. You see the way that girl is upset. She didn't just get that way from nothing."

"Yeah, you'd better start speaking up right now!" another man insisted to Rowland.

"We were in there and the lift to the floors messed up. Then we fell to the floor and she started kicking and screaming at me."

"How was she kicking at you? Were you on top of her, boy?" the man demanded to know in an agitated state. They all started hitting him with a barrage of questions that he couldn't address before another came hurling at him. Then he clammed up as the ladies attended Sarah.

"Honey, where's the button off of your dress?" one lady asked Sarah. She just shook her head, as if she could not reply to any more questions. One man looked inside the elevator to see the button lying upon the floor.

"Here it is," he called out as they all conceived in their minds that the button was more than enough circumstantial evidence to convict young Rowland.

"Call the sheriff," one man instructed, and one of the ladies summoned the sheriff.

"Come on, honey. We'll take you home," one lady said. This meant there was no one left to clear Rowland's story. The only witness, now incapacitated, was being carted away like she had fallen off the top of the building and then hit her head and needed to be rushed off to the nearest hospital. Poor Sarah was truly in a traumatized state, not because of Dick Rowland, but because of the very people she loved and trusted who had deceived her mind like this.

"But I—"

"Shut up, boy, until the sheriff gets here," one man said. "We've heard enough of your lying." *Lying!* Rowland thought. He knew that nothing he would say from this point on would be of any help to him. He only hoped that this would be one of the days when the sheriff was in a good mood and ready to sort out the truth. Word spread fast about the incident in the elevator involving young Sarah Page. It was the very thing that initiated excitement in the biased people of this cowboy town. Also on 'black wall street' this area was the richest black business community in the U.S.

The sheriff took the first initial testimonials from what all the Caucasian witnesses—who weren't inside the elevator but described what they heard. He then took young Rowland down to the station to start prosecuting him. His version of what happened would be sorted out down at the prison, but his story didn't fly with the sheriff or the good ol' boys down at the jail either. Soon more than a thousand agitated Caucasian men had gathered down at the jail along with the ignorant ones shouting out slurs of "Hang the nigger." Yes, the word *nigger* had become a common stigmatized vocabulary word in Caucasian society. As a newspaper article read "Nab Negro for attacking girl in an elevator."

Soon word of a possible lynching had reached the black community of Greenwood. Young Dick Rowland, whom they all held in high regard as one of the more upstanding youth of their community, was in imminent danger of being lynched. The very rope that was to be applied to his neck was to become symbolically really just another thread to stitch and mend the torn canvas fabric of male and female Caucasian relationships. Though the Negro community did not understand the real reasoning behind all these hangings as jealousy, it still sparked a rage in the heart of Negro men, who thought, *Now they are actually trying to hang young black boys for rape; next it will be our young black babies,* the general consensus in the community. Some members of the Klan saw this as another opportunity to convince Caucasian women that the black man was their mortal enemy, from whom they needed protection by Caucasian males once again. They hoped to heal the relationship gap between them, which had arisen from them flaunting the Negro women in their faces during slavery in America.

A group of fed-up colored men came together as a unit to the jail, toting guns. They knew the type of crowd they would encounter, especially a crowd of about a thousand Caucasian men screaming out, "Hang that nigger!" to build momentum for a lynching. It turned into a shouting match, but the Negro men having guns there made the crowd stand at bay. It also made the group of Caucasian men gather in secrecy under the deputized authority of law and commit a criminal act hidden behind the badge. Instead of confronting the black men on equal footing like they had done at the jailhouse, they planned a sneak attack like the Japanese had done at Pearl Harbor. It is often talked about how the Japanese sucker-punched us when we weren't looking, but the residents of Greenwood, Oklahoma, were subjected to the same principles of being rabbit-punched in the back of the head like the United States armed forces were at Pearl Harbor.

The men who pulled those triggers while being deputized in the name of the law burst into the homes of unaware, unsuspecting, unconsciously sleeping citizens to murder in the name of the law, and by the time the chaos had ended, more than three hundred Negro citizens of Greenwood, Oklahoma, had died. All because a young, innocent Caucasian female had been tricked into believing an old mythical superstition that she would turn black to keep her from ever becoming interested in a Negro male. But Klan members' shooting of Negro's was only secondary to their main objective of angering them so that the colored people themselves would run these wayward Caucasian females back home when they saw them crossing over into their neighborhoods.

No doubt after the shooting and killing was over in Greenwood and Sarah Page was resting in the bedroom of her family's home, her mother asked her, "What happened with the black boy in the elevator? Did he try to rape you?"

"Oh no, Mother! He didn't try to rape me," Sarah initially replied. "He just touched me, and I screamed out real loud, 'Don't touch me!' like you always told me, Mother, because I didn't want to turn black." Sarah had been scared straight through the propagation of faith.

"What! What did you say?" her mother asked, her eyes wide open and horrified inside at the unbelievable three-year-old-like remark that had come out of the mouth of this teenager.

"Remember, Mother, you always told me that if I ever touched a black person, I would turn black. So I screamed every time he touched me as he tried to get up from the elevator floor where we fell after I accidentally jerked the elevator controls. Mother, do you have to get me some special medicine from the doctor to keep me from turning black?" Sarah asked calmly, reiterating the ignorant remark again that had been branded into her subconscious mind with conviction since she was old enough to remember. Her belief was so real that every time she saw a freckle or age spot appear, it raised a question in her mind. Could this be the result of touching that black boy in the elevator?

Her mother's heart sank to the floor to know that the three-year-old mentality that she had been instilled with, which was only intended to keep her from eloping with a black man, had just caused more than three hundred colored people to be shot and killed. They no doubt then informed Sarah not to speak of this matter to anyone one ever again as they tried to straighten out the wrongful concept of how blacks affected them in her mind. Of course this would seem childishly unconceivable by most intellectual minds, yet one must understand the biased mind of all hateful men of any color by knowing that their motives are childish and ridiculous in the first place, especially since all are interracial.

A brief investigation reveled by the 2000 commission concluded Roland had a simple accident such as tripping and steadying himself against the girl, but how could that cause her to give out such and adrenalin rush scream that it zapped all the strength out of her instantly or a lovers quarrel was tossed in as a possible wild notion. The Police 'likely' questioned Page. No written account of her statement surfaced. Whatever conversation transpired between Page and the Police, it is generally accepted that they determined what happened between the two teenagers was something less than assault. Afterwards Page told the police she would not press charges. People had no clue how a lie could disrupt a community and cause multiple deaths (like being dropped out a malfunctioning plane in the middle of a different tongue jungle tribe syndrome). Thus because her parents too embarrassed to tell the police the real reason she balled up into a fetal non-responsive blob. They suspected the lovers quarrel scenario and inducted it. Most black people by the time you're ten years old have heard of the "if a black person touches you you'll turn black myth". Most Caucasian people don't know that black people are aware. Except for Sarah and her parents most people don't know that hundreds of people were injured and died in the deadliest race riot in U.S. history, because she believed she was without a doubt going to turn black.

# DIVINE INTERVENTION

Now looking in from God's view from outside a Negro home in Greenwood that fateful night near the twilight hours of the night, where three Klansmen hide in the bushes to attack more innocent victims of this massacre by waiting for the Negro family hiding inside to come out in order to ambush them as they try to exit the house.

"Do you see any niggers trying to escape?" Ed asked.

"Ed, will you shut up before they hear you?" Bobby Joe said. "They's will never come out if'n they is in there."

"Okay! But if'n you see a nigger comin' out, waits till I get an aim before you take a shot, because I wants to get me one, too."

"Okay, just shut up, Ed, and keep a sharp lookout." Just then from behind them an unsuspecting, glowing white figure appeared up high in a tree. It started to descend on them and took on more of a detailed form as it got closer. Halfway to the ground you could tell that it was a deity, an angel to be exact, but it stopped glowing the instant it touched the ground. Once it started to walk toward them, its wings disappeared and its long white gown changed to clothing like that of the men poised outside the Negro home. Its long white hair mostly became hidden away under a hunting-style cap. He walked up behind the men looking at them with a blank stare; none of them even noticed that he was standing there as he looked up toward the heavens as though he were communicating with God, getting some last-minute instructions from him. He nodded as he looked earthward, like he had received full instructions, and then focused his attention on the men lying in wait for the people hidden away in the house.

"What are you doing?" the angel asked of them as they all turned in shock to see the tall white-looking being behind them, the spitting image of Adam, the first man on earth.

"Holy crap! You scared the budgeters out of us," Ed said.

"Yeah! Are you from out of town?" Al asked.

"Yes, I'm from out of town," the angel said.

"My gosh, you sure is pale looking. We might have to start calling you Whitey or something," Ed said, staring at him with the little bit of pure white hair sticking out through the sides of the hat he was wearing.

"What do they call you?" Bobby Joe asked.

"Just call me Whitey like you said," the angel responded quickly.

"Whitey huh? Is all this blood and stuff too much for you, pal?" Bobby Joe asked.

"I'm fine," the angel said.

"Good. We're going to need all the help we can get to take down these uppity damn niggers. Isn't that right, boys?"

"Sure is, Bobby Joe," they agreed.

"Niggers, you say?" the angel inquired.

"Yeah, niggers. I thought everybody knew what niggers were by now!"

"What are they?" the angel asked.

"Niggers are the dirtiest, most loudmouthed, no-good, worthless pieces of trash on the earth, like the ones hiding in that house over there, but we can wait them out."

"You mean the dark-skinned people that some call Negro—you've judged them dirty, loud, no good, and trash? Have you've met the ones inside then?"

"No! I wouldn't want to be near those niggers," Bobby Joe said. "Hey, word to the wise: Don't say Negro—you're giving them too much credit. Makes you sound like a sympathizer."

"Oh!" the angel replied. "How do you know they're niggers if you never met them?"

"How do I know that they're niggers? You must be kidding us," Bobby Joe said as the others started chuckling quietly. "The term must not have caught on yet where you're from, son."

"It hasn't—please explain," the angel in disguise asked kindly.

"Well, a nigger is anyone who has one drop of black blood or more in them."

"You don't say?" the angel replied.

"I do say! And on top of that, anyone who is a nigger needs to burn in hell—right, boys?"

"That's right, Bobby Joe. One drop—you tell 'em, boy," Ed said.

"You're absolutely sure about that—just one drop, not, say . . . twelve ounces or a hundred drops?"

"Nope, it's a law—the one-drop rule, like the Constitution, that's been around on the record books probably even longer than the Constitution—since slavery. That's how we kept them slaves; even if slaves became high yellow or lighter, as long as you can prove black is part of their history, no matter how far back in their family history it started, then they are still legally black and could be bought and sold as slaves. Not one hundred percent pure white like us—huh, boys?"

"Darn toot'n," Al said. "Once part nigger, you're always a nigger—no matter what!"

"I wonder how some of them got to be colored people like that, Bobby Joe," Ed smirked.

"Colored people, that's funny. They used to be black, now they're just colored. Probably through a whole lot of fun, I tell you that. Ha. Ha. Ha!" They all started laughing except for the angel. "Be quiet now, or those niggers will hear you," Bobby Joe commanded as the self-appointed leader of the bunch.

"How comes you don't has a gun, friend?" Ed asked with his face drawn up like a prune.

"I guess I didn't think to bring one," the angel said.

"Well, here's one of my six-shooters," Al said, placing the weapon in the angel's hand. "So's you can get yourself one, but I wants it back before we part tonight, stranger, or niggers won't be the only ones being hunted tonight."

"Are you sure you'll remember me, after the shooting starts?" the angel asked.

"Are you kidding? We've only got to look for the whitest person out here. You almost glow in the dark."

"Yeah, watch out there, friend, some candle flies might start sticking to ya," Ed said as he and Al chuckled while holding their stomachs to keep from bursting out with laughter.

"Quiet, you two. I thought I saw a light flicker," Bobby Joe said seriously to scold them as he studied the house.

"It was probably a reflection off of Whitey here," Al said, and they chuckled a little louder, like junior high school kids.

"Now I mean it—quiet! This is serious business. I thought I saw someone," Bobby Jo said. "Of all the people, I got stuck with you two."

"Bobby Jo, you need a flashlight?" Al asked. "I think we can find you one nearby." They cut up at the angel's expense while holding their lungs till it hurt, but not letting out much of a sound. They turned away from the angel so as not to let him see them laughing in his face. He knew their intentions, but they did not know his. The three men now had their attention focused on the house once again with the angel behind them.

"Now, Whitey, you just do what we tell ya, and you'll be able to get yourself a nigger just like us," Al said. The angel just looked at them.

"When you see a nigger, you just aim and shoot at the closest one," Ed said. The angel tilted his head a little to the side.

"Are you sure about that?" the angel asked. "No plan . . . Just aim and shoot at the closest person who has at least one drop of black blood or more in their veins?" he asked the men as he aimed the gun they had given him at the back of Ed's head. He was about to pull the trigger when . . .

"Wait a minute . . . Whitey might be right. Maybe we should think this thing through a little bit. We don't want one of us to get caught in some friendly cross fire chasing after those niggers in the dark."

"Yeah, maybe you're right, Whitey," Bobby Joe said, thinking it through more clearly. "Let's not just shoot at the first one we see. We need a plan."

"Yeah, Whitey's right. We need a plan," Ed said. Then the angel aimed the gun down at the ground before the three men turned around to face him, without ever knowing that he had had the gun pointing at them.

"I'll take that gun back if you don't mind, Whitey," Al said.

"Sure thing. Here you go," he said, handing the gun back to Al. "I wouldn't think of keeping someone else's possession."

"Thanks. You're all right—we could use a couple more good old boys like you around here to help straighten out everyone's thinking," Al said.

"It would be my pleasure to help you all get back on the right track of thinking," the angel said.

"What now?" Ed asked.

"I think that we should go back and find some others to get things calmed down and organized, because there's been a lot of shooting," the angel suggested.

"Yeah, that's another good idea."

"Come on, fellows. We'll go back and get some more guys to surround the place and then we'll come back," Bobby Joe said, and they all started to head back.

"Follow us. We'll lead the way, Whitey."

"Right behind you," the angel said. They started through the woods when the black family that was hiding inside emerged with the mother leading the way; she had two small children with her, a boy and a girl.

"Where's Daddy, Momma?" the little girl asked.

"Quiet!" her mother said quickly. "There might be some white men nearby. Your daddy didn't make it home. I pray that he is all right." They started out the door of the house headed for the woods on the opposite side of where the armed men were waiting for them.

"Wait, did you hear something?" Bobby Joe said. "Let's go back."

"Perhaps it's just some paper blowing across the yard there," the angel said to divert them while looking behind himself to see his mission completed as the family escaped. It was true: some papers were blowing across the yard that the little boy had dropped out of his favorite coloring book as he fled with his family. The angel hadn't lied.

"Right. Let's head back toward town," Bobby Joe said, leading the way as they walked on for a few feet. Then the angel disappeared. Another twenty yards or so later, they realized that the being named Whitey was gone. He had completed his mission by helping one family escape the sure death that awaited them.

"Whitey's gone!" Ed said.

"What? Where did he go?"

"I don't know. Let's go back and look for him."

"No, come on. We're going to town. Whitey's big enough to take care of himself. Don't worry—he'll find his way back," Bobby Joe said

"I'm not worried about him finding his way, because he can light up his own path," Al said as he and Ed started laughing again about the very pale appearance of his skin.

The angel reappeared in what looked like a part of heaven, standing before a clouded-over throne from which a continual mist of clouds came. A large figure sat upon it, but you could see only the legs on up of the one sitting on the throne, who was covered down to his feet with a silky, shimmering white robe.

"My Lord, I have a report for you," the angel said.

"You may speak," a calm, ancient voice said from the throne.

"The people of the earth are judgmental, exploiting the minority of their lands for their own selfish gains. No matter how light or dark the skin color, they all do the same."

"Man has judged himself with the condemning words from his mouth."

"It is as you say, my Lord. They are all mixtures of black and white blood now, and unknowingly condemn themselves to hell with words like, *Anyone who has one drop of black blood in them should burn in hell!*" The angel was repeating what Bobby Jo had said to him.

"Man is no longer pure in my image as I made them in the beginning, after I put the seed of Cain on the ark with Noah and his family. If he cannot get past his prejudiced mind-set, then he shall be bound and thrown into the pit of hell with the fallen angels. I sent my only begotten son so that through his blood, man could be washed as pure as snow and changed back to righteousness, but man has hardened his heart to listen."

"What else do you require of me, my Lord?"

"Soon the time will be at hand to gather up the harvest. Then I will call on you once again," the voice coming from the throne said. Greenwood, Oklahoma, and Rosewood, Florida, were mirror images of each other with different scenarios, and the same results of segregation were achieved between the races by deceitful men.

"As you wish, my Lord," the angel said as the scene clouded over and faded away.

# PACIFIED HISTORY

Another scene appeared years later after the Greenwood and Rosewood incidents had subsided, in the Deep South once again, inside the classroom of a crowded Negro public school that had received very little funding for classroom expenditures. The books that the Negro children used were ten to fifteen years old and passed on school year after school year. The teacher, a young single Negro woman, knew she was very fortunate to have a respectable job and was very content in her surroundings with the children. She spoke well to be from the South, so she took pride in her speech to teach the Negro children how to speak more affluently in conversation. Grammar was very important to her, and she often corrected children for speaking like backyard hicks to bring them up to a standard that would gain them equal recognition with peers.

"Children, tonight you don't have too much homework. There's just a math paper, and your studies for a history exam tomorrow, so make sure you read your history books tonight. Does everyone understand?"

"Yes, Miss Reed," they answered.

"Okay then, I'll see you all tomorrow. And Travis, you be here early. It's your turn to fill the stove in the morning to get it warm in here before everyone else arrives."

"Yes, ma'am."

"Goodbye then," she said as the kids started grabbing their things to leave. One little girl dropped her book off the desk, and when it hit the floor, it literally split into two pieces.

"Oh, my book!" she exclaimed.

"Millicent, let me see your book," Miss Reed said.

"Here you go," Millicent said, handing it to her with one piece in each hand.

"Ah, there's not much hope for this book," Miss Reed said.

"Can we get another one?"

"No, I'm sorry. You're going to have to make do with this one for a while, so just try to hold the pages together as best you can."

"But Miss Reed, these books are, like, ten years old."

"Fifteen to be exact," she said. "See? This used to be my book, when I went to seventh grade here." Miss Reed flipped pages to the back of the book to show Millicent where she'd written her name on the back cover when she was in junior high school.

"Wow! Fifteen years old. Why can't we get some new books?"

"The school board won't give us enough money to buy new books. We barely get by on heating this place."

"The white children almost always have new books," Millicent said, pointing out a fact that Miss Reed knew all too well.

"Yes, about every three to four years. We are aware of that fact, and we have to pay the same tax rates—dollar for dollar on our land as well as other purchases in the county like everyone else—but the monies are divided up differently when it comes to our schools, honey. Just do the best you can at reading it tonight, okay?"

"All right, Miss Reed," she said. "Bye now."

"Goodbye." Just then the local Negro minister came in the door as Millicent was about to leave. He was lean, light complexioned, clean-shaven, and in his midthirties with a kind face.

"Hello, Reverend Johnson," she said.

"Well, hello, Millicent. How are you doing?" he asked.

"I'm doing good," she replied.

"Millicent!' Miss Reed said in a stern voice, and instantly Millicent knew she had made an error.

"Oh! I'm doing well—Reverend Johnson," Millicent said to correct herself.

"That's better," Miss Reed said. "Don't make me come after you for your grammar." Millicent hurried out of the room with a smile on her face.

"What's going on?" he asked.

"The usual—not enough money for this or that."

"I'll go to the school board again tomorrow, to raise the issue again," Reverend Johnson said.

"Just to get shot down again, you mean."

"Well, it's better than nothing. Maybe their consciences will get to them, after hearing the squeaky wheel for a while."

"You know that wheel could fall off, and their consciences still wouldn't stir," she said. He had to admit that she was right; it seemed that nothing would help.

"God has a way of working things out, sister. We are somehow going to get some new things in here. We've just got to have faith and pray. Come on, right now . . . We are going to pray to God to get that stuff—hold my hand." She looked at him reluctantly, because she didn't think it would work, but she took his hands anyway, and they started to pray together. "Our father," he said. "Come on. You have to get with me in the spirit—our father!" Then she joined in.

"Our father," she said as she started to follow along.

"We come to you with our prayers in this schoolhouse that we know you are going to work out this very hour somehow." Now they were both praying together. Meanwhile, Millicent was walking down the street with another girl from her class to their homes.

"My feet are tired," Gwen said.

"Mine too, Gwen." Just then a school bus came by carrying only Caucasian children, to the same neighborhood that they were walking through to get home. It stopped ahead of them to let some students off.

"Look: the white kids get to ride to school on a bus and we live farther away from school than they do," Gwen said.

"I wish we had a school bus."

"Well, you'd better stop dreaming," Gwen said to Millicent as they walked past the bus that had stopped to let some of the students off. One of the boys in the back of the bus made an insulting comment.

"Why do niggers have to walk to school?" he said loud enough for everyone, including Gwen and Millicent, to hear him as he hung his head out the bus window.

"I don't know. Why?" another student asked.

"Because they'd be too stupid to find the bus stop—if they had one." Most of the kids on the bus started to laugh as the bus driver smirked instead of disciplining him. Most of the children laughed except one, as she departed the bus. She knew Millicent because her Millicent's aunt worked for her parents as a housekeeper. They sometimes played together, although more so when they were smaller.

"That's not funny, you guys," she scolded like an adult. She got off the bus shaking her head, although the driver had yet to discipline the kid with his head out the window.

"It was to us," the boy replied. Once off the bus, she proceeded to catch up with Millicent and Gwen. As the bus sped by them once more, the kid in the back of the bus yelled out. "Niggers!" Gwen and Millicent didn't say a word back to them. They had been schooled very well in not instigating any trouble with the Caucasian children of their community. The bus drove out of sight.

"Hey, Millicent, wait up," the girl who had gotten off the bus shouted out.

"Oh no, look who's headed our way," Gwen said.

"It's just Tammy. She's all right."

"You know I don't trust any white people. You never know what they might do next," Gwen said, picking up the pace a little. "Come on, Millicent, let's go."

"But she is my friend, too."

"Maybe right now, but what about when she gets older? They'll change her whether she wants to or not. They always do."

"Millicent, hold on a minute," Tammy said as she got closer to Millicent, who eased up on her pace.

"Well, I'm out of here," Gwen said as she walked on ahead of Millicent. "See you later, Millicent." Then Tammy started to catch up with her.

"Hi, Millicent. Where's Gwen going? I thought you guys walked all the way home together."

"Well, she had to get home early today, so she kind of walked on ahead."

"Oh," Tammy said with a downhearted look on her face. "It's really because of me, isn't it?"

"Well, no, not really . . . You see—"

"That's okay. I understand how she must feel, after the bus went by and everything."

"Really, it's not you directly, but others indirectly. If you know what I mean."

"Yeah, just like when those stupid guys on the bus were saying that stuff as you guys walked by. I wanted to apologize to the both of you for their ignorance, even though I didn't have anything to do with that." Each girl felt awkward, like they were put in uncomfortable positions because of other people's actions. It was such a common occurrence during this period that many potential good friendships or relations never transpired, just because some others felt it was better for people of a contrasting outward appearance not to associate. It was basically because of jealous emotions of some men in all races who hate to see their women with other men of different appearances, yet this is a double standard practice, for they like to have the other men's women in their arms and beds. This distorted way of thinking is not isolated in any one so-called ethnic group of people; all races have people among them whose thinking is off balance like this.

Usually it is the undesirables within a race who have difficulty competing for the affections of the more desirable members of the opposite sex in their own ethnic group. They certainly realize that their chances of getting a desirable, suitable mate is less than ever before if outsiders come in, and the same goes for some women of this world. This fear of competition has caused the social borders of many ethnic groups to be closed to outsiders like governments who close their borders to immigrants because of race.

"I tried to tell her, but she's starting to mistrust all white people—she's changing, too."

"Gosh! There must have been some time in history when blacks, whites, and everyone else got along in this world as family and friends," Tammy said.

"Well, if we could all remember when, then it would probably help us all get along as a people instead of races."

"It just seems so unfair that people like you and I, who could be real good friends, are being torn apart by society."

"Yeah, just like my history book," Millicent said, showing it to Tammy.

"Wow! That's pretty trashed. Why doesn't your school just get you another like ours does?"

"Because the same board of education that buys things for your school won't give us the money we need for our school supplies."

"You guys have to get the same stuff we do if you pay taxes."

"Sounds like what we learned about the Boston Tea Party last week—that Thomas Jefferson said was wrong of the English."

"The way you say it makes us sound like hypocrites. No taxation without representation. It's even written in the Constitution—all men are equal." Tammy said proudly.

"Oh yeah? You really think it's equal? It takes more than just the words on paper of the Constitution to exact fairness. Like they say in church, faith without works is dead."

"Mostly, yeah. Name one thing our school does that is not fair."

"Okay. How did you get to school this morning, Tammy?"

"I took the bus, why?"

"I live two miles farther from this block than you do, and our schools are on the same block but opposite sides of the street and opposite corners of the block. The school board says that you need to ride a bus to and from school—you're only three miles away. I'm nearly five miles from my school, and they say a good walk will do me good."

"Oh, I never really thought of it like that before."

"I know, and neither do a lot of other people. That's why I have books like these." Tammy paused to think about the situation for a moment, and then she noticed something on the bottom of Millicent's dress.

"Millicent, you have something on your dress."

"Where?" Millicent asked.

"Right there," Tammy said, pointing to a dark spot on her dress."

"Oh, that's just a little bit of coal dust. It was my turn to get the fire going this morning before the school started, to warm the classroom."

"You guys have to start your own fire before school?"

"Yes, but I know . . . you can afford a janitor or maintenance guy to do it, right?"

"No! We have some type of oil heating system that just runs all the time."

"What! Even on weekends?" Millicent asked in surprise.

"All year long, I guess," Tammy said, feeling a little spoiled. "But I'm sure they turn the thermostat way, way down in the summer to save energy . . . I guess."

"All the comforts of home, I see, to help their own kids be their personal best!"

"Well, getting a good-quality education doesn't depend on the condition of your surroundings, if you study," Tammy tried to say in defense of the situation.

"Some comforts do make a difference in performance, though. That's why they give them—to certain people anyway."

"Not really . . . I'll prove it. Give me your torn American history book, and I'll give you my new American history book and we'll compare our next grades. I have a test tomorrow on slavery, and I'll use your book."

"I have a history test on slavery tomorrow, too," Millicent said, and they switched books.

"Good; then it is settled. I'll even talk to my father, who's a member of the board of education, to see if you guys can get some new books for your school."

"Great. Then it's a deal," Millicent agreed as they reached Tammy's house. Then the two girls parted as each went their own way.

"Bye—I'll see you tomorrow then," Tammy said while waving goodbye as she went in through the gate of the white picket fence to her house. She lived in an upper-middle-class neighborhood in a large white house with colonial-style pillars on the front porch. She entered into the house, passing by Millicent's aunt Shirley.

"Hi, Shirley," she said as she walked through the corridor.

"Hello, Tammy," Shirley responded as she continued to dust the fixtures in the hallway. Tammy went directly to her father's office, where he was studying some papers.

"Father, can I have a word with you, please?" she asked.

"I'm really kind of busy right now. I have to go over these papers for the school board meeting coming up tomorrow."

"It'll just take a second, if you don't mind."

"Well, just for a second, sweetheart."

"I was just talking to Millicent, Shirley's niece, after school today, and she showed me her history book. Then she said that her school is not receiving the same type of funds and treatment as our school does from the school board. Is that true?"

"Well, I'm only in charge of making sure the same rules and regulations are applied in all the schools. I don't know about finances. That's Ed Curry's area of responsibility, dear."

"I want to show you the kinds of books that they have to study from, Dad." Tammy lifted the book up for him to see. The tattered book looked like something the cat had dragged in. Of course with the binder broken in two, the loosely staggered pages resembled a deck of playing cards that someone might ask you to pick a card from to perform a magic trick. Her father looked at the book with a drawn-up prune face like it was a sore oozing with infection.

"That is in pretty bad shape, but like I said, there's nothing I can do about those books. It's Ed's department, dear."

"Well, can you at least take this to your board meeting to show it to them tomorrow? Then perhaps Mr. Curry can do something about it."

"I really can't do anything with it. Besides, I'm so busy right now. Can we talk about this later, huh?"

"But Dad." Just then the phone rang.

"Just a second, dear," her father said. "Hey John, I was waiting for your call. Did you get the tickets for the big game this weekend? Great—that's what I wanted to hear."

"Dad!" Tammy beckoned.

"Excuse me for a second, John," he said. "Honey, I'm on the phone now. Please, we'll talk about it later. Okay—go ahead, John." Tammy was disappointed that her dad refused to take up an issue as important as this. How could a ball game be more important to a member of the school board than the quality of someone's education? Wasn't that the reason he along with the rest of the members accepted the nomination to be members of the school board—because they cared and promised to do a better job than anyone else who campaigned for the positions?

She slowly turned and went up the stairs to her room to study for her American history test the next day as her father jabbered away on the phone about the big game. Little did he realize that he was going to get some education from it himself.

The next day came with both girls seated and taking their tests, and the day passed by quickly. Each girl was excited about getting her results back to show the other one.

At Millicent's school Miss Reed walked by, passing back the history exams. She came to Millicent last to place her test score in front of her, and on her paper she saw a big fat F.

"What happened?" Millicent exclaimed.

"That's what I'd like to know. You're my best straight A student," Miss Reed replied with a bewildered look on her face.

"I studied last night," she said while looking Miss Reed in the eyes. "Honest, I did."

"Well, it certainly doesn't seem like it to me."

"Some of the test questions you asked were not in Tammy's book I studied from."

"That can't be. I took the test questions right out of the book." Then Millicent showed her the new book that her friend Tammy had let her borrow. Miss Reed took the book and started flipping through the pages and got to the point of the book where it referred to slavery. There were only two short paragraphs in reference to the slavery ordeal of the Negro struggle, and most of that was about how well they were treated and how they were given medical care when they were sick. There was also the mentioning of some hard laboring work and cotton picking seasonally, but other than that, Tammy's history book implied that it was a lovely time for all involved. "Who's Tammy? This book doesn't mention anything about the real suffering of our people's legacy. It basically says slavery was a good institution for all," Miss Reed exclaimed while closing the book. Then she handed it back to Millicent. "You give this book back to Tammy or whoever you got it from. Then get yours back, and be prepared to retake a real history test on slavery this Monday."

"Yes, Miss Reed," Millicent answered solemnly. Miss Reed took back the test paper, crumpled it up, and tossed it into the waste can with Gwen and the other children looking on.

Over at Tammy's school, the faculty was encountering the same thing. Her teacher passed back all of their exams, except for Tammy's. Her teacher's name was Mrs. Acres. She was in her midforties and reminded you of those stern ladies who ran the orphanages in the *Little Orphan Annie* series print.

"Um, excuse me . . . Mrs. Acres, but I didn't get my test back," she asked while wondering why.

"I know, and your parents are on their way here to discuss it with the principal." The whole class went, "Ooh" and "Ah!" in response to the comment made directly to Tammy, who was taken aback by the remark.

"What was wrong with my test?" she asked. "I got the answers right out of this schoolbook." Tammy held up the haggard old book that took both hands to keep it together for her teacher to see.

"Bring that here!" she ordered Tammy, who quickly came forth with the book. "Where did you get this?" Mrs. Acres demanded inquisitively.

"I borrowed it from my friend Millicent, who goes to the colored school at the end of the block." Mrs. Acres quickly flipped through the loose pages to the section on slavery, and Tammy quickly directed her attention to a particular paragraph.

"See these are the pages I got the answers from," she said, and she flipped back one page to the beginning of the chapter. Mrs. Acre's eyes widened as she read some of the graphic detailed information that the book contained. It was not vulgar in any way, but it didn't cut corners on graphically explaining how African people were changed into colored people, as they were known then. It mentioned savage beatings for discipline, and some other atrocities as well, which opened Tammy's mind to the truth of what really went on during the time of slavery in America.

Mrs. Acres slapped the book shut in abhorrence to the truth. That's when the principal's voice came over the intercom system. "Mrs. Acres, would you send Tammy to my office now, please? Her parents are here." The class started making sounds again, but Mrs. Acres quickly hushed them up.

"Quiet. I don't want to hear another word until I get back," she said. "Tammy, you come with me." Then they exited the classroom; soon they were at the principal's office, where her parents were sitting in wait across from Principal Turner's desk for her arrival. The principal was a portly man who had a receding hairline near the middle of his head. Her mother had blond hair like hers, and still had a good figure for her age.

"Tammy, what has gotten into you?" her mother popped off before she even got all the way through the doorway. "Just listen to some of these answers you put on this test. Name some of the biggest tragedies that occurred during slavery and just after the Civil War ended.

"A. Sometimes black slave women were raped by their white slave master, which changed black people into colored people against their will.

"B. Black men were sometimes castrated on certain plantations, so when the black women became of age and desired intimate companionship, they'd have no choice but to go to the white slave masters for intercourse.

"C. This caused many white women, who felt like 'state prisoners' in their homes, to revolt against their white male counterparts by rallying in 1875 in New York to fight for the right to vote, so they could dictate their own choices and decisions in their lives."

Her mother paused to breathe for a second. "Honey, everybody knows that the greatest tragedy in the South was that we lost the war and had to give up our slaves!"

"It was?" Tammy said, and she compared the answers in her mind.

"Sweetheart, why didn't you put down the answers that were in the book? And where in the world did you get facts—I mean trash answers—like these?" her father asked.

"It appears to me, Tammy, that you have been the victim of brainwashing," Principal Turner suggested.

"Brainwashing!" Tammy exclaimed, her eyes wide open.

"Yes, it's a common occurrence amongst weak-minded people," Principal Turner said.

"That's right, Tammy, because everyone knows that our mothers rallied in 1875 because they didn't want to wash dishes after the slaves were freed—right, dear?" Tammy looked at her mother with bewilderment.

"Yes, honey," her husband said.

"So there! See, sweetheart, you should be unbrainwashed like me!" her mother said, as a matter of fact then the room became silent for a second.

"Tammy, I demand to know who has done this to you, because if it's a member of my faculty, they'll be looking for a new job by the end of today."

"I think I can explain," Mrs. Acres said, intervening as she pulled out the old tattered history book that Tammy had learned the answers from.

"That's the book you showed me last night," her father pointed out. "Tammy told me yesterday that she borrowed this book from a friend of hers who goes to the colored school down the street."

"Apparently you need to monitor who your child hangs out with, Mr. Jeter, because this book contains even more graphic information than the answers she gave in its context," Mrs. Acres said while sounding disconcerted.

"How much of the book did you read, Tammy?" Principal Turner asked.

"All the parts about slavery, but that's what we were studying for," Tammy said in her own defense.

"Oh no! Tammy, I want you to block out all this information from your mind right now!" her mother said.

"But . . . isn't that brainwashing, Mother?"

"Just do as I say!" her mother demanded as she turned to her husband. "How could you let our daughter read a book like this to study for a test? How could you, Harold?" her mother dramatized, as if ready to break down into tears.

"Well, I didn't know what all it entailed, darling. You've got to believe me. She said that the little girl's school was in need of new books along with some other things at their school, but I never thought that . . . you know?"

"Often, not thinking can cause some very serious damage . . . if you folks know what I mean," Principal Turner said, trying not to elaborate but referring to Tammy's mind's eye receiving certain information that could be influential in her decision-making.

"Well, I'm certainly going to do something about this book, being a member of the school board."

"But Daddy . . . yesterday evening you told me you couldn't do anything about their books when you were talking about your big game this weekend, and that Mr. Curry's department handles that stuff," Tammy reminded him.

"Well, now I'm going to make it my job," he said, raising his voice. "Let me have that book, Mrs. Acres. I'll see that Tammy gets her book back as well."

"Now, Tammy, a lot of what you read last night, just forget it. Heck, most of that information isn't even that accurate. Right, everyone?" Principal Turner said.

"Oh, sure you're right, Principal Turner," they all agreed.

"One thing still doesn't make sense to me, though," Tammy said.

"What's that, dear?" her mother asked.

"If they were all black when they came over on the ships, how did they get changed into colored people?" A silence fell over the whole room as each adult looked at the other for an answer, but none could submit one.

"Ah, well, you see, well, it's because of, um . . . well, because it's hotter on the equator, and when they were shipped up here where it's not as hot, they became lighter—just like we might get a tan if we went down there. People's skin features change because of the climate—it's a new theory of evolution they have been working on," Principal Turner said.

"Then why don't all black people have yellow skin—and longer hair changes by now?" Tammy asked.

"Tammy!" her mother cried out.

"Sorry! Inquiring minds just want to know," Tammy said, hunching her shoulders.

"Now just go on back to your class and we'll see about getting you a new book to restudy again for your makeup test on Monday. Okay, Mrs. Acres?"

"Yes, Principal Turner. Now come along with me, Tammy." Tammy went out the door behind her teacher.

"Bye, everyone," she said, acting satisfied, but her teenage mind was not truly convinced.

"Bye," they said back to her in their own way as she departed the room.

"Don't worry, I'll take care of this, Principal Turner," her father said after Tammy left the room.

"Well, you and that school board had better. My God, if more of our children should get ahold of information like that . . . A book can be a dangerous tool. Just look at what all the different Bibles have done."

"Don't give it another thought," Harold said, leaving out the door with his wife, and a specific agenda on his mind. He called Reverend Johnson to ask if he would meet him and some of the other school board members at the colored school the next day, announcing it as an official school inspection. The next day they appeared in the early morning at the colored school with a few other members of the board, including Mr. Curry, who had never even seen the inside of their school, to discuss a few things. Reverend Johnson and Miss Reed found their reception surprisingly open to all their grievances concerning the small Negro facility, especially about how much their school's basic necessities weren't being met, even after numerous placid urges by Reverend Johnson at the school board meetings.

"Well, Reverend Johnson," Harold said. "I will personally see to it that under school regulations and safety guidelines, a lot more of your needs are going to be met from now on. I give you my personal guarantee, and Mr. Curry is going to see that your school gets its funding."

"Yes, certainly. I didn't know that things were in so poor a condition as this or I would have taken care of things long before now," Mr. Curry said.

"Someone would actually have to come inside here to know that," Reverend Johnson said. "I tried to inform the members at the public meetings that conditions were horrendous here, but the children are tough and have endured, thank God."

"Well, they shouldn't have to. Right, Mr. Curry."

"Why, certainly I agree."

"That's why when my daughter first showed me this history book she borrowed, I immediately said that something has to be done about children having to read books like this, so I took the liberty of ordering you all new school books for the colored schools in the county. The new math books even have algebra lessons in it, just like the kids in the white schools have, because I believe in equal exposure to learning for all students."

"I'll have a new oil heating system installed right away," Mr. Curry said. Reverend Johnson and Miss Reed were taken by all the gestures, and Reverend Johnson's eyes welled up. Then he looked at Miss Reed as a Christmas-like smile adorned both of their faces.

"Thank you, Jesus!" he exclaimed while giving her a hug. "We're going to have an extra special thank-you prayer tomorrow before class starts."

"Wait a minute!" Everyone stopped to pause as the two men now had worried looks on their faces.

"What's wrong, Miss Reed?" Harold asked, thinking that she'd inquire about the history book publishing.

"I just realized something."

"What?" he asked on the edge of his feet.

"I don't know how to teach algebra," she said, and the two men relaxed once again.

"Oh, don't worry about that. The teacher's manuals show you step by step how to do it, and if you need any help at all, we'll be more than glad to get one of the teachers from the other schools to give you some pointers, right, Mr. Curry?"

"Sure, why not?" he said with a smile.

"Why, thank both of you," Reverend Johnson said while shaking their hands.

"We won't hold your lessons up anymore today, but we'll be back to make sure all the work is done, so goodbye for now," Harold said.

"We'll be seeing you, and thanks again," Miss Reed said as the men went out the door. The men left the building while Reverend Johnson and Miss Reed were rejoicing.

"Do you really think that they will come through on those promises?" she asked.

"I don't see why they shouldn't, because before, they didn't even have time to talk to us. Now they call us for a meeting. It was our prayer to God. He probably worked it out with a simple instrument we wouldn't think about." Reverend Johnson felt they would do it.

"Are we really going to get some new stuff for our school, Miss Reed?" Millicent asked.

"We'll see, kids," she said joyously. Soon afterward, Harold and Mr. Curry did all that they said and more. The old school got a new face-lift with paint inside and out, the oil heating system was installed, the children got new individual desks instead of the long bench and table they had shared, and everyone was ecstatic about the whole thing. It really didn't even look like the same building anymore, even though the physical structure dimensions had not been changed. Then Mr. Curry and Harold came back with the children's new books in a couple of boxes.

"Here they are—your new school books, just like we said," Harold exclaimed.

"My goodness, you two are so wonderful—praise Jesus! I never thought we would actually get those things we needed so much," Miss Reed said.

"Oh, it's not like it's charity. As school regulator, I'm just following guidelines. Come on—let's open these boxes and get these brand new books passed to the children, shall we?"

"Yes, by all means," Reverend Johnson said, overjoyed with a smile. They started passing the new books out while Mr. Curry collected all the history books. By the time they had finished, the children all had two new books and one old math book still sitting beside them.

"Are there any more of the old history books lying around?" Mr. Curry asked as he looked through the new bookshelves along the sides.

"No, I think that's it," Miss Reed said.

"Oh, you don't have worry about throwing those old books out; we'll do it. You gentlemen have done too much for us already today," Reverend Johnson insisted.

"Oh no! We don't mind," Harold said, intervening before he took the books back from Mr. Curry. "Besides, we have an incinerator that cuts down on garbage costs for the schools."

"Well, do you want the old math books as well?" Miss Reed asked as the two men looked at each other oddly.

"Oh sure, we'll take those as well—just an oversight, you know."

"Kids, pass all your old math books up for Mr. Curry, please." The kids quickly passed all the old books forward and Mr. Curry placed them in the box with the others.

"Thank you all, and enjoy the new stuff. Remember, according to new school regulations, we upgrade books every couple of years, and your new English books are due in next week," Harold said as he and Mr. Curry left with the old books.

After the two men had gone down the street, Miss Reed looked at Reverend Johnson and said, "Isn't this great? Years of nothing, and now all this overnight? I just can't believe it. Everything costs you something, but all this for nothing."

"Well, we do pay taxes like everyone else, so it does cost us something," Reverend Johnson said.

"I guess you're right. All right, children open your history books so that we can finish the final lesson on slavery in America." The kids started looking through the book, but none of them could find what they were looking for.

"What's wrong?" Miss Reed asked.

"We can't find the part on slavery that we were studying," Millicent said.

"What do you mean, you can't find the sections on slavery?"

"It only has two short half pages on the subject, like Tammy's history book that I brought in here the other day."

"What? Let me look at that!" Miss Reed briefly went through the book, looking for the section on slavery. It wasn't to be found, for the new books had been edited to conform to what the Caucasian school's books said.

"Basically all the suffrage information on slavery has been edited from these books," Miss Reed said as Reverend Johnson took the book and looked it over.

"You know, I think your initial suspicion was right," he said. "Everything does cost something . . . and we just paid for it with our legacy. History—little as man knows about his past—should not be discarded. Each piece is like a trail of bread crumbs that will lead us back to where we came from, and if certain pieces of the trail are consumed by foul birds, then the trail is broken, and we may not be able to find out where we came from."

"What if someone did come up with the full truth of man's history all the way back to our beginning of where we came from?" Miss Reed said. "Should it be discarded if it's too ugly for some to digest, just to save face with the few who reject it? No! It should be embraced, because the truth will set us free, making us a better people than those before us. The truth leads us in the direction in which we should go in the future; otherwise we could keep making looped cycles of historical mistakes over and over whenever someone new comes into power."

"Others don't see it that way, I guess," Reverend Johnson said.

Back at the incinerator of the Caucasian school, Harold and Mr. Curry were stuffing all the books into the blazing fiery furnace. The men had to stand back to toss them in because the fire was so hot. The last book thrown in happened to flip open to the page that read "American Slavery," which showed the scene of a chained slave male being whipped while a half naked slave woman pleaded in hand shackles behind them. You could see the fire eating different spots on the pages. Each book consumed by the fire was another missing bread crumb eaten on the trail of ancestral history that causes man's footsteps to trip or wander in circles off the life trail of man's destiny, because the trail guides of history being consumed could lead us all back to our earliest beginning.

"We won't be seeing anymore of these books around," Harold said with confidence.

"Yes, and good riddance," Mr. Curry added. The two men watched as an important part of American history went up into smoke. The only events in the annals of the American Negro race that remained were in the minds of the Negro people and would be carried on through story telling from generation to generation with some accuracy.

Biased community members' influence over the school board system made regulations for all schoolbooks to conform and say what they wanted them to say. If they didn't, somehow schools would be mysteriously burned down, and no local or federal funds would be issued to school whose academics didn't meet the edited regulation.

Most colored folks decided some education was better than no education at all. The main focus of the Negro people now was to get their children educated as doctors, lawyers, police officers, politicians, and judges in order to get some fairness out of the judicial system, but this was met with much opposition along the way in the form of the civil rights struggles, which became the main hurdle for the Negro race to prevail. Their attempts would have been a much longer suffering from injustice if not for the rarely mentioned, heroic, fair-minded Caucasian brothers and sisters who rallied with them to attain the equilibrium of justice that the Afro-American people enjoy today. These Caucasian brothers and sisters rose to the cause to help make a difference in the previously stagnant justice system and often did not get the recognition they deserved, but they have earned that mentioning here on this page of this book. It is truly appreciated by the godly minded Afro-American people who care and thank them for their sacrifices.

# GANGLAND

The menacing ways of the Klan—a sinister gang—would carry on for nearly one hundred years from the late 1860s until the 1960s with the civil rights struggle, dwindling off dramatically, but they were active afterward with some isolated incidents thereafter, but in between that time many hypocritical ventures would come forth trying to bring ethnic cleansing.

They were not the only gang to threaten the ways of civil justice in America. Irish immigrants, who made up the first urban gangs, took control of New York at a place called Five Points, and of Philadelphia. They fought with the Jewish, German, and Italian gangs for control of the organized crime in that area. There was a big shootout at the Rivington station, which caused New York City to hire the largest police force in history to control all the crime. Through Tammany Hall they worked their crimes until the Timothy D. Sullivan-enacted law to end carrying a gun without a permit.

During World War II in California, riots broke out between the Mexican citizens called the zoot-suiters and some Caucasian navy sailors, because the sailors were dancing with the Mexican women on shore leave, and jealous tempers flared. The riots lasted for about three days, starting around June 3 of 1943. The Mexican men were said to be resentful toward the Caucasian sailors for dancing with the Mexican women, as the Klan members had been toward the Negro males in the South dating Caucasian women after the Civil War, but it wasn't as severe, although most men and women have jealous streaks inside them.

Though envious attitudes may have initiated the altercations, most Mexican people thought the Caucasian police arrested only Mexicans while overlooking the faults of the vigilante Caucasian sailors, and they faulted the police actions of not arresting both groups equally as the reason the riots kept going for three days.

Then the Chinese gangs emerged, and the Joe Boys and others had a shootout in Chinatown, CA that killed a large number of people at the Golden Dragon restaurant. The Asian gang involvement mainly involved their own race, but a gang that has biases against their own is just as guilty as one who is biased against other cultures.

Then black gangs, last but not least, popped up on the scene, like the Disciples, the Vice Lords, and other ethnic groups like the Eighteenth Street gang. Gangs have murdered in this country for years. It was not just one group, but each has had their motives for doing what they have been doing—women, money, civil rights, or pure hate—but when one life is lost because of any of them, it is tragic.

Some of these groups claimed to be liberators, protecting the rights of their own, since the governing bodies that were in charge of distributing equality for all citizens were turning their heads and looking the other way when others' civil rights were being violated by the majority in control. This has happened all over the world since the breakup of the one world government. In Ireland they had clashes with the English. Men killed and held hostage members of the English rulers, like William Wallace and others, who here in America they romanticize in books and the media as Robin Hood.

All in all these racial gangs are nothing more than tiny nations within larger nations that have been here since the collapse of the one world government. God came down to scatter the world, which became independent nations like Egypt, Saudi Arabia, England, France, Rome, Nigeria, America, and any other nation that established borders. They are nothing more than large gangs that have established themselves with governing bodies to protect their own human rights.

The only truly innocent people were the nomads, who refused to join sides by wandering around in the world and not claiming any land, but they were swept up by the larger rape gangs and nations that encircled them like a herd of large blue whales, to trap them like plankton in the bubbles of confusion, to be swallowed up. The exception was God-fearing men like Abraham, who had God to protect him from these enormous gang nations like Egypt while they migrated in this world without possessing land. God then deemed that he would give them land, which has been in controversy ever since.

A man named Adolf Hitler came and brought a brilliant mind that was strategically technological, but soundly insalubrious. He thought that he and his followers were the Aryan race, but the Vikings, who would have disowned Hitler as a half-breed black dog, set the tone for prejudice and considered themselves only as Aryans, 100 percent pure human. Soon the world changed with regard to the policy guidelines of human rights across the world. Hitler would lay claim that the white race was the superior race; too bad they were all extinct nearly two thousand years before he was even born or we might have been able to prove that thought!

So unbeknownst to himself and about two hundred million other followers of his belief, they were in fact calling themselves inferior to the Vikings, because Hitler and all of his followers were part black, but as they speculated, part ape. This just goes to show how ignorant man has been since the beginning of his time by falling away from God. We call ourselves masters of the world, but the world seems to be mastering us. We are sometimes as ferocious as the animal that has become a part of us, and what's worse, we often logically think like it when it comes to resolving issues instead of letting the human side settle the dispute.

Hitler did what he thought was right for his people, but isn't that what every aggressive gang leader in the world has been claiming since God came down to see the city that man was building, along with the great tower, before he changed everyone's language?

Whether he was right or wrong, Hitler's quest for world domination and ethnic cleansing was stopped. He took his own life at the failure of his hideous campaign to establish the one world government again, like Cleopatra, Genghis Khan, Julius Caesar, and a host of others, all designated leaders of gangs, whether barbaric, medieval, or somewhat modernly civil. Only God can reunite the civilized one world government once again, and this true depiction of history, which by all means is true, is the beginning of establishing that one world government once again—peacefully.

# FUTURE INSIGHT

Now the scene is set in a near future date, where deep amongst the frozen snowcapped mountains in northern Europe is an expedition team, outfitted for the rugged cold treks through rugged terrain. They had come to the base of a high mountain with very steep cliffs that are almost ninety degrees straight up. The leader of the expedition looked the area over very well as all behind him stopped to wonder what he was doing. After some careful consideration, he spoke.

"Let's dig here," Dr. Trion, leader of the expeditions, said in his native Norwegian language.

"But it seems so dangerous here, because the cliffs are so high, an avalanche could fall on top us at the anytime," Hosea, his most trusted companion, said.

"Yes, I know. That's why it's the perfect place to look for the hundred percent human Viking remains, Hosea," Dr. Trion revealed.

"What fool would have ever lead a people across such a dangerous mountain pass?" Hosea asked Dr Trion.

"An arrogant, prideful, barbaric Viking king," he said, smiling. "Who else?" Hosea, after listening, started smiling. "Besides if my brilliant deductions serve me right, they knew nothing about avalanches if they came from the fallen one world government, from the coast of Africa, through plains of pyramids, and then to these icy mountains. After one bad winter they were forced to head back south. By the time they realized what an avalanche was, some of them were buried in up to forty feet of snow or more. It was like drunken driving; someone had to experience the first accident to warn others of how dangerous it is, right? And who were those first people here?" Then he paused. "The Vikings—the whitest, purest humans left on the earth, so white, in fact, that they could call the blond-haired English, redheaded Irish, and brown-haired Scottish people half-breed black dogs, and physiologically make them feel a complex to wear white wigs."

"You'd have to be pretty damn white to do that, if you asked me, doctor," Hosea said.

"I know. That's why I believe this Red's testimony more and more every day."

"It's a good thing the word *nigger* wasn't invented way back then. That would have really messed up their minds, huh?"

"Don't push it, Hosea. Now set the charges, because it's time to find out if this message from God through this man is true. Are there hundred percent humans—direct descendants of Adam and Eve—buried under this ice?"

"You're going to cause an avalanche?" a woman assistant with blond hair standing nearby said. Her name was Miss Cummings, and she was a highly qualified lab tech in the studies of hematology and genetic mutations. "That means more digging, Doctor."

"Better to cause an avalanche now and do twice the digging than start digging and have to dig our way out of sixty feet of snow and ice." They set the charges, and once everyone was in their places, someone called out.

"All clear?"

"Check point one ready."

"Two ready."

"Three ready."

"All stations clear." Two seconds later the charges exploded and tons of snow came rushing down the mountainsides, roaring like a thundering train until it came to a rumbling rest at the base of the mountain. A horn sounded twice.

"Final blast check."

"All clear."

"All stations clear." Then another blasting cap exploded. It echoed across the valley, but not any snow worth mentioning moved.

"Okay, we're cleared for excavation." Then someone called out. "A Crew north side, and B Crew south side." Heavy excavation equipment with the Caterpillar logo written on its side rolled out while the crew foreman in charge was still calling out strict orders.

"Once we hit ice, all digging has to be done with hand-operated equipment or the hot water cannons. Once any article is found, all digging in that area is to be done with heated low-pressure washers. Is that clear? Anyone not understanding this, speak up. Because if you mess up a find, you might find yourself walking home, as the financiers of this operation gave exacting orders to fire anyone on the spot for not following these strict instructions. Now follow the equipment to your area." They all took off to their assignments, carrying digging tools and backpacks.

The digging went on for the first two days yielding nothing, but then someone shouted out, "Hey, we've found something." It sparked excitement as many people came around to see. It was a Viking helmet with horns that stuck out on the sides. The metal parts of it were rusted with one of the long white ivory horns barely hanging on. Then the doctor came over to examine the artifact, which he held up to eye level for all to see.

"A real Viking helmet!" Dr. Trion said.

"Are those elephant tusks?" Miss Cummings asked the doctor as he examined the item more closely.

"No, they have too much curvature. Normal elephant tusks are straighter than this," he said. "To be more exact, they are the ends of a woolly mammoth's tusks. These people at one time must have hunted the great beast for food, maybe even to their extinction. Keep on digging. I want to concentrate the excavation in this area. Bring a few extra men from Crew A over here in this area." He took the helmet and lifted it up higher to get a good look at it in the sun.

"Usually a headdress of this nature would have belonged to a Viking king or someone of high stature within the Viking ranks," Miss Cummings said.

"You're right, Miss Cummings, and no Viking king would've just left his crown lying around. Some misfortune must have befallen him that he could not retrieve it so easily, like if it fell from a high summit in an avalanche—perhaps with some of his people, too." Then he paused to think. "All right, no more hand-tool digging, just low-pressure hot water cannons in this spot from now on. Is that clear?" Everyone responded yes in his or her own way, and digging commenced once again.

They worked long hours digging into the night, and the heavy excavation equipment loaded huge scoops of ice and snow into a large ten-thousand-gallon metal tank heated by propane to supply hot water for the high-pressure water cannons. The cannons cut through the ice like a welding torch cutting through soft metal. Some men even used flamethrowers to melt pockets of frozen ice. This heat caused constant streams of water to flow from the valley like a babbling brook for the first time in centuries, and steamy mist filled sections of the frozen valley, like the thick London fog in a Sherlock Holmes movie thriller.

"We found something!" a man's voice shouted with excitement as the noise level died down. The power equipment came to a stop as the workers turned in the direction of the man's harking voice. "Over here, we found something."

People started running over to the point of the excitement while asking one another as they went, "What did they find?"

"I don't know yet; let's go see," said others. Soon a group of people appeared to look at the block of ice, and each crowded for a space to see what the commotion was about; inside a huge block of ice, there was an object that was plain to see but hard to make out.

Dr. Trion came walking up to ask, "What is going on?" But no one said a word as he came into full view of the amazing sight. "Can it be?" he asked himself out loud.

"Yes, sir," the crew foreman acknowledged.

"What is it?" Miss Cummings asked.

"It appears to be someone frozen in ice," the foreman said. "The person seems to be kind of bloated up, though, perhaps swollen up with injuries from the fall and then frozen that away." Dr. Trion took out a looking glass to try for a better look into the block of ice.

"Wait a minute!" the doctor said upon closer examination. "This person is not swollen up from injuries. It's a woman, and she has a frozen baby in her arms."

"What?" the female assistant asked. "You really don't think—"

"What? That the prediction is true? I don't know what I believe right now. All I know is that I want this woman in that lab. Thaw out her right arm only, just long enough to get an ounce of blood to perform a DNA and sickle cell test on her ASAP!"

"Right away, Doctor. I'll prepare the lab for her now," Miss Cummings said.

"Good! Make the arrangements." He stood to his feet, turning to face everyone. "I want everyone's attention. If the predictions are true, then there is a Viking prince of about sixteen years of age buried frozen in perhaps the crag of a rock or narrow opening of some kind. He might be wearing a necklace of some sort to mark his royal lineage. He is said to be the hardest one to find, so I want every rock turned over and every crack looked into. Even if it's only the size of your own rear, search it. I want every stone turned in locating him, because he carries the sperm of a hundred percent human, especially that descended of King Nimrod, the first king of all the earth, directly from Adam and Eve—genetically unaltered, he's worth more than you can imagine. I'm talking about true blue blood. A lot of queens will pay highly to sit his offspring on their thrones. It would instantly connect their royal lineage all the way back to the first kingdom on earth."

"Doctor, this funded expedition is supposed to be more of a historical find than a business opportunity. To only sell pure white sperm to any wealthy person in the world who wants to whiten their royal bloodline would be like some paying the dentist to super-whiten their teeth," said Professor Baker, who was in his late fifties.

"Don't worry about the common folks, Professor Baker. If we find any ninety-nine point five percent pure Viking noblemen relatives, then the general population can purchase it with a ten-thousand-dollar secured loan, like one would do if buying a new car. It's sure to turn any brunette-haired woman's child into a life-size replica of a natural whitish-blond-haired Barbie doll at age twenty," Dr. Trion said with a smirk as the air became still and quiet. "Just kidding, Professor." Then everyone started laughing as a relaxed feeling came over them—everyone, that is, except Professor Baker. He felt that the discovery of the frozen woman with the baby in her arms was a very serious matter.

"This is not a laughing matter. I'm here to represent the interest of the godly religious sects from around the world, and as it has been pointed out to us in Revelation 12:4, a woman will bring forth a child and the dragon will wait for it, that ancient serpent called the devil. God will take the child up to heaven, and the women will run into the desert and hide for twelve hundred and sixty days. The dragon will pursue her and he will fail. Then the dragon, enraged at the woman, goes off to make war against the rest of her offspring—those who obey God's commandments and hold the testimony of Jesus. If a pure hundred percent white human egg and sperm do exist, and they are put together in a woman, we might bring forth evil into the world to destroy us all."

"Professor, we don't have time to debate this issue. It's already been debated a hundred times or more already since that man told the world of the possible pure white race. We all then agreed to come here searching under the guidelines of the Human Rights Council, not to bring a hundred percent pure white human beings back to life if we found their existence. It can be done only under the strict overseeing of the council. Are you asserting that someone here intends to break the council's rulings? That I would bring them back like white blood cells to purify the earth's body of infectious human beings with yellow hair or darker through ethic cleansing? I assure you I am not Adolf Hitler."

"No, of course not, but all this talk of making big profits tends to lure one into maybe not doing the right thing, is all I'm saying. A high assembly of church dignitaries convened to consider the important matters of doctrine and Scripture, resulting in the council's decisions that every egg and every sperm needs to be accounted for as council guidelines call for, if these are in fact hundred percent humans. We certainly don't want to see another Hitler-minded maniac creating a pure white army, only to have them contaminating the world's water supply with a growth hormone that will cause everyone with sickle cells in their blood to reproduce at a phenomenal rate to block their arteries."

"Professor, I'm well aware of how sickle cells work, and no one here has any plan to create a hundred percent pure white Viking army to destroy the world with sickle cells. Professor, you have been watching too many *White-Haired Viking Babe* animated cartoon sequels." The crew members around started laughing at the possibility.

"It's *White-Haired Viking Barbara,* if you must know," Professor Baker said. "And the scientific communities around the world have deemed this story's baseline as a real threat, if hundred percent pure white humans do exist and are brought back to life, as possibly warned in Revelation 8:10. 'A third of the waters turned bitter, and many of the people died from the waters that had become bitter.' We all know that people with the Viking mentality are capable of doing such things, even if they themselves are not of pure human form." Professor Baker wanted to warn of the possible dangers. "Now, do we take heed, Doctor? Because if the pure Viking race had been advanced enough in chemistry five thousand years go, it's very possible none of us would be here today . . . Just maybe, we've received a pre-warning from God, who let them be extinct for a reason."

"You are so right, Professor. Every one of us will take all possible precautions against it. Let sleeping dogs lie, they say, if they exist. Now back to work, everyone. We've had enough delays for one day."

Dr. Trion walked away with Jose closely at his side and started to whisper to Jose.

"You know, Hosea, I'm starting to see a vision of prophecy myself."

"You do? What is it, Doctor?" he asked quietly.

"I foresee Professor Baker having an unfortunate accident if we've found the resting place of hundred percent pure white humans," Dr. Trion said.

"You know, I think it might be catching, because I can imagine the same vision," Hosea said, and he gave a sinister laugh.

Hours later, back at the portable lab, Miss Cummings had the woman in ice prepped, and her assistants thawed out her right arm enough to draw a small blood sample.

"Too bad those scientists didn't have the insight to perform a DNA or sickle cell test on Oetzi the Iceman. They could have been rich from his spermatozoa."

"That's hindsight. Let's find out what we have here," Dr. Trion said as Miss Cummings placed a drop of the blood under the microscope, and with anticipation quickly examined it. She studied it for several seconds.

"Well?" Dr. Trion asked her. She slowly lifted her head with her mouth partly gaping open."

"What?" Dr. Trion asked again anxiously.

"I don't see any sickle cells in this blood."

"Yes, we found them," he said in a low but very excited voice. "The whole world laughed at that man, but something inside told me that he knew what he was talking about. Now check the DNA, but don't report to anyone but me, because before we leave from here, this Viking woman is going to receive a hysterectomy. You do have the frozen replacement ovaries on hand, don't you?" She glanced around the room to see who was looking on before she answered.

"Of course, Doctor . . . I have the replacement testicles with the spermatozoa as well . . . in case the Viking prince is found also," she said, speaking discreetly.

"I knew I could count on you. Now let's proceed with caution."

"Yes, Doctor. Right away," she said, getting back to work as though nothing were going on. A little while later the search crews made some more discoveries. They found two more Viking male specimens, and instantly upon cutting them out of the ice, they brought them into lab for inspection.

"Well, what are they?" Dr. Trion asked.

"They are not pure in DNA like the woman. Each of these two men has very minimal trace of sickle cells in their blood and their DNA," Miss Cummings said. "You can't produce a one hundred percent human child if you put their ninety-nine point one percent spermatozoa with her hundred percent pure white human eggs. The best you could get is perhaps a ninety-nine point five percent human, who will have virtually natural-looking pure white hair all of its life. You wouldn't be able to tell it from the real thing without a DNA test after you've mapped the genetic norm, but the child will never be one hundred percent pure human. This is still a multimillion-dollar market with their ninety-nine point one percent spermatozoa that can genetically transform brunette women's children into natural-looking blond women even after they've reached their twenties, and light-complexioned black women's children into a beautiful brunette Wonder Woman lookalike."

"I don't want lookalikes—I want the real thing. I have a fifty-million-dollar arrangement with a queen to impregnate her daughter with an egg and spermatozoa of pure white humans, to make the first pure white royal human heir to sit on a throne in more than twenty-five hundred years," he said. "We need to find the Viking prince!" Others nearby almost heard him and looked in his direction. He quickly quieted down until they looked away.

After careful inspection it was found that the two men were *Homo sapiens*, each only about 99 percent pure human and 1 percent primate. Dr. Trion was obviously upset, because he needed the Viking prince to complete phase one of his plan. The fifty million dollars was payment by an outside source unbeknown to Dr. Trion, who just really wanted to create a pure white army to take over the world by developing a hormone formula that would cause the sickle cells in the body of everyone to reproduce at an accelerated rate to cause strokes in the mixed, partially human species on the planet. He would rule the world after that with the pure white humans by distributing the formula throughout the world's water supply that only they would be able to drink without harmful effects because their bodies had no DNA sequences to regenerate sickle cells.

Professor Baker was right to be concerned about Dr. Trion's actions, because anyone who got in his way usually didn't live. Soon word came that they had discovered another body. It was frozen and wedged between a narrow crag in the rocks, and it ran all the way from nearly the middle of the cleft to the base. The removal was more time consuming than difficult, but after hours of careful excavation, the frozen body was retrieved. They made a careful examination of it once its arm was thawed out enough to draw blood. Miss Cummings drew the blood, and Dr. Trion and Professor Baker were both watching as she did. After grabbing the slide plates, she placed one large drop on two plates and then put the plate under the illuminated microscope. Everyone was a little tense as she lowered her eyes onto the lens. She examined the species' blood for about twenty seconds, and then she slowly lifted her head in silence.

"Well, what did you find?" Professor Baker asked her, on the edge of his seat.

"This boy has no sickle cells in his blood. He's one hundred percent human," she said conclusively.

"Yes!" Professor Baker said, overjoyed. "That proves it: man did not evolve from an ape or how else could there be a five-thousand-year-old person buried in ice more pure human than all of us? Those poor, unfortunate, misguided Darwinist crackpot fools calling themselves scientists are going to have to eat crow and admit that God put the first man on the earth. Praise be to our Lord and Savior Jesus Christ, who died for our sins."

"Ahem!" said Dr. Trion, who considered himself a top scientist in the world.

"Oh! No disrespect was meant toward you or your colleagues, Doctor," Professor Baker said to them. "But being a theology major, this is the greatest news in the life of man since Christ died on the cross to forgive our sins. This joyous news is overflowing in my heart."

"Congratulations, Professor, I am extremely ecstatic for you and your colleagues as well," Dr. Trion said.

"Yes, thank you. This is indeed an overdue joy, if you don't mind me saying so, Doctor."

"Oh no, not at all, Professor. Feel free to enjoy the moment and express your joys of Christianity."

"Why, thank you; that is every noble of you. I'm just trying to contain myself from shouting and praising with joy." He chuckled lightly with happiness. "Well, I must be off. I have to radio some of my colleagues back at the main base about the news," Professor Baker said excitedly.

"You brought your own radio, you say?" Dr. Trion asked, surprised.

"Yes, my theology colleagues wanted me to radio them at my earliest convenience after the discovery. Now, if you'll all excuse me, please, I'll go and relay the good news." This was going to throw a monkey wrench into the fifty-million-dollar arrangement that Dr. Trion had planned, because once the outside world found out about it, he would not be able to get away with extracting the eggs and spermatozoa from the pure white humans for his monumental gain. He knew the news would cause this country's government to send out a security force to make sure all the eggs and spermatozoa were accounted for, so their country's government would control the profit sharing from the sales and proceeds of bringing a pure white human back to life. Greed is in the form of all bodies, even government bodies. Professor Baker left, saying goodbye as he went.

Dr. Trion looked at Miss Cummings with a concentrated stare on his face that made her not even want to know what he was thinking.

"I think I'll go see how Hosea is coming along with his project," he said as Miss Cummings looked away.

Dr. Trion had to arrange for Professor Baker's accident to happen a lot faster than he had expected. Meanwhile, Professor Baker was back in his tent, calling on his shortwave radio to the main base of this frozen country.

"Come in, base . . . This is Professor Baker! Can you hear me?" There was a moment of static and silence. "Base, come in, base, can you hear me? This is Professor Baker." The noise on the radio changed a little, although you could start to hear voices breaking up in the static. Professor Baker was unaware that someone was sneaking up behind him. In his excitement he was focusing only on the radio communications that were mingled with static noise. "Can you hear me?" he asked.

"Yes, Professor Ba-er, we can hea—ou clearly.—an you—ear us—clear—as well?"

"No, but as long as you can hear me somewhat, I'm happy to report that we found the hundred percent pure humans! The missing link, buried in five-thousand-year-old undisturbed ice. Darwinism is dead. Did you hear that? Dead!" he exclaimed happily.

"Let's see if—e heard you right.—ou said that you found—em, hundred percent humans buri—in five-thousand-year—ld ice?" the person asked. But before Professor Barker could confirm, he noticed a shadow looming over him and turned to see Hosea swinging a large pipe wrench that cracked him over his head, knocking him unconscious with the single blow. Professor Baker fell forward and lay slumped over the table. Hosea looked around to see if anyone was watching. He took Professor Baker's hand, which he used to switch off the radio that was still calling out his name.

"Professor Baker, please confirm this report. You say that you found the hundred percent humans? Professor Baker, Professor—."

*Click.* Hosea switched off the radio while they were talking. He then proceeded to drag Professor Baker outside under the cover of darkness. He took him to the edge of a snowy cliff, and then shoved him over the edge, where he fell to the bottom like the five-thousand-year-old Vikings had fallen many years earlier, striking rocks on the way down. The fall was fatal to the professor, and his limp body lay there in the cold. Someone sought power and monetary gain from more than a hundred billion dollars in worldwide sales, but people like this since the beginning of time have let greed stand in the way of making the whole of humanity be complete. Hosea ran off to make up his alibi.

Soon the news of the tragedy of what had happened to Professor Baker reached the ears of everyone in the camp. His body was recovered from the bottom of the gorge to be flown back to the main base. The council called for a meeting to discuss the findings of the expedition. The room was filled with noted scientists and theology majors alike from around the world to hear the first official results on the find of 100 percent humans discussed. Dr. Trion was to offer up the results as well as an explanation of what must have happened to Professor Baker, and he sat at a table with Miss Cummings. Then the presiding council came into the room, a seven-member panel consisting of fair-minded men and women of different ethnic backgrounds either with doctoral degrees in either science or theology, who had been voted in by United Nations members.

"Let the record reflect that the humanitarian council, which has convened for the fact finding and or possible restoration of hundred percent pure white human beings on the earth, is now in session, with Counselor Gordon presiding as chief counselor." A few members were discussing proceedings amongst themselves.

"This meeting will now come to order," Counselor Gordon said. "Dr. Trion, we are here to discuss the results from your fact-finding expedition. Are you prepared to reveal your finds, Dr. Trion?

"Yes, I am, your honor," Dr. Trion said.

"You may proceed then."

"I would like to start out by offering condolences to the family, friends, and colleagues of Professor Baker, who was elated about being a member of this historical expedition. His tragic lost is deeply felt by us all," he said sympathetically, glancing over at the other theological members at the table across from him, who were Professor Baker's closest friends and companions. "Now, we did find members of the Viking clan frozen in ice by an avalanche nearly five thousand years ago, as was suggested by the Smith theory—."

"Theory?" said one of the theology majors.

"I stand corrected. Or possible 'vision,'" Dr. Trion recanted. "However, after careful forensic research, I'm sorry to say that we did not find any hundred percent human beings."

"That's a lie!" one of the theological members insisted as he stood up in protest. "Professor Baker radioed us saying that the discovery of hundred percent human beings had been made before his transmissions ended. We all heard that part of his message clearly."

"Are you trying to convince this council with broken transmissions from an inferior radio prove that I am lying?" Miss Cummings, who was sitting next to Dr. Trion, offered no emotional response as she sat there quietly, taking in the whole debate.

"Order! Order in this court. Now Dr. Trion has the floor. Let him speak. Doctor?"

"Thank you, Chief Counselor," Dr. Trion said.

"Are you saying that Darwin's theory is still the plausible, Doctor?" the chief counselor questioned.

"No, your honor, and if I had been allowed to speak uninterrupted, then I would have offered up some surprising testimony on behalf of creationist Professor Baker and his colleagues."

"Continue," the chief counselor urged.

"The results of the testing did offer up something quite amazing," he said. "The humans we found had unique DNA patterns and virtually no sickle cell traces in their blood compared with the whitest modern-day humans in this century of two thousand. They were in fact nearly hundred percent human—much whiter than anyone on this planet today." Oohs and ahs were heard throughout the tribunal room. "We estimate that they are ninety-nine percent human and one percent primate, which still suggests that they came from hundred percent humans, but probably once the one world government was dismantled, which is now Egypt. Therefore the hundred percent human race was probably already extinct, but the existence of ninety-nine percent humans also dismisses Darwinism, because how could there be people more evolved than us today? Ninety-nine percent humans couldn't be buried in five-thousand-year-old ice, if we evolved from an ape. Ninety-nine percent humans still should not exist for another two hundred million years. This fact combined with the proven fact that the number of natural blonds diminishing on this planet suggests that man is de-evolving or becoming a melting pot, which gives more credit to the Smith version, which suggests there is a creator."

"So we can officially count the Darwin theory as dead?"

"It would appear to conclude that way," he said. "Also the threat of someone raising a hundred percent pure white army to contaminate the world's water supplies with a sickle cell mass reproductive hormone formula is dead as well," Dr. Trion concluded. "We combed the areas well and I believe all the original Vikings that can be found have been found, but I would still like to fund some private digs. You never know—we just might get lucky, and find some."

"And you would report to this council if you did find them, wouldn't you, Doctor?"

"Of course, your honor," Dr. Trion said.

"Just a few more questions, please, Doctor, before we adjourn?"

"Yes?"

"How did Professor Baker succumb to this unfortunate 'accident'?"

"As far as we can tell, he for some unknown reason went into the dark of the night exploring on his own—perhaps out of desperation to prove the church's views right, or because he felt God would lead him by faith in the dark to these people. Then he fell off the edge of that steep cliff."

"Professor Baker was a sensible man. He would never have done such a foolish act!" one of his colleagues insisted boldly.

"Then it seems that we have a complete mystery on our hands, because I have not the slightest clue to his state of mind at the time of his demise, though I do feel responsible for any incidents that occurred during the expedition, since I was personally selected to head the team safely."

"Also, Doctor, there were strict orders given for at least two scientists and two theology majors representing both sides' interests to be on this expedition. Why was Professor Baker the only one representing the religious side?"

"Well, the expedition split into two groups, to cover more ground. I assured everyone that it would be best to split up before the winter weather set in. Everyone agreed, and Professor Baker came with our group. Now from hindsight, I see bad judgment on my part as leader of the exploration, but I must learn to live with the results of my judgment."

"Finally, what happened to the body count? An unofficial preliminary report drawn up in Professor Baker's handwriting and found in the lining of his jacket indicates that five bodies were found, but you and your hired crew reported only two males' remains, ages thirty-five to forty. You turned these over to the council for DNA samples, but the report noted that the spermatozoa had been removed," noted the chief counselor. "Can you explain that, please?"

"I have to admit that I'm at a loss when it comes to the condition of Professor Baker's mind in his final hour. I don't want to draw any conclusions that might lead an investigation astray from the truth, if any should arise from suspicion of possible wrongdoing, but I will cooperate any way I can. In the case of the spermatozoa, eggs, or other reproductive organs that might have been found, I was given salvaging rights to the spermatozoa or eggs, as long as they were not deemed to be one hundred percent human."

"It was also noted that that decision was to be made here in a designated medical facility, not in the field, which you somehow determined to go about yourself."

"A mere oversight on my part."

"I see," Counselor Gordon said, not letting on to any suspicious inquiries within his mind.

"Then it is the official decision of this hearing that the Smith theory or possible vision is a direct replacement of the Darwin theory. This meeting is adjourned." Dr. Trion and his assistant, Miss Cummings, got up and left directly to walk out the door without answering any questions as a mass of reporters shoved microphones and flashed cameras in their faces. Men were still arguing the validity of the discovery without the actually 100 percent human remains.

"Unless I see such a thing as a one hundred percent human, I'm still not going to believe that God put man on this earth, and that's final," one Darwinist objected.

"They found people whiter than anyone on this planet today from more than five thousand years ago. It's got to be true. God is real!"

"Not until I see a hundred percent human, and no less," the man confessed. Dr. Trion smirked as he walked past the two men arguing, because he knew the truth inside, which made him feel like he had ultimate power in his demented way of thinking.

The chief counselor called a security officer who looked like a Secret Service agent as the officer was walking down the hall back to his office.

"I'm authorizing you to have a security detail keep a constant surveillance on our good Dr. Trion, and report every suspicious move he makes back to this board," the chief counselor said as he exited the hearing. "We may have a loose cannon in our midst."

"Yes, sir, right away." The man walked off to get the task going. Outside in their car sat Dr. Trion and Miss Cummings. Reporters were still hounding them after their interview as they left the secured parking lot and passed a guard's station. At the gate they noticed that a huge crowd had gathered just outside in protest to Dr. Trion's testimony, holding up signs saying "God is real!" "Down with Darwinism," and "Put the Bible Back in Our Schools." He began to realize how big this discovery really was, and after they had cleared the crowd, he turned to look at Miss Cummings.

"Call our purchaser to see if he has transferred the funds as requested. Then schedule for him to meet us at the exchange point tonight," he said as they drove out of sight.

# TESTING CONFIRMED

A couple of years later, a woman with two children sat at a bus stop. She was Caucasian with dark brown hair and had two preteenage children with her, a boy and a girl about a year apart from each other. Both children had sandy or dirty-blond colored hair. While they waited for their bus to arrive, another woman with two children appeared at the same bus stop. The woman was a young Afro-American with light golden brown skin—like honey—and shoulder-length hair. She had two Caucasian children with her. She looked as though she might be the children's babysitter or nanny, because by all indications they knew one another well. They all sat next to the other woman with her children at the bus stop. For a second or two, no one said a word to the other. Then the Caucasian woman broke the ice by speaking up.

"Hello," she said.

"Hi," the honey-complexioned Afro-American women responded.

"Nice day out today, isn't it?"

"Yes, it sure is. I was thinking the same thought," the honey-skinned women said while digging into her purse for a mirror. She quickly made sure her makeup was not running, and then placed it back just as fast. "You have some cute children," she said to the Caucasian woman.

"Thank you. They're in their good mode right now, but they can be rascals at times."

"I think all children can be."

"Are you babysitting today?" the Caucasian woman asked.

"With these two, it seems like I'm babysitting every day."

"I'm looking for a good babysitter—do you have any references?"

"No . . . I don't babysit for a living—technically. I'm a stay-at-home mom with my children," the light-honey-skinned women said.

"I'm sorry. I thought you were babysitting these children for someone," the Caucasian woman said, puzzled.

"Oh no, these are my children."

"Yours!" the Caucasian women responded, all wide-eyed.

"Yes, I was one of the first Afro-American women enrolled in that family planning test program to receive spermatozoa from the hundred percent Viking people found frozen in ice. They wanted to measure how much closer to the original genetic norm the cellular transformation would revert, once my eggs conceived, so they could do DNA mapping. We're pictured in their brochure, so we update progression pictures every five years until they're both twenty as part of the contract. That why we're dressed up—we just left there."

"My goodness, they're as Caucasian as my children are!"

"Yes, I know. If you had done it, your children would probably still have all natural-looking white hair on their heads right now—perhaps even until they turned eleven years old," the honey-skinned woman said.

"That is so amazing that we all came from Adam and Eve, altered by the seed of Cain to make this many different human transformations. With pure white Viking eggs or spermatozoa conceived with our own eggs or spermatozoa, we can nearly transform back to the original genetic makeup that we first came from in just a few generations."

"I tell you the truth: when the boy first came out and I looked at him, I said there is no way this child could be mine. I mean, it was just too drastic a change for me to swallow at first, but it was my eggs, and I gave birth to them. When my mother and father came to the hospital for the first time to see their grandchildren—imagine my mother's surprise standing there with all her black friends."

"How did she respond?" the Caucasian lady asked.

"She just kept saying, 'All right! Where's the hidden camera? I know this is *Candid Camera*. Where's the host?'" The Caucasian woman laughed, placing her hand to her mouth.

"I would love to have seen her face," she said. "I was a little taken back myself when you told me they were your children—I can imagine how she must have felt."

"Most people are."

"It just goes to show you that a lot of the things in the past that our races conceived as wrong was nothing more than a plot to keep us apart," the Caucasian woman said. "Like if you touch a black person, you're going to turn black. When I was really small, I believed such things."

"Well, we know now that all that kind of stuff is just a bunch a of boloney."

"How many of you did they test?"

"Six of us in the first program. Three shades of white; a natural blond, a redhead, and a brunette, and then three shades of black: me, the light skinned complexion one; a medium-brown-skinned girl, and a dark-skinned girl. They wanted to produce a scale predicting what mutation change percentages anyone could expect for future purchasers. The dark-skinned woman had the most change, because she had more mutated cells, and of course the blond woman had the least amount of change, because she is closest to the 'genetic norm,' which means half of all your mutated cells get erased in your child if you conceive or impregnate with a hundred percent human—no matter your DNA mutation count."

"How much did it cost you?"

"It was free for all us women in the test pilot program. They selected six hundred female candidates based upon beauty features and IQ scores. I was chosen as the top candidate out of the hundred women who looked like me, but it will cost at less ten thousand dollars per conception for the public. They already have a lot of women on the waiting list. Even some rich businessmen have put up front money for hundred percent human eggs to conceive their children, but they have to hire their own birth mothers. You know a famous pop star is on the list," she joked.

"Yeah, I can see all these redneck women running in, talking about how they want their babies to have blue eyes and natural blond hair in Texas to be cheerleaders at age twenty."

"The children conceived by the natural blond-haired women in the test program came out so white that they think her children will have close to white-looking hair all their natural life, with not a brown speck in their eyes that could be see with the naked eye—they look nearly just like Viking people, but my children, even though they have blue colored eyes, have noticeable brown specks mixed in around the pupils—see!"

"Wow! Do they get sunburned?" the Caucasian woman asked as she looked into their eyes.

"Yes, but she gets sunburned much easier than he does."

"Where did they get hundred percent pure white eggs and spermatozoa?"

"Well, it turns out that this Dr. Trion claims that on a later expedition dig, he found the hundred percent pure human Viking descendants frozen in ice not far from their original dig. Now he's in debate with that foreign government over who actually owns the rights to the hundred percent pure Viking people's remains. But he has also gone on and started testing anyway, and they gave me a certain amount of money to raise my children just above middle-class standards, with prepaid scholarships to our choice of Ivy League colleges. It is rumored that a certain princess who's been in the news and is heir to the royal throne is a one hundred percent human, and has a little brother on the way who is supposedly one hundred percent human also."

"Really!" the Caucasian woman said. "A hundred percent human is on this earth again—I thought that had to be approved by the Supreme Governing council first, so they could make sure these people weren't exploited like laboratory geese that lay the golden eggs, or milked like cows for semen off on some deserted island."

"Yes, but they won't let anyone except for a certain royal physician handle their blood work analysis." Soon a bus came along and slowly rolled to a stop just before them.

"Well, this is my bus," the Caucasian woman said. "Perhaps we'll see you around."

"Maybe. We often go across the way to the city park in the afternoon."

"We do as well, but not often. I'll keep an eye out for you from now on, so our kids can play together."

"That'll be wonderful," the light-skinned woman said to the Caucasian lady and her children as they started to board the bus and then turned to say goodbye. In no time they were seated, and they waved from the window as the bus pulled off to head on down the street while the humble family looked on from the bench as they drove out of sight.

"Mother?" the little blond-haired girl asked her light-brown-skinned mother.

"Yes, dear?" she answered.

"Do you think that that lady would have offered to meet us at the park so that we could play with her children if we hadn't been created with hundred percent human Viking spermatozoa to come out looking Caucasian, but genetically Afro-American looking as you?" the little girl of about ten years asked.

"Well, she seemed nice enough. I certainly hope she would have, but you never know."

"Even though I'm genetically closer to the white race than some other Caucasian people, I'm never going to be prejudiced toward darker-skinned people such as you, Mother," the boy said. "I'll judge everyone by the measured character of a good man."

"That's the way you're supposed to think, but if this process continues to catch on, there may not be any people like me left for anyone to be biased against," the woman said. She hugged both of her children as the scene started to fade to black.

The lost history of the world has been found once again. What will you do to help preserve it forever? Who will realize the absolute truths contained in this book and seek to free the pure white people from their frozen graves? Out of all the people in the world, who will defend their rights before they're brought back to life from the snowy mountain ranges?

Soon the rich and greedy profiteers will go looking for the lost pure white genetic Viking people, who first started out on the earth. They'll intend to milk them for their original genetic material to whiten the blood of the rest of the world for profit like a dentist whitens teeth—genetic scientists and businessmen of the biotechnology revolution seeking large financial gains. Who will head off this potential drunk driving DNA accident by making laws before the genetic "norm" is even found? Or do we just sit back and watch their freedoms stripped and casualties happen, and then decide we need laws to protect them from being like lab rats raised on an island somewhere? Everything indicates a lengthy bureaucracy of red tape and governing laws of man that would not react in time. They would need many official studies done by elected committees of the statistical fatalities—like the drunk driving victims across the world—before they enacted a law to monitor these people's rebirth into the world, an act to save the most precious thing humanity has left to offer—our origin.

*PRELUDE to the upcoming book:*

# WHITE-HAIRED VIKING BARBARA

Now the image of the universe appeared as the stars formed with shining brilliance. Then a meteor passed by in a terrific rush that left a trail of what looked like white shiny stardust in its wake. It plummeted through the Earth's atmosphere and left a red streak like a tracer bullet shot out of an M16 assault rifle in the dark night sky over the polar caps.

Suddenly an upbeat rock-and-roll song blasted out in hi-fi stereo. Then the music faded out, and words could be heard.

"It's time for the adventures of *White-Haired Viking Barbara* and friends!" the announcer said. "Deep in the frozen north of Europe researchers unearthed the frozen bodies of the lost Viking descendants from their frozen graves. Back in an American laboratory, a team of scientists led by Dr. Airrien successfully conceived a one hundred percent human child against the authority of the United Council, who agreed that it would be best for all that prejudice to be eradicated from the earth before such a human being was brought back to life. This would ensure that their minds would not be poisoned with bias-conscious diseases ever again, which would cause them to seek worldwide domination through the use of a hormonally developed formula that would destroy anyone who was not one hundred percent human, and bear any trace of sickle cells in their bodies, by causing all people with it to have congested circulatory system blockage, to induce strokes. Like the evil ambitions of men in the past this Dr. Airrien brought forth a living, breathing

294

hundred percent direct human descendant of Adam and Eve for his evil intentions of dominating the world. The announcer elucidated.

"They conceived and brought a female child to life first, because the conditions of the purchased eggs were poor—questionable at best. They used only semen that would produce a girl, and only one egg conceived—it was a girl, so that they could harvest more eggs from her, like the goose that laid the golden eggs for Dr. Airrien's world conquest.

"They named her Barbara; she was moved to an isolated island far away from the rest of the world, where everyone seen by her had to color all their exposed hair white like the original Viking traits, and wear sapphire-blue contacts. Her education was carefully selected, for she knew nothing of the outside world other than the physics, chemistry, and advanced biological medical training that she'd need to carry out the world domination plan with her people when the time came.

"She grew to young womanhood, and possessed the beauty of Eve . . . the original beauty that adorns every beautiful woman's face, but Dr. Airrien's plans were interrupted when his trusted associate, pretending to be Barbara's mother, fell in love with her after years of service and stole her away from the island just weeks before they planned to start harvesting the eggs from her body, for the child's own good. The Announcer said.

She took Barbara back to America to hide her, while exposing her mind to the rest of the world that she had never known existed. She taught her fairly that all humans were good or bad in all ethnic groups, and furthermore that everyone deserved the right to live on this earth. Barbara and her guardian mother were going to move to New York, where she could accept a job as a curator at famous museum on Viking culture, of which she had extensive knowledge so she could raise Barbara.

"After years of searching for the Viking girl to collect her eggs, Dr. Airrien's men finally found Barbara and her guardian mother. Then they fled in a high-speed chase to escape the clutches of the sinister goons, whom they lost, but their car crashed, and Barbara was thrown from the car. Later, when she awoke, she found that the woman she knew as her mother was unwigged and dying after the crash. Barbara then realized that the hair on her believed mother's head was really brunette and not white like hers, but she still loved this woman as her real mother anyway, who with her last words told Barbara, 'Don't let Dr. Airrien get his hands on your eggs to raise his army. Run to save your life and the world's, because he cannot conquer the world without them. Take my purse and this job in my place at the museum as Annett Summers. You can do it—I know you can, Barbara. Always remember that I love you!' The Announcer explains.

"'No, don't go!' Barbara cried as her mother died in her arms. Soon Dr. Airrien's men picked up their trail and were after Barbara again, but she narrowly escaped again by hopping onto a passing freight train headed east. Days later she found herself in New York City, nearly broke, with one single set of clean clothes on her back and her natural white hair dyed brunette, interviewing for a job with some stiff competition. The Announcer says.

She was interviewed by the head curator of the museum named Mr. Jenkins, a nice, elderly, balding gentleman who thought she was a little too young and casually dressed at first, but going with his instinct decided to give her the job because of her extensive knowledge of Viking history. Her guardian mother felt she should know everything about her people—good and bad—once they left the island. That, combined with a little pleading on her part, was enough to push his decision over the edge.

"She worked hard and fit into the program well, until the day she discovered a Viking warrior king's helmet stored amongst Viking relics in the basement. The helmet was placed upon her head and the sword put into her hands while reciting a phrase from the original native Viking language God gave man in an ancient Viking book: 'I call on the name of God—creator of man in his image—in my Viking tongue, "Valhalla!" Then she was magically transformed into a beautiful Viking warrior princess as her helmet turned solid gold, shining like the sun, which instantly purified her hair back to its natural pure white state. She would have to dye it back to her camouflage brunette color again after each time she was transformed into the warrior princess. Her Viking sword became empowered and glowed white-hot with energy blasts like lightning, adding to her superhuman strength to do battle against all evil forces that would threaten the earth.

"Also in the storeroom was a life-size statue of a white stallion warhorse dressed in Viking armament, which had been transformed into steel, before the conception of the longboat, for helping chase men down on the battlefields, and hunting the woolly mammoth to its extinction. She learned that it would remain this way until its good deeds outweighed its tarnished ones of the past from the ancient journal that said once she placed the original Viking battle cry horn upon the warhorse statue's forehead, it would temporarily transform the enormous relic into a living, flying steed until the midnight hour. It became her closest friend and ally in the battle against any evil that threatened her fellow man. She would keep her identity a secret as she battled the forces of evil while gaining other friends along the way to stop Dr. Airrien and his maniacal, evil plans.

"So begins the saga of White-Haired Viking Barbara and friends to save the world from being taken over by the demented schemes of mad men thinking that they can play God by inhabiting the earth with whoever they feel should occupy it. While battling these evil forces, she will attempt to retrieve the remains of her Viking people to ensure that her people will not be used as lab rats like she was intended to be, for evil purposes. She wants safety for her people to be brought back into a peaceful coexistence with this world the way her noble grandfather Noah would have wanted, living in harmony with all mankind." The Announcer finished.